YOUNG HUNTING

a memoir

Martin Hunter

ECW Press

Published by ECW Press, 2120 Queen Street East, Suite 200,
Toronto, Ontario, Canada M4E 1E2
416.694.3348 / info@ecwpress.com

LIBRARY AND ARCHIVES CANADA CATALOGUING IN PUBLICATION

Hunter, Martin, 1933–
Young hunting : a memoir / Martin Hunter.
ISBN 978-1-55022-852-6
1. Hunter, Martin, 1933–. 2. Dramatists, Canadian (English)—20th
century—Biography. 3. Toronto (Ont.)—Biography. I. Title.

PS8565.U58Z478 2008   C812'.54   C2008-902421-4

Editor for the press: Michael Holmes
Type: Stan Bevington
Cover design: Tania Craan
Printing: Coach House Press on bpNichol Lane, Toronto

This book is set in CartierBook

The publication of *Young Hunting* has been generously supported by the Canada Council for
the Arts, which last year invested $20.1 million in writing and publishing throughout
Canada, by the Ontario Arts Council, by the Government of Ontario through Ontario Book
Publishing Tax Credit, by the OMDC Book Fund, an initiative of the Ontario Media
Development Corporation, and by the Government of Canada through the Book Publishing
Industry Development Program (BPIDP).

PRINTED AND BOUND IN CANADA

Canada Council   Conseil des Arts   Canadä   ONTARIO ARTS COUNCIL
for the Arts   du Canada   CONSEIL DES ARTS DE L'ONTARIO

ECW PRESS
ecwpress.com

CONTENTS

Acknowledgements

ACKNOWLEDGEMENTS

This memoir, like so many others, is based on memories filtered through the imagination of a storyteller. If I have distorted facts, my defence is, in the words of Blanche Dubois, "I tell what *ought* to be true."

This book is dedicated to the friends of my youth, some of them gone, but most of them alive and still kicking somewhat less vigorously against the pricks.

I am extremely grateful for the advice and encouragement I have received from early readers: Stan Bevington, Martin Boyne, Ramsay Derry, Dorothy Jane Needles, Susan Walker, and Jan Walter, and especially from my editor, Michael Holmes.

Must I ride to the East, must I ride to the West
Or anywhere under the sun
To get some good and clever doctor
For to cure this wounded man?

— "Young Hunting," Appalachian Folk Ballad

THE BOYS IN THE TOWER

It was a bright, sunny day in early September when, with a mixture of anticipation and trepidation, I made my way to Parliament Hill to begin my career
as a boy diplomat. I had a vague idea that I might be able to make some small
contribution toward a better world. At the same time I was very uncertain
about my ability to measure up to the high standards of the elite world I was
about to enter.

I was assigned a desk in the large, rather bleak room at the top of the tower
of the East Block. It already had another occupant. Jim, a grinning blond guy
with a California tan and an easygoing manner, greeted me with a sleepy smile
and suggested we go for a coffee. It became clear as we talked that neither Jim
nor I had much idea of what we were supposed to do, but we returned to our
desks to find our in-baskets laden with files, dispatches, and clippings that had
been delivered by Shirley, the *fille d'office*, a seventeen-year-old with straggly
brown hair and no front teeth. She was the only one of the four women in the
division's typing pool who was prepared to climb the two flights of stairs to our
attic office. Jim kidded her about her boyfriends. She blushed and beat a
retreat but a few days later she admitted she had gone out once or twice with
a guy she liked, but didn't know if he'd ask her out again.

After a day or two I was summoned to the office of Arthur Menzies, the
head of Far Eastern Division. He was a small slightly roly-poly figure with a
rather stern demeanour. He informed me that I was in charge of the Southeast
Asian desk and asked me to draft a report on the six countries that were apparently my territory: Thailand, Malaysia, Singapore, Indonesia, Myanmar, and
the Philippines. I returned to my office and told Jim about my assignment.

"Hell, that's not fair. I've only got two lousy countries, Laos and Cambodia."
At the time Canada was part of the International Joint Commission that had
been set up to bring some political stability to the three countries of Indochina
after the departure of the French. The other members of the commission were
Poland and India.

"Okay, but Canada has missions in your two countries and no missions in
my six."

"So why should we care what's going on in any of them?"

"That attitude isn't going to advance your career in this department, my friend."

"Yeah, well I'm not sure how much I care about that. Hey, I hear there are two women officers coming in next week. I can't wait."

"I don't imagine they've been picked for their looks."

"Hope springs eternal."

I knew nothing about Southeast Asia. I got out all the files on my six countries, read them and made notes. All of them seemed to be rife with insurrections and revolts; most of them had many parties whose leaders had unpronounceable names and unfathomable political goals. Except for Thailand and Singapore, which seemed relatively peaceful and prosperous. I set out to make an orderly analysis of the situation in each country in prose that was clear and simple but at the same time as elegant as I could make it.

Jim meanwhile skimmed the masses of telegrams from his two missions, wrote a brief précis of the ones he considered of any importance, and spent the rest of his time reading Kerouac and Camus. Jim had done a graduate degree in California and had mentally aligned himself with the beatniks. Born too early to be a hippie, he was blazing the trail they would follow.

The women arrived and were a pleasant surprise. Lois was attractive in a gangly sort of way. Louise was a real beauty with a splendid swanlike neck, deep blue eyes fringed with dark lashes, her abundant dark hair swept up in a French roll. Though born in the Gaspé she spoke impeccable English as well as French. She wore suits that suggested the hand of a good English tailor, but her style evoked the ambiance of the rue du Faubourg St. Honoré rather than Regent Street. Jim immediately made a play for her; her eyes spoke of her amusement, but her manner was evasive.

As the girls in the steno pool would not come up to the tower office Jim and I had to go downstairs to dictate to them. Jim started to produce more memos so that he could pop into Louise's office to make a few smart cracks. Occasionally she would agree to go the cafeteria for coffee with him but she usually sat with the francophones. Jim didn't give up on her but his invitations to dinner were always politely refused. "It's gonna take time, but she's worth it. Hell, there's no one else worth gunning for."

I completed my six-part essay and took it down to the typing pool. Mrs. Boyd, the chief stenographer, eyed me gloomily.

"I wondered what you were doing up there. I might have known you were going to pull a stunt like this. You realize I've only got two girls working for me and one of them is having a nervous breakdown. She's lucky to get in two days a week. She'd be fired if she wasn't the under-secretary's niece. I can't do it all myself. He keeps me busy eight hours a day."

She gestured with her head in the direction of Arthur Menzies' office. "I'll tell you what. I can do one of the six chapters. Which one is important? That is, assuming any of it's important."

"They're all important."

"Well, if you say so, Mr. Hunter. Okay. I'll guarantee you one chapter a week. How's that?"

"If that's the best you can do."

A week or so later Arthur Menzies met me in the hall. "How's that essay coming along?"

"Mrs. Boyd has it. She's working her way through it."

"Ah, well, no hurry. If you've finished that, why not write a dispatch to our embassy in Bangkok."

"We don't have an embassy in Bangkok."

"Of course not, but pretend we do." His blue eyes twinkled and he was gone. I went to the cafeteria and joined Jim. "I'm beginning to wonder what I'm doing here."

"You and me both. But the pay's good and the work isn't that hard. You want to come to Montreal this weekend?"

"I should stay here and read up some more on Indonesia."

"Brown-nose."

"Okay, what the hell, why not?"

I had learned that many of the senior officers came to work on Saturday morning. They dressed more informally and were more apt to be open to conversation with the juniors. And of course they noted which juniors showed up. I turned up perhaps two weekends a month and was soon on friendly terms with a number of my more seasoned colleagues.

As the weeks went by our group of new young officers began to have lectures from senior civil servants: Rasminsky from the Bank of Canada, Sharp from Trade and Commerce, and our own undersecretary Jules Leger. They were an impressive group. Their clothes bespoke an understated elegance but at the same time a slight shabbiness. Their diction was clear and distinct, often with a suggestion of an Oxford accent. They pronounced grandly on their various areas of expertise, choosing their words carefully and answering questions politely but with a slight air of amused condescension. They had, after all, seen so much more than we young sprats, keen and even promising though we might be. I could understand why they were referred to as mandarins.

One day Shirley came with the mail and lingered a little longer than usual. She moved her hand about and I saw that on her finger was a ring with a tiny diamond.

"Shirley, you're engaged. Congratulations."

"Naah. With my face nobody's never goin' to give me no ring. So I saved up my money and bought myself one." She started down the stairs.

"Poor kid," said Jim. "She should have spent her money on some front teeth."

But Shirley proved smarter than we. A few days later she came by and told us "Guess what? I really am engaged. Last night Dave said to me, 'Hey, Shirl, you got the ring. We might as well tie the knot.'" She resigned at the end of the month but came back two months later to show us her new front teeth. "Pretty nice, eh? Dave bought them for me for a wedding present. And I'm six weeks pregnant. How about that?"

"Shirley. You've got it all."

"That's right. Well, nice knowin' youse guys."

With Shirley gone, Mrs. Boyd decreed we had to fetch our own in-boxes when we arrived in the morning and bring them back downstairs before we left at night. She finally finished my essay. I corrected the considerable number of typos by hand and gave it to Menzies. A few days later I was summoned to his office. "This is really quite a respectable piece of work, Mr. Hunter. If we ever do establish embassies in any of these countries it will be a useful resource. You may know that the minister is going to Moscow in two weeks. The department has undertaken to brief him on every possible issue. I suggest that you boil each chapter down to half a page and we'll include it in the brief."

The whole department bent their efforts to covering every aspect of Canadian policy. I worked away assiduously and somehow Mrs. Boyd managed to get my précis typed up. "Would've made more sense if you'd done this cutdown version in the first place," she grumbled. A week later the entire department was assembled and Mike Pearson addressed us.

"As you know I will be the first Western foreign minister to have a meeting with Mr. Khrushchev. I am honoured and excited. And I am grateful that you have gone to so much trouble. But I must tell you that I will have precisely one hour alone with Mr. Krushchev and I know what I want to say. Thank you, gentlemen."

"Well," said Jim, "so much for briefing the minister. I'm off to Montreal. You coming?"

"Might as well. I'd rather not stay here and listen to the grousing."

In Montreal we went to a Saturday night party at my old fraternity house. We had several beers and while I shot the breeze with some of my old buddies, Jim danced with a girl and then disappeared for over an hour. When he came back he announced he had scored in a bedroom upstairs. We proceeded to go to a strip club where Jim tried to persuade one of the girls to meet him at a bar after her shift. While we waited for her we had more beer and eventually staggered uptown to Dominion Square where we spent the night on a park bench. The next morning we had breakfast in a coffee shop, which did not sober us up completely. We caught a late morning train back to Ottawa. I slept most of the way. Jim snoozed between belts from a mickey of rye. We parted company at the station in Ottawa.

I went back to my boarding house and went to bed but Jim apparently decided to call on Louise. He phoned her and she informed him she was going out and would not be back till late in the evening. Jim phoned again several hours later and discovered Louise had not gone out. She told him to stop bothering her and hung up. He then turned up at her apartment and hammered on the door — until it was opened by Louise, in her dressing gown. He pushed his way into her apartment. Louise called the police, who arrived to find Jim stumbling around Louise's apartment telling her he couldn't get her out of his thoughts. They took him away.

The next week Jim was summoned to Arthur Menzies' office and told he had been judged unsuitable material for the foreign service. Jim was neither disappointed nor apologetic. He told Menzies that he was relieved to learn they were in complete agreement. He climbed to the tower office for the last time, took a mickey of vodka out of one of the drawers in his desk and a handful of notes from another. "This whole thing is a farce."

"I think you have a talent for bringing out the farce in situations, Jim. Maybe you should be an actor."

"No, I think maybe I'll write an exposé."

"Good idea. Send me a copy."

"Sure. Well, thanks for sharing the laughs. Who knows when our paths may cross again?" But they never did.

In early May my father came to town on business; he had a branch office in Ottawa. He took me to dinner at the Château Laurier for my birthday and made a strong pitch for me to leave External and come into his business. Although my Trinity friends saw the foreign service as prestigious my father thought all civil servants were shiftless layabouts who sat around gossiping and drinking coffee on his hard-earned money as a taxpayer. He pointed out that ultimately I would make far more in business.

I think he was shocked that I was living in a boarding house eating stew or macaroni most nights and still wearing the rather threadbare tweed jackets I had sported at Trinity. But most of all he couldn't understand why I didn't own a car. I usually took the train for visits to Montreal or Toronto but for shorter junkets I hitchhiked. The fact was I had no interest in cars and had never even learned to drive. And I didn't want to be a businessman.

Father left town the next day without any commitment from me. He was an extremely determined man but he had learned how to play a waiting game. Well then, let him wait. I could be just as stubborn as he could. I still had some belief in the value of the work I was doing, or at least might be doing in the future in spite of the large element of travesty in my experience so far. I was pleased with myself. I had stood my ground. I only wished I had quoted the lines from a hymn Father had made me memorize when I was in Sunday school.

> Dare to be a Daniel.
> Dare to stand alone.
> Dare to have a purpose firm.
> Dare to make it known.

GOING DOWN HOME

When I tell people I remember the 1930s, they tend to conjure up images of breadlines and swing bands, of Fred Astaire, Charles Lindbergh, and Wallis Simpson. But for me the '30s meant the sweet crunch of biting into a McIntosh apple, the slightly sour taste of unpasteurized milk still warm from the cow, and coal oil lamps glowing in the late summer dusk. I associate these sensations with what my parents referred to as "going down home." Their families were farmers in the St. Lawrence valley near a little town called Cardinal, and they felt it was their duty to go from our house in Toronto to visit their relatives at least once a year. Duty was still a viable concept then. People did something because it was the right thing to do: they prided themselves on knowing the difference between right and wrong, and the payoff was moral rather than financial. Although when my father started to make money, I'm sure he believed it had something to do with the fact that he said his prayers every night, kneeling by the side of his bed. My parents had been brought up as "good Presbyterians." I never imagined there was any other kind; I never heard anybody talk about bad Presbyterians.

By the time I was born, my maternal grandparents were dead, so it was natural that we should go to stay with my father's parents. We drove in Father's Chevrolet, or Pontiac or Oldsmobile. As his financial situation improved, he worked his way up the General Motors ladder but stopped when he reached Buick; he considered Cadillacs ostentatious. My Hunter grandparents lived in a large house made of grey cinderblocks. It had a wide front porch painted dark green, where my grandparents could have sat and watched the world go by, but never did. They were too busy doing "the chores." Chores were the ordinary day-to-day variety and included pumping water, chopping kindling, scattering feed for the chickens, and trimming the wicks for the coal-oil lamps, all of which I learned to do by the time I was five years old. The house itself was ugly, but my grandmother contrived to hide its defects by covering it with vines: deep purple clematis, brilliant blue morning glory, and bright orange trumpet vine that climbed right up to the top of the chimney.

Both my grandparents were keen gardeners. My grandmother grew flowers: iris, bleeding heart, day lilies, and peonies. But her specialty was glad-

17

ioli. She had dozens of different varieties. She put the bulbs in the ground every spring and dug them up in the fall, laying them out in neat rows on the table in the summer kitchen. Each variety got wrapped in a square of muslin tied up with a bright scrap of material. The scrap told Grandma what variety of gladiolus was inside: the dotted pink Swiss was First Kiss, the striped blue gingham was Lady Aberdeen, the yellow cotton check was Flame of Hope. She never wrote any of this down. She had it committed to memory like the good schoolteacher she had been, along with chapters of scripture and hundreds of lines by Sir Walter Scott and Alfred, Lord Tennyson.

Grandma allowed herself one bouquet of gladioli in the parlour if she had visitors staying in her house. The rest went to decorate the church or to cheer the sick, although very occasionally Grandma would present some long-time friend with a bouquet for no reason except that she was a friend. She would get carefully dressed in a good dress with a hat and gloves and a big leather purse, and my father would drive her in his "smart city car." She sat up in the front seat with the gladioli in her arms, a bit like Queen Victoria riding out on her Golden Jubilee. Indeed a gift of gladioli from Grandma was recognized as a signal honour by those chosen few who received them, a recognition of merit, like the prize of a Bible at the end of the Sunday school term for memorizing the most lines of scripture.

My grandfather's province was fruit and vegetables. He grew every vegetable anybody in those days had ever heard of: asparagus and peas, corn and turnips, lettuce and onions, beans and squash, pumpkins and marrows, and even peppers; it was before the arrival of fennel and artichokes and arugula in Canada. He too had his specialties: tomatoes, which he grew from seed in little wooden boxes he set out on the windowsills all over the house in February. And apples. He had an orchard that covered several acres and produced a bewildering variety of fruit that he started to pick in late July when the first Tolman Sweets ripened. Then came Snows and Spies and McIntoshes for eating, Duchesses for pies, and finally russets, which would keep all through the winter.

My grandparents seemed to me even then to be a curiously ill-matched pair. They never sat down and talked together or went out anywhere as a couple. Even at church they were separated, he sitting with the Elders, she with her Sunday school class. They slept not just in separate rooms but on separate floors, she in her big mahogany bed upstairs, sending out rhythmic snores that reverberated through the house; he fitfully downstairs on a daybed, his head buried under many pillows to protect him from light and noise and the world in general. Though to me they were Grandpa and Grandma, they had names of course: Bertha and Than (short for Nathaniel), but nobody ever seemed to use them, certainly not my parents nor my brother and I, except on one memorable occasion I'll get to later.

Grandma was round and "squushy," with softly waving hair and waggling jowls. She was not exactly jolly but endlessly agreeable with children. I could sit on her knee and be read to pretty much whenever I wanted. Or lure her into her musty parlour to look through the stereopticon at three-dimensional sepia photographs of the Grand Canyon, Brooklyn Bridge, and San Francisco before the earthquake. Grandma would say, "When you grow up you'll go to places I've never even heard of," with real satisfaction and not even a hint of envy. She was obviously content to be where she was, totally in control of her garden, her kitchen, and her Sunday school class, and impervious to whatever lay beyond them.

Grandma made cookies, cakes, pies, and candies. She turned the old-fashioned ice-cream-making machine for hours and dipped chocolates by hand, setting them out in tidy rows on waxed paper. She had two stoves: a huge wood-burning one in the main kitchen and an elegant little coal-oil model in the summer kitchen. Both of them always had several dishes steaming away. She produced two big meals a day, often cooking a different dish for each individual in the family, whatever was their favourite: creamed onions for Grandpa; cauliflower for my father, who wouldn't eat onions; cucumbers in vinegar and brown sugar for my mother; fresh tomatoes for me, peeled because I was supposed to be allergic to the skins; and fresh corn for everyone, perhaps the new Golden Bantam that Grandpa had grown that year for the first time. And for dessert three kinds of pie: peach, apple, and her special combination of rhubarb and strawberry. But all this bounty carried with it an obligation. Since Grandma had gone to all this trouble we were expected to eat at least two helpings of everything. We got up from the table so stuffed we could hardly move. That was Grandma's reward. She would sit in her rocker after dinner for half an hour and beam at us while we belched or snoozed. Her gold-rimmed spectacles would sparkle with satisfaction as she knitted, darned, crocheted, and planned the next meal.

Grandpa was less agreeable; in fact he was sour and severe. He had been his mother's darling, the baby of a family of nine and an extremely handsome young man. It was hard for me to imagine this; by the time I knew him he was bald as an egg, painfully thin with a long gaunt face, and he walked on crutches. About five years after he married, he experienced what would later be called a nervous breakdown. He couldn't work any more, he didn't want to talk to anyone, and he wouldn't even walk. My grandmother's family came to visit and told her she was a fool to put up with my grandfather's nonsense. She sent them packing. She knew her duty: she had to bring up her three children and look after her ailing husband. Her fate didn't depress her; she radiated fulfillment even as Grandpa became more and more morose. He, not Grandma, felt cheated and betrayed by life.

Grandpa had wanted to be a Presbyterian minister, but he stayed at home to look after his mother, the formidable Elizabeth Martin, who was lame, cranky, and demanding. She approved of young Bertha Miller, who she felt would be good for Than, helping him run the family's prized 300-acre farm along the lines that she had laid down. (Grandpa's two older brothers had taken off at an early age for the West.) When she died, Grandma stepped deftly into her shoes. I see now that my grandfather felt trapped; his inability to walk was his way of expressing this. Significantly, when Grandma died he threw away his crutches and walked unaided for the last five years of his life, even though he was over seventy by then and had functioned as a cripple for forty years. Like me, Grandpa had allergies. His hands were covered with raw sores and were often bandaged; eventually he had one of his thumbs removed. He saw our common medical problems as a bond and was curious to know what my fashionable Toronto doctors had prescribed for me. Once he told me I must understand that with my tainted heredity I couldn't possibly think of getting married and having children. (I was perhaps seven at the time, and not much concerned with continuing the Hunter line.)

One of his most irritating habits was what he called "asking the blessing." This was a long prayer before meals, sometimes ten or fifteen minutes, and included scraps of scripture and Robert Service, his favourite poet, admonitions to various people seated around the table, and fervent pleas for certain specific kinds of weather. Weather is vital to the vegetable gardener. Grandpa would tell me, "You need hot nights for beans," or "One more day of the drouth and it's all up with the Bonnie Bests." No matter what the weather brings, it's bad for something, so vegetable gardeners never stop complaining.

This made gardening a perfect occupation for someone with Grandpa's temperament and gave him endless material for his discourse with the Almighty. Meanwhile the plates of food in front of us went from warm to tepid and sometimes stone cold as we waited for the wind-up, "Lord bless this food to our use and us to thy service. Amen." Eventually I realized that this performance was aimed at Grandma. He had figured out how to more or less ruin her meals in the name of piety.

Grandpa had one other major way of breaking out. Two or three times a week he would drive into town in his ancient model T, the back seat laden with vegetables from his garden, neatly organized in six-quart baskets. Sometimes I was allowed to go with him and I marvelled at how once he got behind the wheel he seemed almost a different person. He wore a formal grey suit coat and a clean grey felt fedora rather than the holey woolen sweater and dilapidated straw he affected at home. He looked prosperous and his mood was confident. Not that he was a good driver. He never went more nor less than twenty miles an hour and he never stopped for anything. Cars swerved and skidded to get out of his way. He drove into Cardinal over a swing bridge across the canal, and local legend had it that more than once they had started to turn the bridge when they saw Grandpa coming and quickly reversed so that he could sail over it unscathed instead of plunging into the canal.

Grandpa had a number of properties in town and he sold vegetables to his tenants; I think it must have been written into their leases that they had to buy from him. In any case his tenants treated him with respect, and he doled out his beans, tomatoes, and corn like so much largesse, even though he was getting the going price. At the end of the transactions he would count his money with satisfaction and put it carefully into a little leather change-purse. He usually bought me an ice-cream cone and sometimes even gave me an extra dime to save for a special treat. On the way home he sang hymns, not glum dirges but upbeat tunes: "Praise My Soul, the King of Heaven" or "Crown Him with Many Crowns." He had a light baritone and a good sense of pitch. It was a pleasure to hear him, almost the only pleasant memory I associate with him.

When we went to stay with my grandparents, the main activity of the grown-ups was "having a good visit." As males my brother Bill and I were excluded from this activity in the daytime when the women gathered in the kitchen, Grandma imparting to my mother the secrets of pickling, preserving, and, above all, baking. My grandmother had carefully guarded recipes for special cakes and cookies, but the ultimate activity was making pie crust. This was a skill that could be mastered only by years of practice. Under my grandmother's tutelage my mother gradually became an acknowledged master of the art. (She would later teach my wife to make incredibly light and flaky pie crust, one of the very few activities they shared.) My mother was eventually allowed to bake the pies when we went to Cardinal, and this gave her precedence in the family hierarchy, rather like the Princess of Wales being the only one allowed to wear certain royal jewels. Had she wished, she could have, to use her phrase, "queened it over" my father's sister Gladys and his younger brother's wife Gwen, but my mother didn't exercise this privilege. She wasn't interested in that kind of power.

She did like to "visit," however, especially in the evenings after dinner when the whole family sat around the table after my brother and I had been sent up to bed and conversation could include topics "not suitable for young ears." Bill and I heard it all anyway; it came up from below through the round hole in the floor meant for the stovepipe. We collected endless bits of information from sentences that ran something like this: "You mind Nellie Thatcher who lived down by the creek? Wasn't her father your uncle on your mother's side? Anyway poor Nellie's got the TB and they've taken her away, most likely for good." Or "Your Aunt Cora has plumb refused to live with your Uncle George. Got her own place in town. Isn't that a caution?" In Toronto this would have been called gossip, but "visiting" was different. Primarily I think it was a question of tone: gossip involved a certain malicious relish, while information exchanged during a "visit" was always accompanied by expressions of commiseration with those who had veered off the path of rectitude, and even more with the remaining members of the aggrieved families who had to carry on along the straight road of virtue on their own.

Sometimes when we visited my grandparents, the party included Aunt Gwen, the wife of my father's younger brother, Merritt. She had huge china-blue eyes and yellow hair, which she "helped" with peroxide. She made jokes about the family and tried to "tease" Grandpa about his prayers and his driving. She wasn't interested in cooking and gave as an excuse the fact that she didn't want to ruin her nails. She didn't want to sit and visit of an evening; she wanted to drive up to town to see my father's rambunctious cousin Min Gooderich, the family's acknowledged "wild Indian." (But then Min was an only child and had lost her mother at the age of ten, so there was some excuse for her, as they said.)

Gwen was sure my mother would rather have done this too, and she was right. But Mother sensed there would be a moral payoff if she helped wash the dishes and then sat and listened while Grandma expressed concern about the sad state of cousin Olive who'd been told she couldn't have children and was thinking of adopting, or planned what gladioli she should cut for her old friend Maggie Jim Riddle's husband's funeral — Golden Dawn certainly, but would it look better combined with Love's Whisper or Second Chance? They were going to play "O Promise Me" at the funeral instead of "Abide with Me" because Maggie Jim said they'd played it at her wedding and it would remind her of Jim Riddle at his best, which my grandmother thought was "downright *odd*."

Meanwhile Gwen and Merritt were off to town and likely wouldn't be home till all hours, maybe as late as nine-thirty or ten o'clock, creeping up the golden-oak staircase in their stocking feet. My grandmother suspected that Gwen and Merritt and Cousin Min and her handsome husband would be having a drink. I knew my parents drank too, "socially" at parties. My father had even had hangovers once or twice, but he could never mention this to Grandma and Grandpa. Father knew how to keep his own counsel. "Visiting" was all very well but there were certain things that were not to be spoken of.

That was another thing that darkened Gwen's already tarnished image in the eyes of the Hunters. She talked about things that weren't supposed to be talked about — especially sex, which only showed she couldn't keep her mind off it. Once my grandmother had walked into Gwen and Merritt's room at nine in the morning to see if they were sick, as they were so late coming down for breakfast, and there they were, "at it." At nine o'clock in the morning. If Gwen was so keen on sex then where were her children? Gwen never actually said she didn't want children, but she never said she did either. I expect what she didn't want was my grandmother's pity. And my grandmother did pity her, most of all because of her misguided sense of values. Gwen liked to enjoy herself; she put having a good time ahead of everything else and that was her real sin in the eyes of my grandmother. When Merritt and Gwen came to stay, the embroidered pillow shams on their bed said:

I slept and dreamt that Life was Beauty.

I woke and found that Life was Duty.

But Gwen apparently didn't get it. Or maybe she just didn't want to.

If Gwen was a frank and unrepentant hedonist, my father's sister Gladys was a more complicated case. She had large, dark, luminous brown eyes and an air of sensitivity, but she was not totally repressed. She enjoyed a good time, wore smart clothes, read racy historical novels like *Anthony Adverse* and *Gone with the Wind* and played the Hawaiian guitar. Like Grandma she was ambitious and competent: she knitted, dipped chocolates, and taught a Sunday school class. She also made her own clothes and her own Christmas presents, even though she had full-time work, a very good job for a woman in those days, with Shell Oil.

Because Gladys often worked overtime and had a social life (she played bridge with "the girls" every other Thursday, gave showers for her friends, and went dancing with her beaux on the weekend), she never quite managed to get anything done on time. She would be still frantically sewing her dress half an hour before a wedding while my father became increasingly thin-lipped and my mother snickered at his impatience. A typical birthday gift from Aunt Gladys would be half a sock with the needles still in it and a note promising to have the pair finished by the end of the week after next.

Gladys had Grandpa's nervous energy and sensitivity along with Grandma's capability and ambition, but not her staying power. To please Grandma she had qualified as a teacher, but she didn't enjoy it. She had my father's arithmetical mind and she enjoyed the pace and intrigue of business. She gave up her good job, even though she knew that in the depression she had little hope of ever getting it back, when my mother had a nervous breakdown after my brother Bill was born. Gladys recognized that it was her duty to look after my father and his two sons. She moved into our house and Mother moved into Homewood.

During the two years she lived with us, Aunt Gladys encouraged me to read books my parents had never heard of and to listen to music I would never have discovered on my own, at least not until years later. She encouraged what she thought of as my artistic tendencies. She played her guitar and sang to me, took me to movies, and read what she considered suitable books: *The Scarlet Pimpernel* and *The Three Musketeers*, both of which were somewhat over my head but whetted my appetite for romance. She was not an intellectual, but she was the closest thing to an artist in my family and I responded positively to her encouragement. On the downside she could be irritable and curt. There was mutual respect between Gladys and my father, but he expected a good deal in the way of meticulous housekeeping and uncomplaining patience when he arrived home for dinner an hour late and then spent the entire evening working on his accounts. She was used to running her own show, not accommodating a man, and I think periodically she said so, although she must have known my father did not take any sort of criticism easily.

The Hunters were Scots and proud of it. "Good Scots stock," as Gladys liked to say. The Martins were also Scots and had come from Edinburgh, which apparently gave them a certain cachet; the Hunters were only country people from somewhere in Ayrshire. Grandma Hunter's family was Irish, though nobody ever mentioned it and I didn't realize it till long after she was dead. I think she considered herself a sort of honorary Scot. My mother's family, on the other hand, were openly and unabashedly Irish and this put them a few rungs down the ladder as such things were reckoned in Cardinal. I suppose at the top of the hierarchy there must have been a few English families who were Anglicans and received remittances from across the water, but I never heard about any of them. As far as I was aware the Scots were top dogs and the Irish were maybe more like cats, not totally reliable but allowed to live in the barn to keep down the mice.

These observations are coloured by sixty-some years of hindsight and analysis. When I went "down home" with my parents I was aware only that the two sides of my family aroused in me very different feelings and responses. My father's family were stable and secure but stern and forbidding. My mother's family were erratic and unpredictable and totally unashamed of it. They believed in having fun and they wanted my brother and me to have fun as well. They too loved to "visit," but whereas the Hunters cooked and weeded and knitted while they visited, the Byers clan dropped whatever they were doing and gave you their wholehearted attention. It was as though they'd been waiting all year for this moment. They called the neighbours on the telephone and asked them over. They set out pitchers of fruit juice and plates of cookies. They sat on their front porches and heehawed and shook their heads if you cracked a joke. And they entertained you with a show of their own.

All of my mother's four brothers were clowns. Their common skill was mimicry. They had routines they worked on and went into the minute they found any sort of audience. My brother and I loved to sit and watch their antics, not because we understood the content but because the performances were so energetic they were irresistible. They were funny even if you didn't know who or what they were talking about. A full appreciation of the Byers brothers' art depended on knowing the large cast of family characters who were being imitated, many of whom were dead long before we arrived on the scene.

There was Aunt Marth, who came to visit unexpectedly with her dull-witted daughter Verie, claiming to have written ahead, shaking her head and saying, "What's the matter with them Canadian mails anyways," and then insisting everyone sit and listen while Verie played on the piano "one of them famous classics from over to Europe there they call 'The Dance of the Elves.'" There was Uncle Pheme, whose farming efforts always ended in disaster; he once planted an acre of strawberries and harvested only one six-quart basket, exclaiming, "I figure they musta been all he-berries." There was Aunt Annie Holmes, who travelled around without a suitcase, wearing five dresses, one over the other, and three pairs of spectacles, none of which were any use as she was virtually blind. She once sat down on a cat and when she got up it was stone dead. "Poor little thing, it shoulda been more cautious where it set itself down." This may not seem like promising material, but the Byers brothers wrung laughs out of it for decades. Two of them lived to be over ninety and they were still sending up their long-dead kin for the benefit of anyone who would listen.

My mother's second brother, Uncle Earl, was the family bad boy and the most colourful of the lot. He ran away from home at the age of fifteen and reportedly went to Hollywood where he became a friend of Charlie Chaplin. Eventually he returned to Cardinal and married Hilda. They had three sons, the oldest of whom was a cripple and died young for reasons that remained shrouded in mystery. As a result, Hilda became what the family called "a religious maniac." The two surviving sons staked out rival territories. Earl Jr. was a truant and a heavy drinker who acquired a certain local fame as a barroom scrapper. While still in his teens, he married a girl whom he always called "Frenchie." (No doubt she had a proper Christian name but I never learned it.) With her Earl Jr. sired six children. Bobbie, the younger brother, was something of a mama's boy and a teacher's pet; he eventually became a school principal.

We almost never saw Earl Sr. at home; nobody wanted to listen to Aunt Hilda go on about doom and damnation. Instead we visited Earl at work, driving out to the Cardinal train station about a mile out of town. He was the engineer on a locomotive that ran supplies back and forth to Cardinal's major industry, the Canada Corn Starch Company. My brother and I would climb aboard the open cab and be greeted by Earl, black with soot and smiling broadly. He would perform as he took us on a run into town, though we couldn't hear a word over the noise of the churning wheels. In our honour he revved up the engine to its top speed and tooted his whistle as we approached the climax, a full-out run across the iron bridge into town. Every girder rattled and seemed about to shake loose as we looked out over the edge into the canal, which appeared to be as far down below us as the Colorado at the base of the Grand Canyon viewed through Grandma's stereopticon. We were still gripping the rail in terror when Uncle Earl, laughing like a madman, handed us down into the waiting arms of our parents. Our terror, though we didn't know it, was completely justified. Earl always waited till the last minute to toot his whistle. Had the bridge been swung as we approached we might easily have gone crashing down to a watery doom. They couldn't possibly have swung it back in time, nor could Earl have stopped the engine at the speed he was driving. He was a daredevil and loved to take chances. Almost miraculously, although he ran the locomotive for twenty years, he died peacefully in his bed of a heart attack.

Another popular figure with my brother Bill and me was my Uncle George Montgomery, who was married to my mother's eldest sister Aunt Lula. George too was a cut-up; whether he'd learned his tricks from the Byers brothers or joined the clan out of a certain natural affinity I don't know. He didn't look like them, being tall and gangly like some marsh bird, a bittern maybe or a great blue heron, but he knew all the stories and could do all the characters. A sort of honorary Byers brother, he was a particular favourite of my father, who enjoyed no such status with the Byers clan. They respected my father's financial acumen but considered him a dull stick. Occasionally he tried to tell one of the family stories but he had no gift for it. He couldn't imagine what it was like to be anyone else; he could only be himself. So he sat and laughed at the antics of his brothers-in-law sometimes till tears came to his eyes. Deep down I think he hankered to connect with their caustic, chaotic spirit, but he just couldn't manage it.

I suppose it was this impulse toward the intuitive and spontaneous, the zany and uncontrolled, indeed everything that he wasn't, that had attracted my father to my mother. She and her sisters also were mimics and they did their own variations on the stories. They didn't, however, compete with the men. My grandmother Byers had given her sons preferential treatment, and her girls were inculcated with the notion that men had to be cooked for, house kept for, and, as my mother would have put it, "catered to." As a twin with a sickly brother in the middle of a family of nine, Mother had claimed very little attention from her mother and sometimes said that she had been brought up by her father, who had died when she was eleven. She went to work when she was fifteen, saving up enough money to put her two younger sisters, Bessie and Effie, through high school, before all three of them were trained as nurses by the grey nuns across the St. Lawrence River in Ogdensburg, New York.

Mother had done her part to help her sisters; that was part of her family's understanding of familial duty, though it didn't square easily with her rather volatile personality. She was fond of her sisters but often told them off. They all had sharp tongues and didn't spare each other's feelings once they got going. The Byers brothers and sisters were funny; that was their distinguishing talent, but their humour was based largely on other people's inadequacies and misfortunes. They were observant, but they could also be mean. Whoever was not present was lampooned mercilessly. Indeed, anything or anybody was fair game if it got a laugh. Except of course for religion — or sex. The first was avoided less out of reverence than from a superstitious fear of retribution, the second not because of moral compunctions but out of a prurience also based in fear. None of the Byers family ever got "into trouble." They could be reckless when it came to hurting people's feelings, but they didn't have the type of bravado that indulges in erotic or emotional abandon. Even the Hunters were more openly demonstrative than the Byers family. But then the Hunters had confidence rooted in their consciousness of virtue and their position in the community, which was less grounded in their social or material status than in ethical probity. They knew what was right and they did it.

When we visited our Byers relatives we played with our cousins, swam in the creek, hunted birds' nests, or helped bring the cows home. At our Hunter grandparents' house we were sent out by ourselves to play. On one of these occasions, in the old carriage shed where Grandpa stored his apples, we sampled every variety set out in bins and were eventually sick to our stomachs.

We were scolded for our foolishness, but an appetite for food was understandable so we were not severely punished, merely put to bed in Grandma's best guest bedroom where all the furniture was painted mauve. She brought us porridge, specially prepared cream of wheat, to settle our stomachs, and indeed it did combat our incipient diarrhea. My brother was soon asleep, but I lay awake long into the night, worried that when he gritted his teeth he might be going to have some kind of seizure. To take my mind off this frightening possibility I would count the number of cars of the freight trains as their wheels hit a join in the track somewhere out in the vast darkness. Even then, a part of me wished I were on one of those trains speeding away from my family to unimaginable adventures. I loved my family, but from a very early age I wanted to get away from them and their expectations — expectations that I instinctively knew I would never be able to fulfill.

On rainy days our favourite pastime was exploring the storage room in Grandma's attic. There we found the strap she had used on her pupils when she was a primary school teacher before she was married. We took it down to show her. She smiled ruefully as she looked at it. It was hard for us to imagine her putting it to use, but she said yes, she had strapped even the biggest boys when they were bad. "Spare the rod": her generous mouth took on a formidable firmness that underlined her kinship with my father. Years later I would sometimes look at him and see Grandma: the determination, the certainty of knowing what was right and believing that by sheer force of will this right could be made to prevail. Eventually my father turned into Grandma. He even looked like her, only of course he didn't wear a dress.

A few days after we discovered the strap, we were in the storage room rummaging through bags of Grandma's discarded bloomers and corsets. We forced the lock on the big trunk that contained her wedding clothes, a cloche hat decorated with silk violets, crocheted lace, old letters, pressed flowers, and scented gloves. We found a portfolio of drawings that Grandma must have done in high school, and with it a pencil box containing rusted steel pens and a bottle of India ink. The ink had dried up, but we put some water in it and tried writing with the rusty pens, predictably spilling ink on the drawings, the lace, and the ancient kid gloves. When Father found us we were trying to clean up the mess we had made and only making it worse. I was wearing a pair of bloomers and Bill was wearing the cloche hat. My father took Grandma's strap and gave us ten sharp smacks on each palm. Grandma continued to cry as she watched, but she didn't move to stop him. This punishment seemed so successful to my father that he took the strap back to Toronto and used it on us with gradually diminishing effect until we were in our teens, by which time it was evident that withholding our allowances or confining us to the house on Saturday nights were infinitely more effective punishments.

Our adventure in the storage room did lead to an event in which Bill and I managed to crack the citadel of Hunter rectitude through the application of Byers mockery. The occasion was my grandparents' fortieth wedding anniversary, which occurred just after Christmas. It must have been 1941. We were all going to Cardinal for the holiday, the four of us and Aunt Gladys in my father's Oldsmobile. Uncle Merritt and Aunt Gwen were driving up from Montreal. There had been much talk about suitable gifts. Gladys was knitting an angora bed-jacket for Grandma, the fluff getting up her nostrils until she thought she'd go mad, and argyle-patterned gloves for Grandpa, only seven more fingers to go. Father had bought Grandma a handsome cameo at Birks, and for Grandpa a gold tie pin. He and Mother had an argument over whether Grandpa ever wore a tie and father said of course he wore a tie for funerals. But what were we kids supposed to give them?

Mother had a brainwave. She tried the idea out on Aunt Gladys and gained her support before telling Father, but he was not enthusiastic. He didn't like the idea of my dressing up, which I was too prone to do anyway. And what if my grandparents took it the wrong way? The three of them hashed it out over a Sunday dinner at our house which was also a rehearsal for the anniversary dinner they were going to make two weeks later in Cardinal: French-Canadian-style pea soup; roast beef with gravy, chili sauce and Lady Ross pickles; scalloped potatoes (one of Aunt Gladys's specialties), combined peas and carrots; and pumpkin and cranberry pies, topped with whipped cream. Aunt Gwen would be allowed to pass around a pound of "Lauras" (Laura Secord chocolates) after dinner.

My father held out until dessert but, sated with pumpkin pie, he wavered, and Gladys prevailed by pointing out it was something we boys could do ourselves, preferable in Grandma's eyes to our buying something with money he doled out to us. We retired to the living room to begin rehearsals, Aunt Gladys at the piano and Mother coaching us. The event was only two weeks away; there was no time to lose. My mother had no theatrical experience. She simply did her imitations of Grandma wrinkling her nose, and Grandpa asking the blessing or looking down at us over his glasses, and we copied them. We worked hard over the next two weeks. Mother was not easily satisfied but we wanted to please her, especially when she bribed us with icebox cookies. On the Saturday before Christmas we all piled into the car in coats, scarves, and galoshes because the heater was erratic. Wrapped presents were piled all around us, most of which would be unwrapped in Cardinal and brought back home again. Aunt Gladys was knitting fingers in the backseat as we set out.

The Christmas feast was sumptuous. It was finished off with mince pie, butter tarts, and four kinds of Christmas cake. Even Aunt Gwen had made one: a bit doughy but at least she'd made an effort. There was a tradition that each piece of Christmas cake made by somebody different eaten between Christmas and New Year's brought one month of good luck in the coming year, so as Aunt Gladys observed, we were off to a good start. Only eight more cakes to go. The Christmas presents were on the whole a success. I received a chemistry set (perhaps to whet my parents' ambition for me to be a doctor; in any case it was to be the source of serious trouble when I did an experiment that permanently blackened the walls of the recreation room and filled our entire house with smoke, but that lay in the future). Bill got a tricycle, which my father had somehow managed to conceal in the trunk without either of us knowing. Mother got a black Persian lamb jacket. (As soon as we got home she took it back and changed it for another one.) Aunt Gladys got gold earrings that had belonged to my great-grandmother Miller and cried as she put them on.

The next day was Gladys's birthday. Another big meal with another cake, but this one was a sponge cake so it didn't count as one of the twelve. We'd been up to town in the afternoon to see relatives, so the count was now at seven, and Aunt Hattie had sent some of her cake over from Ogdensburg with Cousin Marion. We could have a small piece before we went to bed. It was American cake but it still counted. The next day was not a special day in the Hunter calendar, so we went to visit Aunt Lula and Uncle George: another huge meal with turkey pie and four-coloured jello pudding and three more kinds of cake. Aunt Lula's mother-in-law had made a cake of her own: a dark cake, suspiciously smelling of liquor, but then her family were English. Eleven down, one to go.

The next day was the big day. Grandma was banned from the kitchen. She sat in the parlour in her good dress, the cameo pinned to her bosom, and read to us from *The Idylls of the King* before the minister came to call and take tea. He prayed with Grandpa, who was wearing a tie at Father's suggestion so he could show off his new tie pin. The minister had never heard of the cake superstition but gallantly ate a piece of each kind offered, including Aunt Hattie's. Then Grandma's old friend Etta from the Women's Missionary Society arrived with a substantial slab of her cake, so that made up our twelve. Aunt Gladys produced her shortbread, which was pronounced to be the shortest anyone had ever eaten, surpassing even Grandma's, which was renowned all the way to Brockville. Grandma generously congratulated Gladys on her culinary skill.

Then it was time for our contribution. The whole family was seated on the uncomfortable Victorian chairs and sofa of the front parlour, except for Aunt Gladys who took up her post at the piano. She played a medley of songs she'd learned to please her parents — "In the Good Old Summertime," "Shine on Harvest Moon," "After the Ball Is Over" — before launching into the verse of "Daisy Bell" or "A Bicycle Built for Two." As Bill and I came down the staircase and rounded the golden oak newel post, all the Hunter eyes were on us. I was first, wearing plus fours, made by stuffing the legs of my trousers into long socks, Grandpa's white linen wedding vest and his grey fedora. Bill wore a pair of Grandma's bloomers and her cloche hat. Mother had supervised these costumes upstairs in the trunk room and had even stolen a pair of Grandpa's old spectacles to perch on the end of my nose. I carried a set of handlebars and mimed the act of bicycling; Bill rode his tricycle behind me. We circled the front parlour once, narrowly avoiding running over someone's toes. Then we began to belt out the lyrics:

> Bertha, Bertha, give me your answer, do
> I'm half crazy, all for the love of you

Lascivious eye rolling on my part as Bill tried not to giggle. Guffaws from Aunt Gwen.

> It won't be a stylish marriage
> For we can't afford a carriage
> But you'll look sweet
> Upon the seat
> Of a bicycle built for two.

We circled the parlour once more as Aunt Gladys rolled out the chords of the chorus and indulged in some flashy arpeggios. I turned to see how the audience was reacting and Bill remembered his line:

"Than, keep your mind on the road."
"O Bertha, you know I can't keep my mind on anything but you."

These lines devised by Mother and Gladys were corny, but it was a wedding anniversary after all. Then I had an inspiration.

"Bertha, before we go on, I'll just ask the blessing."

I looked out over my glasses and intoned unctuously.

"O Lord, bless this vehicle to our use and us to thy service. Amen."

We wheeled around the newel post and made our exit, stopping on the stairs to peer out between the pilasters of the railing. There was clapping; but more than that, there was laughter. Mother was smiling with satisfaction; my father was chortling, barely making any effort to control his mirth; Uncle Merritt's face was wrinkled up like a chimpanzee's; Aunt Gladys was giggling; Aunt Gwen was practically braying. In the middle sat my grandparents on their straight-backed horsehair sofa. Both of them had tears rolling down their cheeks. Grandma's jowls were shaking and her nose was wrinkled up with pleasure as she dabbed at it with a lace hankie. Grandpa grinned broadly, twitching like a grasshopper as he tried to control himself. In his confusion he actually grabbed Grandma's hand and squeezed it. So unexpected was their pleasure it was almost like an evening with the Byers family.

I wonder now if my mother saw this event as some kind of breakthrough. If so, she was to be disappointed. I don't remember another occasion when the Hunters all got together and really laughed. They're all gone now, even Uncle Merritt, who reached the age of ninety-two. The easygoing one, he lasted longest. He remained amiable; it was hard to tell him a joke in his later years because he couldn't hear it, but he laughed anyway. As for my brother Bill and me, we've gone our separate ways but we still get together and talk about the two families and wonder where the various attributes of our children come from. My son, Ben, is a mimic like his Byers uncles; Bill's daughter, Elizabeth, has her Grandmother Hunter's precision and methodical ways; my daughter, Sarah, has my father's determination. And both girls look rather like Aunt Gladys.

And so the weaving of the family mythology goes on: some threads cut, new ones introduced, the patterns repeated with variations into the dimly discernible future. Bill and I watch to see how it will turn out. Like good Hunters we husband our assets and plan for the future, trying to do our duty for the good of the clan. We look on at accomplishments and mishaps, goals achieved, ambitions abandoned. And the Byers spirit within us can't help having a good laugh.

THE REBELS OF GOLFDALE ROAD

I first met Dick Williams playing in a puddle in a vacant lot a few days after we moved to Golfdale Road. We were five years old. We splashed around in the mud together, and eventually the water ran over the top and down inside our rubber boots, giving us what was called, and still is, a "soaker." I knew I should have gone home, but when Dick asked me to go to his house, I readily agreed. We went around to the side door and climbed the four steps up to the kitchen where his mother was laying out cookies on a sheet. She got us to take off our socks and boots, which she put on the radiator to dry, gave us milk and her freshly baked cookies and let us go up to Dick's room to play with his electric train.

Even at that young age, I think I recognized that Dick's mother was a beauty, with her dark hair parted in the middle and caught up at the nape of her long, graceful neck, ballerina-style, and her wide slanting eyes, which gave her an exotic, slightly Oriental look. Later I would hear her compared to Wendy Hiller, and she did indeed share with the famous actress an almost elfin appearance, although Kay Williams' ethereal sensibility was tempered by a wide range of practical skills and an enormous capacity for hard work. At the same time she was highly intuitive and even knew how to read palms. She predicted for me a long and colourful life full of changes. When I later went back to her for more details, she told me she had one day divined that one of her friends was soon to die. She didn't tell him, but he was found murdered a week later. She never practised this black art again.

Dick had the same large, slanting eyes and the same pixyish look as his mother. In fact Kay's whole family, the Bells, had it. They were six siblings, the sons and daughters of an English carpenter who worked till he reached a ripe old age in a shop at the back of his house on Dufferin Street. He instilled in his children a respect for craftsmanship, which they applied to various fields, most of them arts-related. The best known was Kay's brother, Ken Bell, who became a celebrated photographer, perhaps best known for his work as a war artist. The Bells were industrious, ingenious, and long-lived; when I went to Kay's funeral (she was ninety-three), four of her siblings had survived her. Dick would prove to be equally meticulous and painstaking in his work, demanding of others but even more so of himself, as I would learn over the eight years in which we were schoolfellows and increasingly close friends. At one point that October afternoon, I must have gone to the bathroom, passing Kay's workroom. She was sitting at her drawing board, outlining the figure of a stylish matron wearing one of those fanciful hats that women sported in the '30s. I learned that Kay was a commercial artist who worked at home, creating advertisements and illustrations for magazines. I had never before encountered a real, working artist.

When I went home at suppertime, my mother interrogated me with a mixture of curiosity and disapproval. What would this neighbour think of my upbringing if I didn't know enough to come home with my dirty socks and muddy boots? Dick should have known better than to invite me to his house. Worse still, it was a grave breach of suburban etiquette to go to the bathroom in the house of a stranger. My praise of Dick's mother, far from deflecting my mother's annoyance, increased it. Perhaps there was a tinge of jealousy when I said how good Mrs. Williams' cookies tasted. (My mother was justly proud of her own culinary skills.) But more than anything she was intensely suspicious of a married woman who worked for money, even if she did it in the privacy of her own home. It was during the Great Depression, and middle-class women were not supposed to compete in the working world with men who needed to support their families. The seeds of suspicion were sewn in my mother's mind, and from that day on she never wholly approved of Dick or his mother, though she came to regard them both with a sort of grudging admiration.

In fact, I think my mother envied Kay Williams more than anything. Mother had been a nurse and resented giving up her profession when she married, although she wouldn't have admitted it. She wasn't a beauty like Kay, but she was stylish, interested in clothes and cooking, though not really at ease in urban society. She missed having an independent income and she missed having patients who depended on her. When I was young she tried to turn me into her patient, using my allergies to convince me I was sickly and needed her ministrations. It worked for a while, because I enjoyed the attention. And it shielded me from some of the minor brutalities of Golfdale Road.

Golfdale Road was to be my home until I escaped into the navy and university thirteen years later. It was a curious little world, peopled by more or less successful businessmen and their wives. All of these people were what would now be called upwardly mobile; they'd grown up on farms or in small towns, had finished high school and come to the city to get ahead. They were eager to absorb city ways as best they could — learning to drink cocktails and play bridge — but solid country values of thrift, hard work, and moderation underlay their newly acquired sophistication. And a good deal of deep-seated suspicion. They knew they didn't quite belong, and they eyed each other warily. The women visited each other's houses for lunch or card parties and checked out the furnishings, the food, the housekeeping — and then compared notes. They competed as cooks and house decorators; the men competed as handymen and gardeners. Their houses had over-decorated living and dining rooms that were not in daily use. They were fronted by beautifully manicured lawns, and once the war started there were "victory gardens" of vegetables, carrots, beans, and tomatoes in the back.

Dick and I were a bare six weeks apart in age. Our closest young neighbour, Ted, was about six months older. Where Dick and I were skinny and nervous, Ted was stocky and phlegmatic. He would prove to be a natural athlete, though not much of a scholar. Ted's mother and father were the most aggressive of the three sets of parents. Aus (short for Austin) was loud, red-faced, and a bit of a bully; Babe was blond, buxom, and a committed busybody. Reportedly she sat on her upstairs toilet peering out the window through a pair of binoculars and observing the comings and goings of the neighbours. She and my mother often spent an hour talking on the phone together in what was supposed to be their afternoon "rest." They certainly exchanged more than recipes.

Mother distrusted Dick from the beginning, but they shared a sharp sense of humour. Dick could make Mother laugh, and she enjoyed his quick intelligence and outrageous imitations. Babe, however, saw Dick as a threat. I was no good at sports and therefore was no competition for Ted, but Dick could catch a baseball as readily as he could come up with a smart retort. He was fast on his feet and utterly contemptuous of authority. He made fun of Babe and her Pekinese dog, Tootsie, sometimes to her face, but he sassed her once too often. She once picked him up and shook him like a dishrag while the rest of us looked on. Dick never forgot this public humiliation and awaited his chance to wreak revenge.

During our public school days, Ted, Dick, and I habitually walked the half mile to the school together, home and back again at lunchtime, and back home at three thirty. We played various games along the way: tag or follow-the-leader in the fall, snowball fights and slides on the ice in the winter, and "alleys" (marbles) in the spring. When my brother Bill was old enough he tagged along with us. One day he fell in a puddle and I took him home to change his clothes. This charitable act received so much commendation that the next day I pushed him into a puddle. So much for brotherly love.

Inevitably Dick, Ted, and I had quarrels, scraps, and sometimes outright fights. For a week or so, two of us would gang up on the other one, then our allegiances would shift. This went on for several years, encouraged no doubt by the bombardment of news of the Second World War that was beamed at us in the classroom, from the pulpit, and on the radio. We played war games on the way to and from school, hiding in the bushes and suddenly leaping out, firing imaginary guns. Later we played more elaborate all-day war games with other neighbourhood kids, mostly older boys, down in the nearby ravine in the summers. We split up into teams, spread out, and then tried to capture each other. The captured ones were tied to trees and left alone, sometimes for hours. Our parents knew nothing of these adventures. Our mothers were happy to have us out of their hair for hours at a time and asked no questions.

Eventually these teams turned into gangs. Dick became the leader of a gang, to which I belonged, although I also operated as a spy and infiltrated a rival gang. (I was reading Somerset Maugham's *Ashenden* at the time.) Eventually Dick's gang went after Ted and terrified him to the point where he was afraid to go to school. Babe went to the principal, and Dick and I were summoned to his office and threatened with a strapping. We agreed to leave Ted alone. Our parents had a powwow and decided we should all go to different high schools, but I'm getting ahead of my story.

I don't know when I first realized that Dick could draw. According to the prevalent psychology it was natural enough; he took after his mother. Certainly Kay taught and encouraged him. His early efforts were almost always cartoon figures: Donald Duck, Bugs Bunny, and Goofy were favourites. Dick's drawings of them were just as good as those in the comics and Big Little Books we went through by the dozens. Kay took us to see all the Walt Disney features as soon as they came out: *Pinocchio, Bambi, Dumbo, Fantasia*. The last two were my favourites, particularly the pink elephant sequence and the Greek gods in Beethoven's Pastoral Symphony. Kay also introduced us to *The Thief of Baghdad* with its flying carpets, magical horses, and wicked viziers. It was the first and best of a number of oriental fantasy films that lodged in our imaginations.

But more than anything we were hooked on comedy, some of it sophisticated, much of it not. Kay introduced us to Danny Kaye's *Up in Arms* and *The Secret Life of Walter Mitty*. And at Saturday matinees we discovered the Marx Brothers in *A Night at the Opera*, and Olsen and Johnson's *Hellzapoppin'*, both of which we saw several times. We spent a lot of time making faces and doing weird voices. We competed, egging each other on to see who could be the silliest. We recited such immortal verses as:

Hasten, Jason,
Bring the basin:
Oops, plop,
Bring the mop.

Our consumption of popular entertainment was not limited to cartoons and comic performers. We marvelled at the exploits of Superman, Batman and Robin, and an underwater superhero called Submariner. We went to all the Tarzan movies and followed the adventures of Terry and the Pirates and the Lone Ranger on radio. We both identified with Terry, living a life of ongoing danger unencumbered by parents. But Dick, always ahead of me in his commitment to imaginative fantasy, became convinced his uncle was Superman. For a while he wore a blue cape Kay had made for him everywhere, even to school. Eventually on a dare he climbed up on a rose trellis and announced he could fly. He leaped into the air and crashed to the ground, breaking his wrist. "Serves him right," said Babe, who had a field day telling this tale.

As soon as we learned to print, we wrote a play. It was called *Cat and Dog* and was a comic adventure story for two actors (us). Sadly, this early masterpiece has not survived, but it was the first of many dramatic entertainments we devised. Wherever we went, whatever groups we belonged to, we immediately put on a show. My father bought and pitched a tent in the vacant lot next to our house, and here we staged a domestic drama for some of the neighbours, in which Dick and I featured as naughty children. There was a backlash when Babe let it be known that our behaviour reflected our home lives, and further shows of this nature were banned.

About this time we joined the Cub Pack at the church my parents attended. Dick's parents didn't go to church, but Ken Williams, Dick's father, became

Cub master and encouraged our theatrical efforts. Ken was a salesman for Brigden's, a large printing and design company. He was handsome, smooth-talking, outgoing, and an amateur magician. He could make coins and playing cards appear and disappear. He took us to see Blackstone the Magician for Dick's seventh birthday, and Dick brought home a rabbit pulled out of Blackstone's top hat. It lived in a little shed in his garden until we fed it a special treat of whipping cream and it died of indigestion.

Soon after, we proceeded to stage our own magic show in the tent. We planned it for several weeks, determined to make it worth the quarter we planned to charge. We would use the money we made to extend our repertoire and buy more magic apparatus at Eaton's. They had a resident magician, John Giordamane, who sold trick decks of cards and rubber roses that could be made to squirt a stream of water at unsuspecting spectators. Giordamane could be hired to perform at birthday parties. No one on Golfdale Road ever bought his services, but we were invited to a grand birthday party for our classmate Mickey Sifton, and there Giordomane was with all kinds of tricks up his sleeves.

To augment the few sleight-of-hand tricks we had actually mastered under Ken's instruction, we devised several tricks with my toy chemistry set: turning water to "wine" by dropping some chemical into it (potassium permanganate, if I remember correctly) and making a minor explosion with smoke and a rotten egg smell from some other admixture of chemical ingredients. We couldn't get a rabbit, but Dick caught a pigeon to produce from my father's opera hat. My father of course never went to the opera; he had bought the hat because he was asked to be best man at somebody's swanky wedding. He also bought a full set of tails and I was allowed to wear the coat, but only on the day of the performance. To make myself truly exotic I added a red sash and one of my mother's rhinestone earrings. Blackstone had had several scantily clad female assistants to hand him handkerchiefs, saws, and other magical paraphernalia, so we persuaded Beverley, a neighbourhood girl, who, though not a beauty, had definitely entered puberty, to be our handmaid. From somewhere or other Dick managed to produce a two-piece bathing suit and he persuaded her to wear it.

When the big day arrived, our tent was filled half an hour before the performance. We decided to cut off the front of it and put chairs outside. We collected $16.25: wealth beyond the dreams of avarice. Dick's card tricks were moderately well received and so was the water-to-wine routine. But the explosion was a bit much: for maximum effect we had tripled the ingredients and the rotten egg smell drove every one from the tent. We decided to move outside for the grand finale. Beverley appeared with the opera hat and the crowd went wild. A number of teenage boys began to chant in unison, "Take it off, Beverley." The poor girl turned beet-red and fled down the street and into her house. The pigeon escaped from the hat and flew out over the audience, splattering them as it went.

My father was not amused. Our tent was wrecked, his opera hat was filled with pigeon shit, and the chemical explosion had burned a hole in the corded-silk lapel of his tailcoat. Worst of all he had to go down the street with the entire neighbourhood looking on and apologize to Beverley's parents. At first he wanted me to go with him, but after taking in my smoked-up face and bizarre outfit, he thought better of it. "What do you think is going to become of you?" he spluttered, his voice shrill with exasperation, and stamped off down the street on his own. This was the last of our performances for Golfdale Road, but it had not exhausted our appetite for show business. We proceeded to find other venues in which to exploit our theatrical ambitions.

Cubs was one such place. Dick and I performed shows of our own invention. I wrote the scripts and played the straight man to Dick's comedy routines. I remember one of these shows was called *Road to India* and was more or less based on the movies that Bob Hope and Bing Crosby were turning out at the time. A very good-looking boy called Billy did a turn as Dorothy Lamour, but this was unusual. Most of our shows didn't have female characters, except perhaps grossly caricatured harridans inspired by Babe. We both wanted to be clowns and imitated the acts we had seen at the circus or in the movies. On our way home from the meetings of our Cub Pack on Friday nights, we dared each other to commit ever more outrageous pranks. We went into apartment buildings along the way, ringing doorbells and pitching snowballs at whoever answered, then ran away before the irate tenants could catch us. Or we pretended to be spastics walking out into traffic, laughing hysterically as cars swerved and screeched to a stop.

In our last years of public school Dick formed a Woman-Haters' Club, to which I was only marginally connected. We both had problems with the women in our neighbourhood, who let it be known that they thought we were "odd." The word "sissy" was used, though I don't think it was meant to imply sexual deviance. Sex was not mentioned or even hinted at in the presence of us kids. However Dick the Woman-Hater must have worked his way through most of his negative feelings toward females, because he was soon to become very much involved with the opposite sex.

When Dick went off to camp at the age of nine sex became a conscious element in our lives. On his return he explained the anatomical details to me and sang a few mildly dirty songs:

> Won't you tell me, dear,
> The size of your brassiere —
> Twenty, thirty, or forty?

We sought out whatever smut we could find. Before the advent of *Playboy* and *Penthouse*, porn was hard to come by, but we explored *Esquire* magazine and the novels of Thorne Smith. We started to compose a dirty novel called *The Perils of Penelope Plank.* All I remember is the opening sentence:

> "Poor Penelope. The money went plink and she went plank."

We indulged in a bit of mutual masturbation but this didn't prove very satisfying, so we moved on. We managed to get our hands on a female mannequin. It didn't enlighten us much about anatomy. Of course we'd seen our mothers naked but we didn't allow ourselves to fall so low as to discuss their relative merits. Whatever Freud might have had to say about it (not that we'd ever heard of him), we had no conscious incestuous drives, merely a curiosity about the opposite sex, which might have been more easily satisfied if either of us had had sisters. Fortunately there were other activities that claimed our attention.

Sometimes Dick and I were in the same class at school, sometimes not. But in grade seven we were both in the class of Mr. Martin, the school's art teacher. By this time Dick was drawing with exceptional skill, and this, I think, inspired Mr. Martin to devote an unusual amount of time to art projects. He taught us to make marionettes using light bulbs and plasticine to fashion the heads, coating them with papier-mâché and painting them. We made bodies of cloth stuffed with tissue paper and attached articulated arms and legs. The puppets were manipulated by strings attached to the head, hands, and knees. We wrote playlets and put on shows in class.

Not surprisingly, Dick's first puppet was Donald Duck. His mother made and clothed the body. Kay was a gifted seamstress who made all her own clothes and even her hats. (In fact at the age of sixteen she had been apprenticed to a milliner, who recognized her abilities as a draughtsman from the sketches she made and insisted she go to art classes at Central Tech, thus paving the way for her career as a commercial artist.) Kay's puppet bodies were extremely skillful concoctions, and before long she and Dick had created a range of Disney characters. Dick and I worked on a script based on various comic-book scenarios. Once again we were in show business together.

We were joined by a classmate, Richie Brown, who had a strongly idiosyncratic sense of humour and a gift for doing cartoon voices, especially Donald Duck. We were asked to perform at a birthday party and put on a show that we believed rivalled anything John Giordamane could come up with. Before long, Dick and Richie had a business going that was to keep them in pocket money for the next five or six years. I was only briefly involved in this venture because I found another outlet for my theatrical ambitions. My parents also discouraged me from too close an involvement with Dick and his schemes. Once it was decreed that we should go to different high schools, they hoped Dick would be a diminished influence in my life, but that was not the way it turned out.

Being at different schools and involved in different organizations did mean we spent less time together, but we still hung out on weekends. At some point in our early high-school days we became interested in what was then called Dixieland jazz. We discovered Bessie Smith, Louis Armstrong, Johnny Dodds, Sidney Bechet, Billie Holiday, and Bix Beiderbecke: all the great performers of the '20s and '30s. Their early recordings were being re-released on the newly invented LPs, and we bought as many of them as we could afford. We listened to them late at night, mainly in the basement room at the Williams house, which Dick now occupied. It had a separate entrance through the garden shed, and consequently he could come and go as he pleased. I envied him this freedom and sought to emulate it, using a window in our basement playroom for occasional late-night outings. Eventually my father caught me coming in after midnight and the window was nailed shut. But there was another basement window.

Just as Dick borrowed routines from *A Night at the Opera* and *Hellzapoppin'* and made them his own, so too he wanted to make jazz himself. He acquired a cornet and taught himself to play, crudely at first, but with great energy and verve. I was learning to play the piano but I didn't have Dick's quick ear or ability to improvise and our attempts to play together were short-lived. Instead Dick found some other would-be musicians at his high school, Northern Vocational, and formed his own band. They played at noon hour or after school. Dick took on an invented persona as the leader of the band, calling himself Ivan Yurpee. It was inevitable that he and I would decide to produce a full-length evening of music and skits. The Ivan Yurpee Show was loosely inspired by a revue that Olsen and Johnson had brought to the grandstand at the Canadian National Exhibition a year or two earlier. We stole some of their gags as well as material from *The Milton Berle* show, which we watched on television at an appliance store on Yonge Street, long before our families bought their own sets.

I devised sketches for The Ivan Yurpee Show into which Dick interpolated some favourite gags and routines. There was a Sherlock Holmes skit and a mock game show. I sang a duet of Jerome Kern's "All the Things You Are" with an overweight soprano, using revised lyrics. We enlisted the help of a couple of sexy girls, one of whom ran across the stage in a grass skirt pursued by a guy with a lawnmower. She also walked across the stage with a handsome young guy, both of them in pyjamas; when they reappeared they had exchanged pyjama bottoms. There was a skit in which Dick entered a beauty contest wearing an outrageous blond wig and exaggerated lipstick. And of course he led the band, tooting his own horn for all he was worth. Dick had become a celebrity at Northern Vocational.

But he was also having problems. We had moved beyond the gang stage after a narrow scrape with authority. We had built an underground fort on the path leading down into the ravine where we met at night, crawling through a narrow tunnel to a room where we sat around and smoked, told dirty jokes, and planned outrageous pranks. We were rapidly becoming mini-terrorists. Then one night we found our fort smashed in. The people in the house closest to the ravine had called the police, who came and wrecked our secret hideout. Dick and I swore revenge. We bought half a dozen cans of brightly coloured enamel paint and stored them in Dick's basement room. One night at about 2 a.m., Dick and I took the paint and decorated the house of the squealers with erotic drawings. They were sufficiently crude that no one would suspect the work of an accomplished draughtsman. Next day, a Sunday, the whole neighbourhood turned out to inspect this act of vandalism. Dick and I went and gawked with the rest, feigning astonishment and horror. The police conducted an investigation. We were never found out, but it put the fear of the law, if not of God, into me. I gave up smoking. But Dick was less cowed by this incident than I: he continued to hang out with some fairly rough characters, learned to shoot pool, and devoted more time to his cornet than his schoolwork. His grades slipped and he was in danger of failing. Ken Williams decided it was time to take action.

Ken was not Dick's real father. I think Babe had first wised us up to this fact, not that Kay or Ken tried to hide it. Kay had married young to another artist, Leslie Lane. Once she became pregnant with Dick, Lane abandoned her. Shortly after he left, she was visited by another woman who was in the same condition. "At least you've got a name for your kid," the woman said. Kay decided she was well rid of Lane and sued for divorce. Soon after, she was courted by Ken. They married, and Ken adopted Dick, who took his surname. For a while this seemed like a good arrangement all round. Dick benefited from Ken's support and Ken was proud of Dick's talent.

But Ken was not as easygoing as he appeared in public. At home he could be severe, demanding, and bad-tempered. Gradually Dick turned against him, resenting his restrictions, his outbursts, and particularly his treatment of Kay. Ken was proud of her and loved to show her off to his friends, but at home he expected to be indulged and catered to. Kay often cooked elaborate meals for his two closest friends, who were somewhat older homosexuals. They were a witty and cultivated pair. Initially we didn't suspect their orientation, but once the light dawned, Dick believed that Ken was also, in the parlance of the time, a pansy, who had used his mother to hide behind.

When Dick was nine, Kay became pregnant with Ken's child. Dick felt that Ken wanted to keep Kay dependent on him and had used this means to make sure she continued to look after him, keeping house, cooking meals, and caring for Baby Tony when she might have pursued her own artistic goals. Kay was an accomplished illustrator. She did beautifully detailed watercolours in the manner of Arthur Rackham and Edmund Dulac, but she was so busy with commercial work and housework that she rarely had time for these more esoteric projects.

As I got to know Kay I came to realize she had a strong masochistic streak. She discussed her personal relations, and indeed everybody else's, in a frank and analytical manner that was unusual at the time. She was perceptive and also permissive in anything that had to do with our artistic ambitions, but at the same time rigorous in her judgment of our work and her own. She was demanding in her studio, her kitchen, and her garden. Not only did she have artistic skills that the other women on the street could not even begin to emulate, but she surpassed them in the preparation of unusual and compli-cated dishes that were a feast for both the taste buds and the eyes; they were sometimes photographed for food magazines. She made and wore clothes decorated with exquisite embroidery, and grew flowers that the rest of us had never heard of. She listened to Mozart and Tchaikovsky, and knew about Sergei Diaghilev, Pablo Picasso, and Dorothy Parker. She was not a popular figure with the other women on the street. Kay was just too damned accomplished.

I suppose I was a bit in love with Kay, and so was Dick. I think this love made him jealous of Ken, and Ken jealous of him. Once Dick moved into his teens, their house became a hotbed of conflicts that were less tamped down and concealed than was usual in our neighbourhood, where there were rules that had to be followed and physical retribution was swift and unsparing if they were broken. No serious questioning of the accepted norms was tolerated. We had been taught what was right and wrong and were expected to live by the code that had been handed to us.

By the time we were teenagers, Dick was definitely considered suspect by the denizens of Golfdale Road. He was pronounced "wild." It was often said he had inherited bad blood from his real father. Far from being hurt by this judg-ment, I think Dick set out to live up to his reputation. And at the same time he was determined to escape. The summer after he turned fifteen, he climbed on a bus and went to California. He looked up a connection of his parents who worked as a draughtsman for Walt Disney. Disney was not about to put a fifteen-year-old on the payroll but allowed Dick to stay for the summer and learn whatever he could. He seized the opportunity and made the most of it. He came back in the fall and told his parents he wanted to apply to go to the Ontario College of Art. In keeping with the educational rubric of the time, this prestigious institution did not open its doors to anyone who did not have a high-school diploma, but when they saw Dick's work, they allowed him to enrol in commercial art. Dick was well on the way to leaving Golfdale Road behind.

Dick flourished at art college. He was skilled, quick, and hard-working. His outrageous humour and gifts as a mimic made him popular with other students. He liked to party and hang out with the guys; he was also attractive to women. Under the influence of Jim Burke, an aspiring writer he met at the Y, he began to read a wide variety of modern work and shared this new-found literary interest with me. On Jim's recommendation we discovered Joyce Cary's *The Horse's Mouth*, Truman Capote's *Other Voices, Other Rooms*, and J. D. Salinger's *The Catcher in the Rye*. Jim was a paraplegic but his brain was extremely agile. He was married to a pretty and charming CBC radio commentator called Laddie Dennis, who happily supported him financially so that he could work on the great novel he had in progress. She and Jim invited us to parties at which young intellectuals gathered. I recall one evening when Marshall McLuhan, who had just published his first book, was loftily inveighing against the commercialization of sex in the media. Jim turned in his wheelchair and shot out, "Then why did you call your book *The Mechanical Bride*?"

We began to listen to classical music: Stravinsky, Bartók, Aaron Copland, and above all, Beethoven. Encouraged by Jim we also tackled the big figures in the arts: Beethoven and Brahms, Shakespeare and Tolstoy, Michelangelo and Rembrandt, and especially Goya, whose savage depiction of war and madness Dick found powerful. Not that Dick abandoned telling jokes or listening to jazz. He continued playing his cornet and rapidly became a skilled musician. Before long he was part of a small combo of the art college students that included Michael Snow on piano and Graham Coughtry on trombone. The three would remain friends throughout their student days and long after.

Dick introduced me to these new friends, who accepted me as an equal, and we sometimes partied together on weekends. At the end of Dick's first summer at OCA, he and I went to New York together. I had saved money from summer jobs and I guess my parents felt that if Dick could get himself to California and back on a bus, we could manage a week in New York. We set off for Buffalo by Greyhound but hitchhiked the rest of the way to save money. We stayed at the Chelsea Y and visited art galleries. At the Museum of Modern Art we saw our first real Van Goghs, Rousseaus, and Matisses. I still get a quiver of excitement when I stand in front of these canvasses fifty years later: *Starry Night*, *Sleeping Gypsy*, *Dance of Life*. We also heard Billie Holiday at some dive in the Village and saw Tennessee Williams' *Summer and Smoke*. It was not my first introduction to Williams, but his acute sensitivity to pain and his wild humour would haunt and inspire me over the years.

The purpose of the trip for Dick was not only to experience art but to see if he could track down his natural father, who was supposed to be living and working somewhere in Manhattan. From one of his teachers at OCA Dick had discovered the addresses of people who were supposed to be friends of Leslie Lane. One of them, a man I remember as Yudel Kyler, invited us to dinner in Greenwich Village. I remember walking through twilit tree-lined streets full of nineteenth-century houses and being served a Middle Eastern meal of hummus and baba ganouj and pilaf, none of which I had ever heard of. We stayed late into the night as Yudel smoked Gitanes and told tales of life in Rome, Athens, and Beirut, and played us Arab music that had been recorded by his friend Paul Bowles. We walked back to the Y, aware we had caught a glimpse into a world of unimagined sophistication, but we learned nothing about the whereabouts of Dick's father. That would come years later after Dick had left home. Leslie Lane would be delighted to discover that he had a talented son whom he had not had the trouble of bringing up, but Dick would conclude that Lane was a jerk. He would not play a significant role in Dick's life.

Dick continued to live at home. For some time he had earned pocket money doing puppet shows for kids' birthday parties, but a new source of income soon opened up. Television production was beginning in Toronto. There was a demand for animated commercials, and, thanks to his summer at Disney, Dick knew how to animate. He became connected to Graphic Associates, a studio north of Toronto at Kleinburg, a partnership led by George Dunning and Jim McKay. These two had been students at the Ontario College of Art in the late '30s, when they picked up extra pocket money travelling around for Paddy Conklin doing caricatures at country fairs, before they were recruited by Norman McLaren to be part of his stable of animators at the National Film Board.

They broke away and set up on their own in the early 1950s, building an unusual house with separate living quarters for each of them radiating from a central work area. They employed various artists like Dick, Michael Snow, and Joyce Wieland, who all came and went. The studio was presided over by a gnomic octogenarian Asian houseman with the improbable name of Yet Yung. It was a hangout for artistic types who lived nearby: a young but already somewhat pontifical Pierre Berton, and a straggly-bearded polymath named Lister Sinclair, who pronounced on a wide variety of topics from Celtic poetry to

Athenian politics to the mathematical discoveries of Niels Bohr. There was also a striking, sharp-tongued, carrot-topped woman called Steve, who flirted with both of us. Underneath the intellectual sparring and edgy repartee of this little society we sensed the throb of sexual dalliance. In the early '50s Kleinburg had a faint echo of Bloomsbury.

Dick began to make real money animating commercials and soon acquired a car, a red Mini Morris. It was a second-hand convertible with no heater — extremely cold in the winter. Often Dick drove me to school. After a while the only way to start the car was by pushing it out of the driveway and down a hill. It would normally start about halfway down and I would climb in through the hole in the back of the canvas roof as we drove off. Needless to say this spectacle caused a good deal of comment and provided ideal material for Babe's continuing diatribes about Dick's craziness and his negative effect on me. One result of this continuing barrage was that I vowed I would move out of my family's house at the first opportunity.

When he was about sixteen, Dick acquired a girlfriend, Stephanie, known as Tep. She had a Botticelli delicacy, with corn-gold hair and china-blue eyes. Although superficially demure in the style of the time, she was sharply observant and quite capable of barbed comments. She helped Dick with his puppet shows and had a shrewd appreciation of his artwork. Not an intellectual, she was nevertheless able to keep pace with Dick's musical and literary interests and won the respect of his friends. She and I got on well enough and we occasionally double-dated, going to movies or jazz hangouts, although I did not have a steady girlfriend. In no way did Tep try to come between us, but Dick's desire to spend an increasing amount of time alone with her meant that he and I saw less of each other.

The summer before his last year at the art college, Dick went with a fellow student to Mexico for part of the summer. He stayed with his friend in the third oldest house in North America and soaked up the strange flavour of a culture new to him but with ancient roots. He was strongly influenced by pre-Colombian art, but also by the great Mexican muralists, particularly the social realist José Clemente Orozco and the brilliant colourist Rufino Tamayo. Dick went back to school and transferred from commercial to fine art. He had decided he wanted to become a serious painter. He worked closely with one of his teachers, Fred Hagan, and produced some very complex lithographs, particularly two large-scale works, one of a Mexican brothel and another of an evangelical revival in downtown Toronto. He also began to draw portraits and revealed a particular gift for getting a likeness and catching the essence of a sitter's personality. This would be another source of income in the next few years.

Because he had switched courses, Dick didn't graduate from the Ontario College of Art with a diploma, a point he rammed home when the college held a tribute dinner in his honour many years later. Dick was always one to get his revenge when the time was ripe. However, when he finished at OCA we cele- brated his non-graduation at Old Angelo's, the only Italian restaurant in Toronto at the time. We drank Chianti with our spaghetti and meatballs and thought ourselves very cosmopolitan. Dick went off to Spain with his friends Mike and Graham, where they painted all morning, swam every afternoon, played jazz in the evenings, and lived for a dollar a day on the tiny island of Ibiza. I wished I were there with them.

A year later, he came back for a month and married Tep at her parents' summer cottage. Dick looked very respectable in blue blazer and white flannels but made a predictably outrageous speech. He had asked Graham to be his best man and I was a bit piqued, but we were going in different direc- tions: Dick was to be a serious painter in Spain while I imagined I was going to London to be an actor. Both ambitions were short-lived, but we would remain in touch over the next fifty years, connecting in London, New York, Los Angeles, and occasionally in Toronto.

Dick would go on to become an accomplished animator, arguably one of the best in the world. He set up studios in London and Los Angeles, produced dazzling titles for films including the *Pink Panther* series, *What's New Pussycat?*, and *The Charge of the Light Brigade*, working with some of the leading directors of the 1960s and '70s: Woody Allen, Richard Lester, Mike Nichols, and Tony Richardson. Both his animated version of Dickens' *A Christmas Carol* and *Who Framed Roger Rabbit* would win him Academy Awards. His style was simple yet vigorous, powered by an impudence very much in tune with the London of the swinging '60s that carried over well into the egomaniacal '80s.

In the early 1990s, Dick closed his studio in London and moved with his fourth wife, Mo (short for Imogen), to Saltspring Island on the West Coast of Canada. He had retained his Canadian citizenship and a love of the land, though his comments about Toronto remained scathing. ("Living in Toronto is like being in an attic above an apartment where a wonderful party is going on.

You hear the music and the noise, and open the door, and somebody staggers halfway up the stairs and pukes on your shoes.") He and Mo produced two children, Natasha and Lief, made friends with their bohemian neighbours, and enjoyed the pine forest. Dick found some like-minded musicians, and they played jazz together several nights a week. He began to work on a new film based on Aristophanes' comedy *Lysistrata*, about Athenian women deciding to hold out on their husbands until they agreed to stop making war. We had first read the play as teenagers and it had all the elements of Dick's signature work: satire, bawdy humour, and an underlying moral concern. To augment his shaky finances he agreed to write a book, *The Animator's Survival Kit*, published by Faber and Faber in 2001.

In February of that year, Dick and Mo came to Toronto on a tour to promote the book. We met for a drink at the Hyatt (the old Park Plaza). Dick looked the same as ever: the big blue elfin eyes, the hair thinning a little bit but hanging in a lock over his forehead, the irrepressible grin, the sudden chuckle, the hands gesturing expressively, the barbed quips about Toronto, the Americans, the British. Mo joined us and it was obvious she was in charge of this outing. She was brisk and efficient but also warm and protective. Dick, like Henry VIII, had made some bad choices over the years in the consort department. Like Henry he didn't repeat his mistakes; he made different ones. It seemed to me that Mo wasn't a mistake. Before long she drew Dick's attention to the time. He explained, "I'm giving a little talk somewhere. I don't know whether anyone will show up. I'll set aside some tickets for you if you like."

Thank goodness he did. The Bloor Theatre, one of the few surviving old movie palaces left in Toronto, was surrounded by buses bringing students from Ryerson, OCAD, the Film Centre, Sheridan College, wherever animation is taught. Kids were hanging from the rafters when Dick came onstage and spoke for ninety minutes, supported by clips from *The Little Island*, *The Pink Panther*, *The Light Brigade*, *Guinness* commercials, and *Roger Rabbit*. In one minute he grabbed the attention of his youthful audience. He moved about the stage with energy and grace, gesturing extravagantly and cracking jokes. It was a performance worthy of Groucho or Milton Berle. At one point he was illustrating different kinds of walks: a muscle-bound athlete, a tottering drunk, a prostitute, a prissy schoolmarm. Suddenly he grinned and said, "This is a friend of mine. I think he's here tonight." He became an uncontrolled spastic, waving his arms wildly and I recognized myself at the age of ten on the way home from Cubs, running out into the traffic at Dick's instigation, cars screeching and skidding around me. I laughed and wondered what comic heights I might have scaled if I'd still had Dick to egg me on.

A TENDERFOOT IN GOTHAM

By the time I was nine years old I had begun to have a double image of my parents, though of course I wouldn't have phrased it that way at the time. This was particularly true of my father, who was trying to refashion the values of a farmyard fundamentalist to the demands of suburbia, still resolutely wearing the whole armour of God, though even I could see the chinks in it. One of the first signs of backsliding was the way we observed the Sabbath. In the morning we went to church at Glenview Presbyterian. After a light lunch (Campbell's soup and Ritz crackers), Father and I retired to the library; he prepared the lesson he was going to teach his Sunday school class of obstreperous twelve-year-olds while I learned my memory work, some twenty-five or thirty verses from the Bible. Like Father I had a keen memory; each year I won the prize for memorization of scripture. Father took pride in this: he heard me recite, and once I was word-perfect he allowed me to read the *Books of Knowledge* until it was time to drive back to Glenview. While he pondered the meaning of the parables of Jesus, I ogled black-and-white photos of Greek and Roman nudes.

Then came Sunday dinner, which was supposed to be followed by Evening Service, but in the '40s this rite was abandoned. Supposedly we were saving gas as part of the war effort. But actually, Father wanted to stay home and listen to Jack Benny on the radio, followed by Charlie McCarthy, and, my favourite, Fred Allen. My father's allegiance to the strict behavioural practices of his forbears slowly eroded as he succumbed to the lures of the American entertainment industry. He could resist the glamour of Garbo and Dietrich, and even Betty Grable, but he got hooked on radio comedians.

There were other signs of city sophistication supplanting my parents' simple rural godliness. I have no doubt they had signed the Pledge back in Cardinal, but now they occasionally took a drink, "socially." They played cards, and as my father emerged as a first-rate bridge player, they did this more and more frequently — at least once a week. They went to see entertainers my father liked: Al Jolson, Bing Crosby, and Will Rogers. I clamoured to be taken to these entertainments and was rewarded one snowy Saturday afternoon when my father took me to Shea's Vaudeville while my mother shopped at Eaton's. (She was buying herself a new girdle, which required some time for try-ons, and it was considered unsuitable for me to hang around the ladies' lingerie department.)

The show at Shea's included a rather feeble dog act, a comedian who told some coarse jokes (most of which I got but understood I should pretend not to), a contortionist who also juggled Indian clubs that lit up in the dark, a soft-shoe number with two very old performers hoofing their way through "Shine on Harvest Moon," and a stripper who went as far as peeling off everything but her corset, did some high kicks, and threw kisses to the crowd as she made her exit to wolf whistles. I thoroughly enjoyed the whole spectacle, not because I thought it was very accomplished, but because I was so stage-struck I found anything to do with theatre exciting. My father was more critical: he apologized for the quality of the performance and said it might be better if I didn't mention the stripper to my mother. He loftily opined that Shea's spectacle certainly didn't measure up to what he'd seen in New York.

My parents weren't socially ambitious, but they did want to be accepted by people like our next-door neighbours, Aus and Babe, who, like my parents, accepted New York as their social arbiter, setting standards of dress and repartee. They had gone to the World's Fair in 1939, seen the Dodgers play, and eaten at Toots Shor's. But my parents had visited New York in 1930 on their honeymoon, grandly staying at the St. Regis for three nights in the blistering heat of August and sitting in the top balcony to see Ray Bolger in *On Your Toes*. My father had since been sent to New York on business three times and had taken my mother along. While he went to meetings, she shopped at Saks, Fifth Avenue, and Altman's. Together they had eaten at Sardi's, seen *Abie's Irish Rose* and *Oklahoma!*, and been to the Stork Club.

In 1944, even though there was a war on, father's business partners thought it important that he maintain contacts with their suppliers, who every year attended a convention in New York. My mother was having a bad patch of nerves and didn't feel up to going. To my amazement he asked me one night at dinner if I would like to go with him. I almost choked on my macaroni and cheese as I spat out my ecstatic acceptance. I bragged about my good luck to Ted, who stopped softening up his baseball mitt long enough to warn me that his parents said New York was full of pansies, so I'd better look out or I might turn into one myself.

We got on the train at 11 p.m. at Union Station. Father's hand on my elbow steered me firmly toward the platform as I marvelled at the echoing voice bouncing off the vaulted ceiling, calling out the times of departures and arrivals. Our luggage was borne before us by a black porter, who put out his hand for a tip, revealing a white palm. I remarked on this to my father, who whispered dismissively, "All darkies are like that."

"Why?"

"It's the way God made them." End of investigation. We were to sleep in a Pullman car, Father in the lower berth and I in the upper. I was sent down the narrow aisle to the washroom and then, on my return, hoisted up to the top berth by the porter, along with my suitcase. "Sweet dreams," he said. I shook his hand, which I think surprised him. It felt just like anyone else's hand. Maybe he'd expected me to slip him a quarter, but he grinned back at me and pulled the curtains shut. I undressed awkwardly, lying on my back and wriggling out of my trousers and into my pyjamas.

The train clattered out of the station and rolled on through the darkness. I lay looking out the little window for a long time, listening to the double rhythm set up by the speeding wheels and the passing telegraph poles, marvelling at the billowing smoke and shooting flames of the Hamilton steel plants, then the winking lights of the Buffalo skyline. Eventually I fell asleep, and when I awoke we were already in Grand Central.

I pulled my clothes on fast, scrambled down, and followed Father as he strode through the vast hall of Grand Central and hailed a cab. I gawked at the busy streets as we drove to the Roosevelt Hotel, waited in line while we registered, squeezed into an already full elevator, and then combed my hair and brushed my teeth in the bathroom adjoining our room. Ten minutes later we were sitting in the Grill ordering eggs over easy and hash browns, neither of which I recognized by those names, though when they came they were familiar enough. "Americans have different names for a lot of things, but you get used to it. Basically they're pretty much like us. The main difference is they blow their own trumpet more." Even then I knew my father well enough to realize this was not an original observation, but the accepted opinion of the businessmen he consorted with.

"We'll come back tonight and hear Guy Lombardo and his Royal Canadians. He grew up in London, Ontario. Went to school with Babe." I'd heard Babe brag about the Lombardo boys, who had been considered pretty hot stuff back in London. "They're Eyeties, of course. Maybe that's why they fit in so well in New York. There's a real hodgepodge of different races here.

Wops, and niggers, and Jewboys," my father said in the unabashed racist terminology of the day. "Somehow or other they seem to get along, though I don't know that it can last. I'm not sure the good Lord intended everybody to be all mixed up together like that." Like the good Canadian farm boy he was, my father admired the aggressiveness, ingenuity, and sheer success of his American cousins but thought New York was travelling too fast, hurtling out of control toward inevitable doom and destruction.

"Maybe they're all good Christians," I said, thinking of the coloured leaflets we got at Sunday school showing Jesus sitting talking to kids of every race: a kinky-haired black kid, a slanty-eyed Asian, a brown girl in a sari, though for some reason never a feather-bonneted North American Indian. Little prig that I was, I hoped this remark would win me points with Father, but he merely snorted. "Jewboys aren't Christians. You'd know that if you tried doing business with them."

After breakfast, he told me he would be going to meetings all morning. He'd meet me for lunch at one o'clock in the lobby of the Empire State Building. Everyone knew where that was. So at 9:30 on a bright, sunny Monday morning in late March, I found myself with a dollar in my pocket all alone on the sidewalks of New York. I made a quick tour through the lobbies of the Waldorf and gawked at its elegant mirrors and chandeliers, then made my way over to Fifth Avenue, stopping to marvel at the imposing Greek facade and splendid lounging lions of the Public Library. I thought this must be what the Parthenon looked like in its heyday. I walked over to Times Square to gaze in awe at the towering signs advertising beer and cigarettes, and then returned to Fifth Avenue. Classical echoes rang in my head: Italian palazzos and French chateaux were replicated on a grand scale, sometimes covering an entire city block or perched on top of a thirty-five-storey skyscraper. In between were churches that rivalled or probably outdid Notre Dame and Westminster Abbey. The classical allusions were not lost on me, thanks to the *Books of Knowledge*.

I made my way up past the Plaza and stared at the imposing mansions that lined the park, wondering what sumptuous treasures were within: life-size marble statues and crystal chandeliers as big as Buicks, perhaps. I longed to see inside but did not dare venture past the splendidly uniformed doormen, whose costumes suggested Serbian cavalry officers or Prussian field-marshals. I was delighted by the eclectic pastiche and fakery I found everywhere in New

York. As I explored Manhattan's wonders — the celestial blue light filtered through the stained glass in St. Patrick's Cathedral, the three-storey replica of Niagara Falls on a Times Square sign, the gilded baroquerie of the lobbies of the Waldorf and the Astor — I didn't object to the phoniness but revelled in the sumptuous theatricality.

I was forty-five minutes late meeting my father at the Empire State. He was tense with anger and we ate our hamburgers in silence; as my punishment, he did not take me up to the top of the great building. But because he didn't mention it, it never occurred to me that his anger was grounded in his fear that something terrible had happened to me. He was loath to let me go off on my own again in the afternoon, but he didn't want to take me to his meetings. So, as a compromise, I was allowed to spend the afternoon in the Library. He would pick me up there at five sharp and no nonsense. We were going to have dinner with some business associate, and he hoped I would remember my manners and not try to show off.

The afternoon passed pleasantly enough. I went up the grand staircase and looked down on the lobby below. Then I went to the washroom, where I was approached by an older man. I think probably he was in his early thirties. I was aware that he was looking at my penis and I thought of Ted's warning. But the man who introduced himself as Bobby made no attempt to touch me, so I put myself back in my pants and agreed to go upstairs with him and look at the paintings on the top floor. He seemed to know quite a lot about history and told me about George Washington's wooden teeth and Dolly Madison saving the White House from fire. He asked me home for tea, but I looked at my watch and told him I had another engagement in twenty minutes. I said I'd meet him the next morning at ten thirty, and then I went downstairs to wait for Father.

Dinner was at a small French restaurant that sported red-and-white checked tablecloths and poker-faced waiters with long white aprons. Father's business associate was waiting for us with a woman who immediately seized my total attention. She was thin almost to the point of emaciation, with colourless straight hair pulled back in a knot and a long, pale face dominated by a thin-lipped mouth painted a brilliant shade of orange-red. Her dress was a clinging, cream-coloured satin, and her hands and ears glittered with diamonds. Her mouth widened slightly as she fixed her large, slate-grey eyes on me. The man leapt up and shoved a hairy paw toward Father. "Kenny, good to see ya. Howsa boy?"

I had never heard my father called Kenny. My grandparents called him Kenneth, and my mother and a few chosen friends called him Ken. Almost everybody else called him Mr. Hunter. Father said, "I hope we're not late, Sandor."

"Nah, perfect timing. We're just ready for our second martini, aren't we, Birgitta? So this is junior, huh?"

"This is Martin."

The woman held out her hand to father but kept her eyes on me. "My favourite uncle was called Martin," she said, with a little twitch of her brilliant lips.

"It's not a very common name." This was my best attempt at making conversation.

"It is in my country."

"Birgitta's Austrian. She got out just in time, two days before the Putsch. They let her keep her diamonds but she lost everything else. Hey, let's get something to drink. *Garçon, trois martinis, s'il vous plaît, et pour ce jeune homme* — What you wanna drink, kid?"

"Orange crush?"

"They don't have that here. *Faites-lui un petit apéritif. Quelques gouttes de Dubonnet avec beaucoup de soda. Et pour commencer, quatre douzaines de huîtres.* Hey, I should be getting you to order, Kenny. You Canadians all parlez-vous, dontcha?" Father shrugged. "So whaddya think of this town, kid?"

"I love it."

"Attaboy."

"He wandered around on his own this morning and turned up for lunch three quarters of an hour late. I thought he'd been kidnapped."

"Could happen. You wanna be careful, kid. There's some desperate characters wandering around out there. They say Gotham's got more organized crime now than Chicago even." This was stated with obvious pride, as Sandor lit one cigarette from the butt of another.

"Tomorrow you must spend with me," declared Birgitta. "We will find something amusing to do while they talk about their boring old business. Would you like this?" Her grey eyes widened again, challenging me.

"Sure."

"That's very kind, but you must have things you want to do. Shopping . . ."

"Shopping? The stores are full of hideous rubbish. Padded shoulders and those silly little hats. Who would wear such things?"

The drinks arrived. Mine was fizzy and bitter, but I decided I quite liked the taste. Then came the plates of oysters on the half-shell. Sandor explained that they were genuine Malpeques and that it was a mistake to kill their flavour with Tabasco sauce. Rather, we should bring out the full flavour with just a hint of vodka. He splashed a drop or two of his martini on one of my oysters and said, "Try this, kid. It'll knock you out."

I could tell Father was horrified, so I gulped it down fast before he could protest. The oyster slid down my throat, smooth and satiny like Birgitta's dress. "Wow," I said, and Sandor laughed delightedly.

"He is quite the little man, your son," said Birgitta, and Father relaxed enough to smile back at her.

Father tried to slide the conversation to business, but Sandor was having none of it. He ordered filets with sauce *marchands de vin*, followed by a salad of dandelion leaves, which I could tell astonished Father as much as it did me. To my Father, dandelions were instruments of the Devil. One of his passions was weeding our large lawn by hand with a kitchen fork, working his way up and down until he had completely eradicated every dandelion, plantain, or shoot of crabgrass. As soon as he finished he started over again at the beginning. Only the coming of the snow halted this activity, which I think somehow for him was emblematic of the good Christian life. Weeds, like evil, were everywhere; only constant vigilance could overcome them, even temporarily. So to see him munching gingerly on dandelion leaves and listening to Sandor's increasingly raucous comments was an object lesson in forbearance and control, qualities I would see him exercise with varying degrees of mastery over the next fifty years.

"So what's your pleasure? The night's still young."

"I promised to take Martin to a show."

"Too late for Broadway. We'll have to do that tomorrow. We could still catch the ten o'clock show at Billy Rose's place."

"You don't think it's a bit raw for . . . ?" Father nodded his head in my direction.

"Nah. Nothing to worry about there. I bet the kid's seen gals shakin' their titties before now."

"Dad took me to Shea's Vaudeville and they had a stripper," I volunteered.

"What'd I tell you? Okay, let's get the cheque and shove off."

Birgitta smiled at me. "Sandor, if you don't mind I think I'll go back to the hotel while you boys go out on the town. So, I expect you tomorrow, ja? We're at the Plaza. Shall we say about nine thirty? We can have breakfast together and then we will do something amusing. Goodnight." She gave me a kiss on the cheek and walked away, her satin swaying sinuously.

Billy Rose's Diamond Horseshoe offered a show whose main attraction was a chorus line of long-legged ballerinas. *Oklahoma!* was the hottest show in town, and ballet was in. After a martini and two glasses of wine Father was as relaxed as I'd ever seen him. "Look at the gams on that, Kenny," Sandor said, ordering double Scotches as Father grinned appreciatively.

The show was a parade of sequin-spattered costumes, platinum-blond hair, false eyelashes, and net stockings. Lights flashed, music played, jokes were cracked, and legs kicked high in the air in a riotous blur to which my Dubonnet aperitif along with Sandor's splashes of vodka and a couple of sips from Birgitta's wineglass must have contributed. It was like a sped-up moving collage of all the wonders I'd seen in the day. When it was over, Sandor ordered another round of drinks, but Father insisted he had to get me home. We lurched to a taxi, drove back to the Roosevelt, and fell into our beds.

The next morning at breakfast Father said Sandor had promised to get us tickets for a Broadway show. I asked him how he knew Sandor, and he told me the first time he'd come to New York on business, Sandor had really shown him the ropes. Now he was handling a new product, a label with a peel-off back that he wanted father's company to take on. Sandor was a bit of a "blowhard," but underneath he wasn't a bad fellow. (Father had a scale of epithets for people of whom he disapproved: blowhards were the least objectionable, followed in descending order by highbinders, four-flushers, bad actors, and finally rascals.) Father had a busy day ahead of him and used that as an excuse to avoid more detailed discussion of Sandor's good and bad points. He put me in a cab, told me I'd better be on my best behaviour, and we set out for the Plaza.

When I arrived, I asked at the desk for Mrs. Simon and was told I could go up to her room. I knocked on the door and her voice told me to come in. Birgitta was sitting propped up on pillows with a breakfast tray on her lap. She was wearing a chiffon nightdress through which her small breasts could be plainly seen; they had enormous, apricot-coloured nipples. "Come and sit on the bed and have a cup of tea." She poured me some; I didn't usually drink tea but thought it impolite to refuse. "Now, what shall we do today? Have you seen the Frick?" I didn't know what the Frick was. "It is the most beautiful house in New York. Designed by the wife of Somerset Maugham. You do know who he is?"

"Yes, I read *Ashenden*. I liked it a lot."

"Did it make you think you would like to be a spy?"

"Yes, sort of."

"It is not so glamorous, believe me."

"You're a spy?"

"Don't tell Sandor."

"He doesn't know?"

"Can you keep a secret?"

"Of course."

"You have secrets from your father?"

"Yes," I admitted, slightly uneasy.

"I was sure of this. Well, it is the same with me. I have secrets from Sandor. And he has secrets from me."

"How do you know?"

"I know. It is good to have secrets. Secrets give you power. They are weapons. When you live with someone you need this."

"Even when you're married?"

"Especially then. But Sandor and I are not married."

I couldn't resist asking, "Why not?"

"He already has two wives. Sandor has been very nice to me, but . . . I don't want to be married. I need my freedom. And now I need my bath. Take this tray, will you?"

I took the tray off her lap and saw through the chiffon the hair between her legs. It was dark and bushy, quite unlike the pale thin strands of the hair on her head. Then I realized she'd seen me looking and felt embarrassed, but I needn't have worried. She took off her nightgown and headed for the bathroom, saying, "Come, come, you mustn't pretend to be shy."

I followed her to the doorway of the bathroom and watched as she got into the tub, which was already full. "Why don't you take off your clothes and join me?"

"I don't know if I should . . ."

"Please. Just for me?" Her eyes widened beguilingly.

She watched with unabashed interest while I took off my clothes and climbed in a gingerly fashion into the tub. I sat facing her. "I think you are going to be a handsome man. Women will want you. You must get used to being with them. Will you come over here and let me soap you? I would like that."

I was already in the tub, naked. I moved over and sat in front of her between her legs. I felt her breasts brush against my shoulder blades as she rubbed soap on my back, my arms, my chest, my belly, my legs. "I had a little boy who would have been about your age." Her voice was level and unbroken. I didn't know what to say. She took my penis and pushed back my foreskin. "I am not used to this. We are Jews, as you must have understood from our conversation last night."

"No."

"I went to England to visit my sister a few days before the Nazis marched into Vienna. I left my mother, my husband, my son. I wanted to go back, but my sister persuaded me not to. She said instead they must come to me in London. But they could not get out. I talked to them on the telephone but I never saw them again. I worked for British intelligence. Then I became sick. My sister was married to an American and arranged for me to come here. I met Sandor in hospital and he took me to Chicago. And now I work there for the museum. Come, it is time to get dry."

We climbed out of the tub. Birgitta dried me off but left me to dress myself. I stood and watched as she did her makeup with a brush, like an artist creating a masterwork. She put on a mannish suit and hat. "All my clothes are what I had in Vienna. They were made by a very famous designer. I do not like American styles. They are vulgar."

We walked up Fifth Avenue together. It was different from the day before, less busy and more elegant. Well-dressed middle-aged men and women walking their dogs greeted each other politely, the men lifting their hats, the women acknowledging the greeting with tiny gestures of their gloved hands. We came to the Frick and went in. She led me through the house, pointing out various things she liked. "Now, I shall give you a little lesson in art history. We will look first at the Lelys. You see that all these women look something the same. They are pink, rounded, with big eyes and mouths that are ready to take a bite or perhaps to be bitten. They are like ripe fruits. This is their style. Then we look at the ladies of Gainsborough, painted one hundred years later. They are thin, pale, graceful as willow trees, and a little bit distant. You cannot bite into them. You see the difference in their quality? This is what we mean by style. Do you understand what I am saying to you?"

"I think so. I think you have style."

She laughed delightedly. "I should hope so. Style is to me very important. I think it will be important to you also. Come now, we will have lunch. And then, because I am told you are an actor, we will see a play."

We ate at an Italian restaurant on Madison Avenue: marinated eggplant and pasta with oil and herbs. Birgitta had a glass of white wine and let me have a couple of sips from her glass. We caught a cab and got to the theatre minutes before the curtain. I hadn't asked what we were seeing, but the curtain rose on a tawdry house with an iron staircase running up to the second floor. Two women sat on the steps and two workmen came onstage. One wore a sweat-stained T-shirt and hollered, "Hey there, Stella, baby." I sat mesmerized, watching this rough lout yell at his wife and her sister, a woman in a chiffon dress.

At the intermission, Birgitta told me this was a play by a new playwright from the South, and it had received a great deal of attention. It was, of course, *A Streetcar Named Desire*. Birgitta did not want to discuss it until we had seen the whole thing. In the second act I identified with Blanche: she was refined, delicate, and sensitive. The man Stanley was like some sort of animal. He scared and fascinated me at the same time; he was repulsive yet strangely attractive. I didn't completely understand what I was seeing, but I was held by the raw emotion of the actors.

Afterwards we took a cab back to the Plaza and had tea in the Palm Court. "Well, what did you think?"

"I don't know what to say. They were like real people. Stanley reminded me of a man who lives on our street in Toronto. And some of my relatives. I don't expect people in plays to act like that. What did *you* think?"

"It is crude, but I think perhaps it is a very great play. You will remember it, yes?"

"I think so."

"I am sure of it. I watched you almost as much as the actors onstage. Now we must say goodbye. I would ask you to my room, but I think it will be better not. It has been very nice to spend this day with you. You are a very nice young man and I wish good things for you. A pleasant journey back home and into the future. *Gute Reise.*" Her big mouth trembled into a smile and she was gone.

I did not tell Father about the play. I didn't know how to explain what I had experienced, but instinctively felt he would disapprove. We had an early dinner at Longchamps, which he said was like the New York version of our Toronto Honey Dew chain, but it seemed much more glamorous to me. We had steak and baked potatoes, and no alcohol, and we were at the theatre fifteen minutes before the curtain went up. The audience was very dressed up; the men in dark suits, the women in black dresses. "That's New York style," Father said.

"Birgitta talked about style," I told him.

"That's funny, because she's out of style herself. Her clothes look like she's had them for the last ten years."

"I think she has. She brought them with her when she left Vienna. She couldn't go back. She's Jewish. Is Sandor Jewish too?"

"I've never asked him."

"I thought you didn't trust Jews."

"Sandor isn't a bad fellow," my father repeated in a tone that I knew meant this was not to be discussed. It was typical of my father, I later realized, that although his ideas were shot through with racial prejudice, he actually responded to people individually. He either liked them or he didn't, and his judgment of them was immediate, emotional, and usually irreversible.

The musical show for which Sandor had got us tickets was called *Let's Face It.* It had songs by Cole Porter, but this meant nothing to me at the age of ten; I'd never heard of him, though twenty years later I would idolize him and realize that I knew every word of the songs I'd heard endlessly replayed on the radio since before I could remember: "Just One of Those Things," "Night and Day," and "Begin the Beguine." They were played at high-school dances while hormone-charged couples swooned across the floor clutching each other hungrily in a parody of the romance these songs celebrated, a romance that was in itself a joke that their world-weary creator appreciated and relished to the full. But there was little of this kind of music in *Let's Face It.* The closest thing to a ballad was something called "I Hate You, Darling," whose lyrics were humorous but tinged with a cynical acceptance of the claims of the heart. I can't claim that I understood or responded to their calculated cleverness.

But I was instantly taken by the performers, a bunch of smart-cracking youngsters led by a skinny blond guy whose facial expressions were manic and who would spit out his lyrics so fast he seemed about to explode. At one point he spurted about three minutes of gobbledegook, all the time mugging, capering, and gyrating, twisting his rubbery body into ever more improbable positions like a demented windup toy whose spring was about to pop. I thought he was the funniest thing I'd seen since the Marx Brothers. My laugh rang out and I felt Father's restraining hand on my knee and looked over. His face was puzzled; he was trying to appreciate the show, but I could tell he just didn't get it. At intermission I asked, "Who *is* that guy?"

"No idea." He consulted his program. "Somebody called Danny Kaye."

A year later, that same Danny Kaye would make a movie called *Up in Arms* — and I would see it seven times. I saw every movie he made in the '40s, but Father never warmed to him. He was more taken with a blond girl in *Let's Face It*, whose husky voice had a metallic, sarcastic edge to it. She too would surface again in our lives when my father began to listen to a new radio show called *Our Miss Brooks*. Was he thinking of her as our cab drove back to the Roosevelt? I was rehearsing the lyrics of "Let's Not Talk About Love," which I would use as a party piece to impress some of the more sophisticated adults I encountered in the next three or four years. I particularly liked the bitchy quality of the lines:

Let's speak of Lamarr, the Hedy so fair
Why does she let Joan Bennett wear all her old hair?
If you know Garbo, then tell me this news
Is it a fact the navy's launched all her old shoes?

Back at the Roosevelt, I reminded Father that he had promised Babe that we would say hello to the Lombardo boys. In the Grill, couples were dancing, alternately jitterbugging or dipping and swooping in Astaire-inspired glides around the floor. We sat near the back and Father ordered a Scotch and soda. He wrote a little note and gave it to the maître d'. When the orchestra took a break, one of the brothers — Carmen, I think — came over and sat at our table. He had a high, rather whiny voice and flabby, drink-sodden jowls. Father relayed Babe's greeting and he looked a bit blank, but then he grinned.

"Yeah, Babe, now I remember. She was quite the hot little tomato. Freddie, our piano player up there, thought she had the cutest little ass he'd ever seen. He took her out one night and tried to get her to pull down her pants so he could at least get a look at it, but I guess she was too scared. Finally he took her home and it was pretty late. Her old man was waiting for her on the front porch. He was so mad he put her over his knee and pulled down her panties and walloped her right there on the porch. So Freddy got a good gawk at it after all." He guffawed and ordered another drink, which he carried back onto the stage, slopping it down his shirt front as he wove his way back to the stage.

We stayed for one more number, "Don't Sit Under the Apple Tree with Anyone Else but Me," then trudged up to our rooms. "I don't think I'd tell your mother that story about Babe. Sometimes it's good to keep things to yourself. I have secrets I'll carry with me to my grave."

I remembered what Birgitta had said about secrets, but I didn't say anything to Father. I lay in bed and wondered what secrets Father was talking about. Secrets were something we had lots of in my family. There were things I couldn't tell Father because they would make him mad, and things I couldn't tell Mother because she would use them against me. Secrets were weapons. Babe was an enemy and now I had a weapon. I'd know how to use it when the time came. But it never did.

THE REMARKABLE MRS. G.

When I was six I was taken to see my first play, *Cinderella*, at Margaret Eaton Hall. I remember parts of it clearly: the funny bits with the ugly sisters squabbling and pulling each other's hair, and Cinderella's drunken father being taken home after the ball in a wheelbarrow. And the magic. Cinderella being touched by the wand of the Fairy Godmother and her rags being transformed into a beautiful gown. The gilded coach appearing and Cinderella being borne away behind prancing horses. (I later realized that this part was largely supplied by my imagination.)

Sitting beside my mother in the darkened theatre, I knew I wanted to be part of that magical world. At one point she looked over and realized my seat was empty. I was on my way up the aisle to become part of the show. She stopped me that time but I continued to pester her not only to go to see more plays but to let me be part of them. Eventually I was able to get an audition with the director, Dorothy Massey Goulding. My mother came with me. I remember a small group of nervous kids meeting with a tall, rather austere woman. She commanded us to do certain simple things: walk, sit, speak a given line of dialogue, express an emotion: surprise, perhaps, or rage. I was uncomfortable and afterwards felt I had made a poor showing. So did my mother.

But two weeks later the telephone rang. It was Mrs. Goulding; one of the actors in her Christmas play had become ill. Would I be able to replace him? I was to play a sailor doll. My mother offered to take me to the first rehearsal. Mrs. Goulding made it clear she would prefer me to turn up alone. Of course I did not realize it then, but Mrs. Goulding had sensed that my mother was an inhibiting influence. Mrs. Goulding was adept at dealing with the parents of her child actors. She spoke to them at length on the telephone and sometimes enlisted them as backstage helpers. But she did not tolerate their interference in her work.

I arrived at the first rehearsal with a sailor doll I had owned for several years. This might have made me a subject of ridicule, but it impressed Mrs. Goulding as evidence that I was serious about researching my performance. The play was called *Mr. Bunch's Toys* and involved a window full of dolls who came to life after the shop was shut. They included a French doll, a Dutch girl doll, a Dutch boy doll, Mickey Mouse, a teddy bear, a Golliwog, a soldier, and me. Each of us got to do a little turn of some kind. I danced a hornpipe, which I never felt I really mastered. It gave me a specific task to work on, something I would later come to realize was a good way to help an inexperienced actor overcome self-consciousness.

The story of the play involved the separation of Dutch girl from Dutch boy when a poor girl could afford to buy only one of the dolls. It was resolved by the courageous intervention of Mickey Mouse and ended happily with the two Dutch dolls together. I was untouched by the sentiment but thrilled to be on the immense stage of Eaton Auditorium in costume and makeup. Sitting rigid with anticipation on the stage, I heard the stage manager say, "All clear." The curtains parted, and I looked out past the red, white, and blue footlights to where a thousand spectators sat in a hush of expectation. It was an experience that would make me quiver with excitement every time it was repeated over the next ten years.

I had entered the magical world of live theatre through the Toronto Children Players. As I made my way in an enchanted and at the same time intensely rigorous and practical organization, the other child actors in *Mr. Bunch's Toys*, particularly Jimmy Armour who played Golliwog, would become my friends and companions for a decade, and in some cases for life. We were presided over by a figure whom I instinctively both revered and feared. I see her still in my mind's eye: feet firmly planted on the ground, arms akimbo, taking charge, leading her young players, intent on her quest for the best that her actors could give. I see her in profile, her clear grey eyes alert and watchful, like some kind of great bird ready to swoop or soar, an eagle or a raven. A raven in a circle was the symbol of the TCP in the first twelve years of its existence. For me it was a symbol of enchantment and mystery. In one short play I had totally fallen under the spell of Dorothy Massey Goulding. Though she rarely talked about herself over the next ten years, my fellow players and I collected scraps of information about her past, her preferences, her philosophy. We were endlessly curious and fascinated by the woman we customarily referred to, with her full approbation, as Mrs. G.

Dorothy Massey was born in 1898, the third daughter of Walter Massey and Susan Denton, a Bostonian woman of commanding character. Dorothy's grandfather Hart Almerrin Massey had built the family business Massey-Harris into a huge industrial empire that manufactured and sold farm machinery in Europe and Asia as well as North America. Dorothy's father, Walter Massey, was seen to be the most promising member of his generation and became president of the company in 1896. He died prematurely in 1904, a victim of typhoid, contracted from contaminated water he drank while travelling in a railway car. His widow mourned him for the rest of her life but accepted the obligation of carrying on many of his interests. The family were wealthy by the standards of the day and acknowledged social leaders, prompting the poet Frank Scott to pen these lines:

> In Canada there are no classes,
> Only the Masseys and the masses.

The Masseys were devout Methodists. The Massey children were not allowed to engage in frivolous activities on the Sabbath but they did evolve a form of charades on Sunday afternoons. These tableaux, based on biblical stories, were acted out by the Massey children and had to be identified by the adults. Dorothy participated in these dramatic scenarios with her sister Madeline, her brother Denton, and their cousin Raymond, who lived across from them on Jarvis Street. Raymond was an isolated child; his mother died when he was seven, and his brother Vincent was ten years his senior. He became almost like a member of Walter's family and was particularly close to Madeline and Dorothy, whose lively imaginations sparked and complemented his own.

In the 1890s, Walter Massey had purchased a sizeable tract of land east of Toronto where he established an experimental farm. Here he tested the machinery made by the family firm and built up a dairy herd of some 200 head of Jersey cattle with the aim of providing the city of Toronto clean milk to be distributed by his City Dairy Company. After his death, Susan Massey ran the farm, which had been named Dentonia in her honour. The children spent a good deal of time there, riding on wagons and sliding down haystacks when they were young, and later playing tennis and golf on the courts and nine-hole course that Walter had laid out. In his autobiography, Raymond Massey recounts how they played imaginative games devised by his cousins Madeline and Dorothy. One game was called "Adventures" and involved forming teams and setting out through the woods trying to find the mysterious "Leaf Men," who travelled in "sky wagons" (space ships?) and could stifle human breath as they slid through the woods disguised as leaves. This science-fiction fantasy preceded any knowledge of Frank Baum, never mind Ray Bradbury or Isaac Asimov.

A photograph of Dorothy at the age of seventeen shows an alert young woman, her eyes, one slightly larger than the other, looking into the camera, inquiring and challenging. She has the prominent, not quite aquiline, nose she shared with her cousins Vincent and Raymond, a determined chin, and a tumble of curly, if slightly unruly, hair. She looked much the same when I first met her twenty-five years later, the hair frizzier and a bit greyed, her air self-possessed and commanding. She was always well turned out in tailored suits or skirts and simple blouses with elegant flat shoes, silver earrings and bracelets, and a handsome watch surrounded by diamonds. Everything about her bespoke understated quality.

Following *Mr. Bunch's Toys* I was cast in two other shows in my first season with the TCP. The first was called *The Shepherd's Purse* and was written by Mrs. Goulding's youngest daughter Dorothy Jane, or, as we all called her, "Dorf" (her own baby name for herself). The heroine was a beautiful princess who had five princely suitors but was attracted to a shepherd boy. She set her admirers a riddle: they had to give her something that was beautiful, cost nothing, and belonged to them. The princes brought various ridiculous offerings, but the shepherd boy solved the puzzle by bringing her the flower of the plant known as "the shepherd's purse." Each of the princes had one dominant characteristic; I was Prince Fizil and my trait was stupidity. I discovered it was easy to play dumb and get an instant reaction from the audience. I would make something of a specialty of comic dullards in the next ten years.

The costumes were modelled on the eighteenth century. We wore white wigs and turquoise satin coats and knee breeches. These were manufactured by Patricia Card, an invariably cheery woman with a fondness for the bottle. She presided over an atelier near Carlton and Yonge that was a gloriously disorganized welter of exotic fabrics and tasselled outfits. We would go there for "fittings" between rehearsals. She would drape us with material and advance uncertainly toward us, flashing an enormous pair of scissors. That we escaped unscarred seemed a minor miracle. I was happy in this part: all dolled up and getting laughs, but I was soon to learn that this was not what Dorothy Goulding thought acting was all about.

The other play that season was *Pagan Magic*, another script by Dorf. It was a sort of neo-Grecian fantasy in which a young girl is caught between a group of good spirits and evil spirits who try to separate her from the boy she loves. The conflict is resolved by a faun who plays a magic melody on his pipe, freeing the girl from the baddies. The faun was an actor named Bobbie Jackson in spotted tights, emulating Nijinsky. I was an evil spirit swathed in black-dyed cheese-cloth over black underpants. We chanted some lines in verse and moved to the fluid strains of Debussy's *Arabesque*. We were meant to be grotesque, and this also turned out to be in my range: something else I would recycle in the future. After the initial performances at Eaton Auditorium we gave a special perform-ance in a sunken garden behind a women's club on Prince Arthur Avenue. In the middle of the performance there was a huge downpour: the audience ran for cover but we finished the show as we knew Mrs. G. would expect. After the show we evil ones were covered with black dye. We were given money to buy our supper at the Honey Dew (one of Dorothy Goulding's favourite haunts), but they wouldn't let us in. The good spirits, whose white cheesecloth had left them unscathed, bought us hot dogs, which we ate while giggling in the rain on the steps of Philosopher's Walk before we took the streetcar to our homes. It was a moment of camaraderie that would build over the next few years.

After one more play I didn't hear from Mrs. G. for a year. I pestered my mother to phone and eventually she did. I was reinstated and handed an unex-pected challenge. The new play was *The Christmas Star*, one of Dorf's most successful works. The story centred on a group of street kids on Christmas Eve. As they played their games they fantasized about the presents they hoped to get but knew their parents couldn't afford. One of the boys, Dan, was lame and had trouble keeping up, but he was game and, in spite of having to use a crutch, tried to play tag with the others. Various passersby ignored the chil-dren, but a stranger stopped and talked to them. He told them about the Christmas Star, which appeared only on Christmas Eve but could grant one wish to someone who really deserved it. On this occasion, Dan was to be granted his wish: to be cured of his lameness.

I was cast as Dan, a vote of confidence that pleased and somewhat surprised me. The early rehearsals were awkward, and Mrs. G. told me I didn't have much feeling for the role. "Feeling" was one of her key words but initially I didn't understand what she was talking about. My idea of acting was pretend-ing to look like someone else; it had never occurred to me that acting could involve an inner connection with the character. Then I had the bright idea, or perhaps it was really Mrs. G.'s idea, that I should borrow the crutch and use it as I travelled to rehearsal and home again on the streetcar. People waited for me to clamber up the steps into the car; they stood aside and gave me their seats. They felt sorry for me and I didn't like this. I didn't want their pity; I felt I was stealing their sympathy. Somehow, in a way I didn't understand, this began to shape my performance: I felt both defiance and shame. It was the first time I had ever experienced an emotional connection with my character. And I realized the audience was not merely laughing at my antics but was genuinely moved.

In time I would come to understand that Dorothy Goulding was more intuitive than analytical, more tuned in to emotion than to logic. For her, feeling was the key. She was governed in her choices as a director by her *feelings*: for people, for behaviour, for historical periods. She knew when something *felt* right. Most of her plays were set in a particular period: the Middle Ages (*The Pied Piper of Hamelin*), imperial China (*Rival Peach Trees*), eighteenth-century France (*Cinderella*), ancient Egypt (*The Temple of Horus*), Victorian England (*Beauty and the Beast*), the Baghdad of the caliphs (*Aladdin*). For her, each of these times and places had its own feeling. She conveyed to me and to others a sense of this, and I came to see it as a valuable gift, one that I would use in my own work when the time came. Partly it was a matter of taste, but it was also the development of a certain sensibility that I absorbed over the years I worked with her, by some means that I didn't entirely comprehend. She showed us pictures, she demonstrated certain kinds of movement, but she never lectured us. She approached each play as a new adventure and carried us along with her.

Dorf would later maintain that her mother was not really much of a teacher and that she and her sisters often had to show the other actors how to do things. Certainly she was not academic in her approach. She had little grounding in mathematics and was a poor speller, but she was clear about what she wanted, and her efficient running of both her house at Dentonia and the TCP attest to her skills as a manager. When I try to recall her actual words, the phrases that come back to me are inclined to be "Martin Hunter, you're a floor sweeper" (because I looked down at my feet a lot), or "Martin Hunter, if you do that again I'll slap you." Not, of course, that she ever did slap me, or anyone else, but she was a rigorous disciplinarian who demanded — and got — our full attention and concentration on the work. She was interested in us as people but she rose above the personal. She challenged us to be the best we could be and we knew she would settle for nothing less. Her praise was sparing, but when it came, it meant something. I would realize later that there are many ways of teaching. As she wrote in one of her rare statements about her work, "Actors have different personalities and require different ways of approach."

In 1947, Mrs. G. mounted *The Pied Piper of Hamelin*. Arthur House, an adult actor with a sonorous voice, was the narrator for the Browning poem. The show involved a huge cast of forty actors ranging in age from twenty-five (Arthur) to seven (Jamie Cunningham making his TCP debut as the lame boy). The set was architectural, with a number of intersecting ramps that allowed for various processional effects, leading up to the climactic moment when the Piper takes the children away and only the little lame boy is left behind. Based on the paintings of Piero della Francesca the costumes would be recycled for other shows, particularly our felt boots, which were stored in shoe-boxes with our names on them. By the age of thirteen I had grown taller and was cast as Clerk of the City Corporation along with the bigger boys. I devised my own character, scribbling furiously with a quill pen as the others talked and argued. I had a huge book of records that seemed larger than I was and devised comic business, flipping through the pages or stumbling and almost dropping the book as I tried to follow the others and still keep writing. I got several laughs and was pleased with myself.

Mrs. G. had done a good many short pantomimes before this, playlets acted out without spoken dialogue to the accompaniment of music. As early as 1934, she devised pantomime versions of *The Three Bears*, *Jack and the Beanstalk*, and *Little Black Sambo*, which would be repeated several times in the years to come. The music for them was played by Babs MacKay, who became one of Dorothy Goulding's closest collaborators. Together they chose and arranged the music to suit the storyline. The music for *The Pied Piper* was an eclectic mix of Haydn, Schubert, and English folk tunes, with different motifs for the children, the Piper, and the Corporation of Hamelin. The ingenious combination owed much to Dorothy Goulding's musical knowledge and sensibility.

The Massey family had always had a keen interest in music. In the 1890s, they built Massey Hall and gave it to the city of Toronto. Dorothy Massey attended concerts with her mother and sister, sitting in the family box. In 1910,

Dorothy and her sister Madeline visited New York with their mother to see their older married sister Ruth Tovell and attended *Parsifal* at the Metropolitan Opera. Dorothy became a lifelong devotee of opera and in the 1940s and '50s listened religiously to the radio broadcasts of the Metropolitan Opera. Also in 1910, Dorothy started piano lessons. She showed an immediate aptitude, quickly mastering the early pieces she was given. She would evince a particular affinity for modern works: Debussy, Ravel, Stravinsky, and Gershwin, but she also loved the Romantics, particularly Schubert and Schumann. And of course Wagner. In 1912, Susan and her children sailed to Europe, visiting Ruth and her husband in Paris and travelling in Germany. Friends took them to the theatre, where Dorothy saw the Sergei Diaghilev ballet. She saw Vaslav Nijinsky and Anna Pavlova and the story ballets *Scheherazade* and *Petrouchka*, which would have a profound influence on her future work.

Later, music was a passion shared by her husband, Arthur Goulding, an accomplished pianist. In their teens, both dreamed of careers as concert virtuosi. Arthur Goulding was the son of a successful haberdasher, and although his family could not match the wealth of the Masseys, they were on a par socially. Arthur attended Lakefield College (from which he ran away twice) and later Ridley. Ten years older than Dorothy, he was a good friend of her cousin Vincent and of Hume Wrong. With them he was a member of the Seven Seekers, an intellectual society, and in their company he went to Oxford. He read history and practised the manly arts of self-defence: boxing and fencing. When war broke out he enlisted in the Royal Flying Corps and flew reconnaissance missions over France. At the war's end he returned to Canada preceded by a telegram, "Intend getting married," to find on his arrival that wedding plans were well under way. He had apparently been courting a young woman in New England, but he and Dorothy married in 1918.

In *The Pied Piper* I began to acquire the confidence to work with music and let it lead me, in spite of my awkwardness and inhibitions. But this production was important to me for another reason. Mrs. G. telephoned a week before rehearsals began and asked me to work on properties. She was concerned with how to represent the rats. She had made them out of papier mâché — but how to move them up the ramps and across the stage? I suggested stringing them in rows on fine black fishing twine. I could stand in the wings with a fishing reel and pull them across the stage. This idea proved workable and immediately established me as a sort of technical wizard. The actual work of stringing the rats was accomplished by Cook, Mrs. G.'s chauffeur, gardener, and all-round handyman. In the summer he maintained the lawns and trimmed the hedges at her house in Dentonia Park. In the winter he made most of the sets for the plays, setting them up and taking them down and often standing behind them to hold them up. He also drove Mrs. G. to and from rehearsal in an old wood-panelled station wagon, the back filled with props and costumes, with Mrs. G. making lists as Cook drove. It was typical of Mrs. G.'s aristocratic style that this old vehicle had no heat in winter but was driven by Cook wearing a proper chauffeur's cap.

Cook had started to work at Dentonia as a gardener's boy on her mother's estate from the age of thirteen, before transferring to Mrs. G.'s establishment. He was a gentle, rather shy man with a high but husky voice. It was obvious he would do anything that Mrs. G. asked him without question or complaint. He was unfailingly cheerful and pleasant to the actors, and particularly to those of us who worked backstage. His daughter, Betty, a tall handsome girl with a ready sense of fun, was part of the company and occasionally assisted Dorf in stage management, as did several other girls, particularly Ruth Comfort. Mrs. G. called him Cook in the English manner, as did her daughters. Ruth Comfort called him "Cookie," but, as we worked together manipulating the rats with our fishing reels, I was at a loss about how to address him. I asked him about this and he said, "Why don't you just call me Bill?" We became friends in the way that people who work closely together sometimes do, and he patiently taught me what little I know about carpentry and repairing things. Bill Cook could fix anything.

I never knew why Mrs. G. asked me to do props, but it quickly became my specialty. I think once again she relied on her intuition and a certain shrewd ability to assess individuals. She may have seen in me the vestiges of a sense of responsibility, and this vote of confidence certainly did a great deal to develop this quality in me. It gave me a certain status in the company, which I knew my acting skills could not command, and the freedom to go back and forth backstage laying out my props on special tables in the wings stage right and left, and sometimes helping Bill Cook shift scenery.

I was called upon to deal with technical problems in other shows. I had to make the roses grow up out of the ground in *The Snow Queen*, again employing invisible stings pushed through holes in the set while I stood behind and pulled them on cue. And I had to make a sudden appearance as Manitou in the

Indian spirit legend *He Who Makes Music*. This involved turning on a high-powered flashlight concealed in the folds of the blanket that was my costume, so that I was suddenly illuminated from below, giving me a truly spooky look and casting weird shadows on the set. These were my glory moments, more so than what I achieved in performance as an actor. Mrs. G. loved ingenuity and could be very inventive herself, creating wigs out of raffia and flexible masks out of support hose. On one occasion she wanted an effect of animals going up into Noah's ark, and so she consulted with Benny, the lighting man at Eaton Auditorium. He suggested all kinds of special equipment, but she arrived the next day with cut-outs that she had mounted on a piece of wire coat hanger. "Get me a goosenecked lamp," she commanded. She mounted the hanger on the lamp and when she rotated it the shadows of the animals did indeed seem to move up the ramp. "And I can make them come down again," she boasted. She rotated the coat hanger in the other direction and down they came.

My role as prop man also brought me into a closer intimacy with Mrs. G. About a week before rehearsals began for a new show, she would telephone me to discuss the prop plot. These conversations often lasted an hour and she would go on to discuss the music, the costuming, the style of movement, and the casting. She did most of the talking, with long pauses while she considered a problem, but I became in some sense a sounding board for her. Though I didn't realize it at the time, this was training in the basics of stage direction. Years later, when I became the artistic director of Hart House Theatre, I would hear myself saying something and think, "That's the voice of Dorothy Goulding speaking through me." (To complete the circle I found myself directing two of her grandsons, Dan and Reed Needles.) I never knew whether Mrs. G. was conscious of the training she was giving me, and by the time I was aware of the extent of her influence she was dead. I spoke of this not long ago to Dorf, who said, "Of course she would have no idea about that. She was simply looking for someone to listen." But I'm not so sure.

She had an uncanny knack of detecting capabilities in people and bringing them out. She drafted some of the parents of the actors to help her keep order backstage, particularly Mrs. Dalton and Mrs. Turner, both of whom had daughters in the company. They wore blue smocks embroidered with the initials TCP and provided an unfailing oasis of calm when kids had sudden attacks of the jitters and thought they were going to throw up or got their costumes tangled. These mothers laid out the makeup on the big table, helped clean up at the end of the day, and straightened out any confusion about who was assigned to which dressing room. Most of the actors stayed in their dressing rooms and were not allowed to wander about. One of the senior actors gave the calls — "Fifteen minutes, please," "Five minutes, please," "Beginners, please" — and the actors made their way to the wings and collected their props from my prop tables.

Perhaps Mrs. G.'s most remarkable discovery was Jack Medhurst. Like me he started at the age of nine; unlike me he quickly established himself as a natural. He had a real aptitude for mime and moving to music. Mrs. G. once stated, "I believe that mime is the fundamental of all acting. . . . It can be understood in all languages. Mime should be learned before speaking." It was basic to the work she did and closely allied to her appreciation of dance. She had not studied dance herself, but all of her daughters had ballet training and many of the girls in the TCP also studied with Bettina Byers, Mildred Wickson, and Boris Volkoff, the primary teachers of the day. Jack and one or two of the other boys also took dance classes, which of course enhanced their ability to move to music. I never considered it. I was aware of my poor coordination, but I knew my father would never have tolerated anything so sissy.

Acting was suspect enough as an activity for boys in the '40s and '50s. I was aware of a homoerotic undercurrent in the TCP but there was nothing overt in my experience. I would realize later that a fairly high percentage of the male TCP actors were homosexual, and apparently there were fumblings in the darkened wings of Eaton Auditorium and the woods at Dentonia. Dorf claims her mother was unwilling or unable to see and come to terms with this phenomenon. Certainly Mrs. G.'s husband Arthur Goulding tuned into it. He would occasionally say that one of the great problems of the modern world was that men were becoming more like women and women more like men. He once made a pronouncement that homosexuals were "rare, incurable and dangerous." Today he would be called homophobic. The fact that he had a sibling who was raised as a girl and then decided to lead an adult life as a man no doubt influenced his judgment.

For Mrs. G. I think the opportunity to be associated with young boys was stimulating and filled a gap she felt at not having sons of her own. Those of us who took primarily comic roles were able to laugh and joke with her, and our relationship was easier than for those who played romantic leads: the princes, shepherd lads, and younger sons. They were often beautiful boys who came under the spell of a strong and commanding woman, a kind of contemporary Snow Queen relationship. If the boys were gay, and most of them were, the relationship had a sort of built-in safety factor. It was erotically charged but nothing sexual was going to happen. It was a bit like the courtly love paradigm, where the Lady was already married and so high above the troubadour that consummation was unthinkable. Mrs. G. would not have seen it in these terms. The effect on the boys may have been more damaging, or so some of her actors would later theorize, but Mrs. G. was not concerned with their future lives or careers. She worked and lived in the present, and when her actors moved on, she moved on. Except in the case of Jack.

Jack was not only the uncrowned king of pantomime; he was also the master of makeup. I had supposed he had studied it somewhere, but when I spoke with him recently he told me, "There was nowhere to study. Mrs. G. simply told me she wanted me to design the makeup for *Little Black Sambo*. She gave me a little book and some sticks of Leichner, and I started to experiment." By the time I began with the TCP, Jack was in full command. We were expected to learn how to do our own makeup and Jack taught us, starting with what he called "the glamorous or corrective straight," which was designed to enhance one's best features and disguise the worst. We began with a mixture of Leichner 5 and 9 and blended a skin tone all over our faces, then used eyeliner and added colour to our cheeks and lips: pinkish for the girls and a sort of terracotta colour for the boys.

Later we would learn to do character makeup, adding wrinkles for age, perhaps a scar for a pirate or very elaborate special effects if we were playing Orientals or Indians, or as we might now say, Asians and Natives. It was serious business. We customarily arrived backstage at about eight in the morning, checked our names off on the call sheet, stripped down to our undershirts and began our makeup, while onstage the auditorium's four grand pianos were being tuned, the repeated notes ascending through the silence as we worked. Idle chatter was not permitted. Nor were we ever allowed to go into the audience or the lobby in costume and makeup. We went by a backstage passage to eat our lunch in Eaton's employees' cafeteria, and then returned to the theatre and did touch-ups for the afternoon performance. Friends and family were allowed to come backstage and watch us take off our makeup; each of us was allowed a single Kleenex. Mrs. G was nothing if not frugal. Then into our street clothes, a quick goodbye to Mrs. G., who would be gathering up props and costumes with the help of Bill Cook, and off to the Honey Dew to rehash the near disasters of the day's performances, as actors seem to need to do the world over.

For the next few years I was involved in every show as a prop man and was usually cast in the show as well, probably because I was going to be on deck anyway. I played a series of more or less comic roles. I was a silly courtier who danced with both the ugly sisters (played by two clever comediennes, Anne Comfort and Eileen Torrans) at the ball in *Cinderella*; a comic robber in *The Snow Queen*, where I played opposite Denise Pears' drunken robber wife and snored for her because she was too delicate to make such vulgar sounds; the adipose Sultan in *Aladdin*, vastly padded and tended by scantily clad dancing girls Betty Keir and Susan Sanders, all of whom became friends. I was also cast in a number of singing and dancing choruses in *The Master Cat* (Dorf's lively adaptation of *Puss in Boots*), *Rumpelstiltskin*, and *Jorinda and Jorindel*. In these plays, six or eight of us would double as courtiers, mowers and reapers, shepherds, or whatever incidental characters were required. We would sing short songs and perform rustic or stately dances, and although I had no great aptitude for this I improved with practice. I could carry a tune and more or less mastered the minuet, the gavotte, and the Morris dance. I was also cast in smaller roles in pantomimes, the woodcutter in *Little Red Riding Hood*, a doctor in a circus story devised by Jack Medhurst called *Under the Big Top*, and, the most fun, one of the tigers in *Little Black Sambo*. I could see virtually nothing and poured with sweat in the tiger mask that Jack had devised from chicken wire covered with papier mâché, but once again my comic instincts were given free rein and I made the most of the opportunity.

I felt I had penetrated the inner circle of the TCP. At its centre was Dorf. Mrs. G. had largely given up on the British plays she had favoured in the early years and concentrated on producing pantomimes with music and Dorf's plays, some original, some her reworkings of such classics as *Cinderella*, *The Snow Queen*, *Aladdin*, and *Sleeping Beauty*. Dorf stage-managed the plays, and sometimes appeared in them, especially if one of the actors was suddenly taken ill. On one occasion player Eleanor Jackson ran into the wings and started to throw up. Dorf ran out onstage, improvised her lines to the end of the scene, and rushed back into the wings to cue the curtain. When I was first in the plays, Dorf still lived with her parents at Dentonia. By her own admission she more or less ran the house for her mother. She also taught kindergarten. At the end of the war she married William Needles, who had been a TCP actor and was to become a mainstay of the Stratford company.

I attended Dorf's wedding at Holy Trinity. The whole affair was, not surprisingly, a triumph of stage management. I remember Dorf driving up in the huge Packard that was taken out only on very grand occasions. She sat in a cloud of tulle beside her father while Cook drove in full chauffeur's uniform. We waited inside the church as the guests assembled. At exactly the right musical moment Mrs. G., in a long turquoise gown, came down the aisle on the arm of Jack Medhurst, resplendent in tails. Jack joined nine other ushers who marched down the aisle followed by the TCP's ten prettiest girls in pink bridesmaid dresses, arranged according to height, the shortest in front. Their hair was wreathed in orange blossoms and they carried lit candles. Then came Dorf in a splendid gown on the arm of her father. She was delivered to her groom and turned to give him a ravishing smile, which she "cheated out" a bit for the benefit of the spectators. Dorf had then, and has still, a most winning smile.

Dorf and Bill lived in a house on St. Clement's Avenue and within a year their first child was born. She was brought to the theatre in a basket and stayed in the green room under the supervision of Mrs. Dalton while Dorf stage-managed. Dorf nicknamed her "Feathers," a soubriquet which didn't stick, perhaps fortunately, as there is nothing fluffy about the adult Jane Needles, who has become a highly competent stage and theatre manager. Before long, Dorf embarked on a new career in broadcasting. She created *Kindergarten of the Air*, a fifteen-minute program that she did five days a week for the CBC. She wrote the scripts, played the piano, sang songs, and told stories. Later, when I was an undergraduate, some of my friends and I used to catch her program in the Junior Common Room at Trinity College. We sang along with her as she trilled through "Baa, Baa Black Sheep" and "Mary Had a Little Lamb," acted out at her instructions for "Jack, Be Nimble, Jack, Be Quick" and "Hi Diddle, Diddle," and when she said, "Now. Let's all pretend to be fairies," the antics can be imagined. When I told Dorf about this, she laughed appreciatively. Like her mother, she always had a lively sense of humour.

Dorf was accomplished as a dancer, pianist, performer, playwright, and organizer. She was also highly ambitious. She eventually produced five children, and while maintaining a large house in North Toronto, she bought and operated a farm near Caledon, complete with chickens, cattle, and a huge vegetable garden. She continued to do *Kindergarten of the Air* but spent half the year on the farm, half in Toronto, moving the kids from a sophisticated urban school to a small rural one from the beginning of May till the end of October. Bill spent an increasing amount of time at Stratford, but she brought up her children according to her own progressive theories and they all undoubtedly turned out to be colourful individuals. She continued to collaborate with her mother, but a certain amount of tension developed over time. This was perhaps inevitable, since Dorf had so many irons in the fire and her mother had become somewhat more rigid in her later years. At one point Dorf confronted her and said, "You know, Mother, you're not making it very easy for anyone to follow after you," to which Dorothy Goulding replied, "No one is going to follow after me. The TCP is mine and when I'm finished with it, it's over." And so it would prove.

I must confess I had mixed feelings about Dorf. I was impressed by her energy, creativity, and sheer productivity, but I was also intimidated. I did not consider her as original as J. M. Barrie or as witty as A. A. Milne, but I had the judgmental arrogance of the young who, having accomplished nothing themselves, are therefore hypercritical. I now realize she wrote crisp, effective dialogue that held the attention of her child audience in a way that clever British wordplay did not. She had a clear grasp of character, understood dramatic structure, and knew how to tell a story. She was in some ways doing what Disney had just started to do: take traditional fairy tales and adapt them for an audience of contemporary children. She would no doubt have been horrified by this comparison, and Mrs. G. even more so. At the time all the literati thought Disney was a cheap populist; they did not foresee that he was going to influence and eventually dominate the world of popular entertainment in North America and, indeed, far beyond.

I had my own ambitions as a playwright, but I never succeeded in writing a play that Mrs. G. thought suitable for production at Eaton Auditorium. I had more success at Dentonia. Here Mrs. G. held summer classes at her home during July and August for about twelve to twenty members of the company. Several of us would meet at Yonge and Bloor for the long streetcar ride across the Bloor viaduct and along the Danforth. We would walk up Dawes Road and into the park, skirting a rather stagnant pond with large golden carp swimming below the surface, then along a wooded drive, across a wide lawn past a little summer house and the deserted tennis courts to a small terrace centred around a pool with water lilies, guarded by four enormous cedar trees, and finally — up a steep flight of stone steps and onto the lawn at the south side of the house, where Mrs. G. would be waiting on the porch. We would set up camp stools and classes would begin.

For us Dentonia was a magical world, remote from our everyday lives. Susan Massey had given Dorothy and Arthur a substantial piece of property on the edge of the farm at Dentonia when they married. Here they built a house, originally intended as a summer residence. It was a roomy building, half-timbered in the Elizabethan style, with mullioned windows, gabled roofs, and a large brick chimney beside the wrought-iron-hinged front door. It was dominated by a spacious living room, lined with Arthur's impressive collection of books, and featured a Bechstein piano. A huge fireplace was flanked by chintz-covered sofas and a splendid Oriental carpet covered the floor. In the centre of the room was an old German refectory table with carved wooden legs. The walls were hung with pictures: German paintings in the manner of Breughel, black-and-white portrait photographs, and reproductions of the paintings of Van Gogh. The house was simple, elegant, and original, in stark contrast to the elaborate neo-rococo decor that was fashionable at the time.

Here Dorothy and Arthur entertained their contemporaries and relatives: Ruth and Harold Tovell, Vincent and Alice Parkin Massey, Dorothy's girlhood friend "Queenie" Meredith, and the painter Lawren Harris (of the Harris family, who were Massey partners), among others. The young couple was not entirely in tune with the ideas and outlooks of their contemporaries. After one dinner party, Dorothy observed in her diary, "My family are very nice but I wish their ideas about art were not so dashed *commercial*." They would continue to have evening parties at Dentonia Park; some of their musical friends, such as Freddy Manning and the Hambourgs, would play classical music, and Dorothy would direct her daughters in short plays. The four Goulding girls (Helen, Ann, Susan, and Dorf) had already impressed their cousins and neighbours with their imagination, energy, and daring. Vincent Tovell recalls that he and his brothers referred to these cousins as "the Power Pack."

By the time I was invited to Dentonia, Mrs. G.'s classes had evolved in scope and complexity. Usually we would start with simple technical exercises involving stage falls, trips, turns on the stairs, all of which we would be taught to execute in a precise and stylish manner. Then Mrs. G., using a gramophone, would give us perhaps twelve bars of music and we would be expected to walk in a circle, reaching the starting point at the exact end of the music. The exercises would become more elaborate; we would be given a pattern of movement such as this: enter down the stairs, find an object, sit on a bench, get up, start to go back up the stairs, stop, pause a moment and then exit. We would be expected to fill out this pattern to tell a story (or as we might say now, motivate the moves). Mrs. G. would comment on the believability of the work and sometimes the other actors would also comment. Then we would be given a longer section of music, perhaps forty bars of Schubert's *Marche Militaire* or Ravel's *Empress of the Pagodas*, one of Gershwin's *Preludes*, or the gavotte from Prokofiev's *Classical Symphony*, and be asked to tell a story in mime to the music. These would be rehearsed three or four times before they were presented to the class. Another exercise would involve doing some action such as brushing our teeth, putting on our shoes, or opening an envelope in such a manner as to express a particular emotional state: anticipation, perhaps, or weariness or disgust.

I recall my friend Jimmy Armour, when asked to express fear, asked, "Do you want me to be horrified or terrified?"

To which Mrs. G. replied coolly, "Both. Start with horrified."

Once Mrs. G.'s daughter Susan visited the class and asked us to express every emotion we could think of. Several of us managed ten or twelve. Then Susan did every emotion she could think of and came up with an impressive total of forty-three. Susan had been one of the most accomplished performers in the TCP in the early years. She had dominated her mother's production of A. A. Milne's *Toad of Toad Hall*, an adaptation of Kenneth Grahame's *The Wind in the Willows*, with her performance of Toad, who is one of the great characters of children's literature: the conceited, flamboyant, devious but lovable hero, half prankish schoolboy, half arrogant playboy. She went on to become the leading actress of the company, though her mother would not have acknowledged this and sometimes cast her in small roles to prevent her from becoming too full of herself, an attitude that betrayed her Methodist upbringing. But Susan's performances as the wicked stepmother in *Snowdrop and the Seven Dwarfs*, the reluctant dragon, Queen Elizabeth, the wolf in *Little Red Riding Hood*, and the mock turtle in *Alice's Adventures in Wonderland* were remembered by the older actors of the TCP with admiration and something approaching awe.

The day she visited our class with Mrs. G. Susan capped her virtuoso emotional workout by performing a monologue she had written in the manner of Ruth Draper, which was to be part of a one-woman show she would tour in the late '40s. She left as we applauded and we repaired to the covered porch to sit on our camp stools and eat the sandwiches we had brought in brown paper bags while Mrs. G. supplied us with milk (shades of her father's City Dairy) and Dad's Cookies. Sometimes Dr. Goulding would join us for a few minutes and ask us what we were reading. In the early days of their marriage, when he was a medical student in Boston, Arthur had been very much his young wife's intellectual mentor. Tall and handsome with a head of thick, curly hair and a dashing moustache, he was a bit of a dandy, even in middle age. I remember his brightly striped athletic blazers and black velvet smoking jackets. He was also something of a polymath, well versed in science and mathematics, and a voracious reader of novelists from Dickens to Tolstoy, history from Gibbon to Spengler, and philosophy from Nietzsche to Bertrand Russell. Dr. G. was influenced by Fabian socialism as propounded by George Bernard Shaw and the radical psychological writings of Sigmund Freud. He pronounced on contemporary literature, played the flute, and wrote poetry. Dorothy picked up on his enthusiasms, and many of her ideas were influenced by his caustically phrased opinions. She worked to keep up with him, reading the *New Statesman* and the *New Yorker*. To us teenagers he would recommend ever more challenging works: if I was reading Dickens's *Nicholas Nickleby* he would suggest *Dombey and Son*, if Dumas's *Three Musketeers* then Dostoevsky's *Crime and Punishment*. He practised one-upmanship before it became fashionable, and although I always got on reasonably well with him, I could understand why some of the other boys referred to him as "Old Piss and Vinegar."

In the early evening after our supper we would go up on the hill behind the house for a session of what Mrs. G. called "Free Acting." Two or usually three of us would be given a clue unknown to the others. It might be that we had just stolen something and were looking for a place to hide it, that we had had a fight with our parents and decided to run away from home, or that we just wanted to get away from everybody and be alone for awhile. Mrs. G. would signal us when it was time to enter. We would then interact with the other actor or actors, inventing our characters, reacting to what they told us or didn't tell us as a story emerged and was finally in some way resolved. This was my favourite activity of all. It certainly did a great deal to build our skills as actors and in my case ultimately as a writer. It was the need to relinquish control and let the story take shape that was the biggest revelation. I don't know how Mrs. G. stumbled on this exercise in the 1940s. I never heard her mention Stanislavsky, but I now realize we were doing a very complex form of improvisation long before it became part of fashionable theatrical training.

These sessions were customarily held on Tuesday and Thursday. Then on Saturday we would assemble at one o'clock and be divided into three groups of four or perhaps five actors and assigned a location: the little bridge over the creek, the woods below the hill, the steps leading up from the lily pond to the south lawn. We would then work together in our group to devise a short play. We would invent some dialogue and choose our characters within the demands of the story. After two or three hours of rehearsal we would head off to the wing of the house that had been the servants' quarters. In the small bedrooms in brightly painted bureaus and chiffoniers were stored pieces of costumes: jester's caps, fur coats, gypsy skirts, tall silk hats, capes and riding breeches, and diaphanous gowns. We would pick whatever seemed most appropriate and then have our supper on the porch. After eating we would go down into the big basement room, do our makeup and get dressed. Each group would perform its playlet for the other two. There was not a great deal of criticism or discussion of this work afterwards. The point was the doing of it, and we would head home with a satisfying feeling of accomplishment and exhilaration.

At the end of the summer there would be a final evening at Dentonia when we presented some of the playlets that Mrs. G. considered the best of the summer, often considerably reworked. There was an invited audience of our parents, various friends of the Gouldings, and the actors. The evening had an air of festivity, with Mrs. G. suddenly appearing in a long dress and Dr. G. in his velvet smoking jacket. There were refreshments; I don't think liquor was served, not that the Gouldings were teetotallers, but it would have been considered inappropriate because of the children involved. Mrs. G. often directed a special production she particularly wanted to do but considered inappropriate for the season at Eaton Auditorium. I remember costumes inspired by Velasquez for a dramatization of Oscar Wilde's *The Birthday of the Infanta*, with Molly Golby in the role of the imperious Spanish princess and Bobbie Jackson as the hunchbacked dwarf whose heart she breaks; and a sort of medieval pageant called *The Six Saints of Healing*, which invoked the paintings of Flemish masters like Hugo van der Goes and Hans Memling.

The last two summers I was at Dentonia I wrote several short plays, two of which were considered good enough to be performed at the final evening.

Both were comedies, and in both I penned a good part for myself. In *François*, two older women bring flowers to the grave of a former lover. They do not recognize each other, and when they discover they are both there for the same reason, they begin to wrangle over who was his favourite. At this point François (my character) rises from the grave and explains that he loved them both equally so the only way out of his dilemma was to shoot himself. He reconciles the women, who go off together to devote the rest of their lives to his memory. The other play concerned a wily priest (played by me again) who manipulates the families and friends of two young lovers who are opposed to their marriage in order to get money to build a bell tower for his church. In the end the lovers are united and the bell tower is funded. This piece had six characters and I had some trouble with the plotting; at one point Dorf took the script and did a rewrite. I resented this but learned something about dramatic construction in the process. And I had a minor success in the role of the priest.

Two productions stand out in my last years with the TCP at Eaton Auditorium. *Pirates!* was one of Dorf's most successful entertainments. A group of children and their exceptionally proper governess are kidnapped by a raffish bunch of brigands, but, of course, eventually manage to outsmart their captors and escape. The piece was closer to *Peter Pan* than *Treasure Island* and was a great favourite with audiences. I played Jem, one of the pirates, who was allowed to be both funny and grotesque, my two specialties. I made Mrs. G. laugh, even in rehearsal, not an uncommon accomplishment but gratifying nonetheless. Almost my last role was the stranger who tells the children about the Christmas Star in a remount of the play in which I had played Dan, the lame boy. It was a brief appearance, but in the first performance I remember the absolute hush as I told the story and the whole audience hung on my words. It was as though I sent out a wave of feeling into the audience and they sent a sympathetic wave back to me. After the performance I told Mrs. G. about this and she said, "I know. I felt it too." At later performances the effect was not quite as strong, but it was there. I am not a particularly religious person but this experience had a sort of spiritual quality, one that would happen for me only one more time in the theatre, after I had left the TCP.

In my last year of high school I was still very much part of the TCP, but I sensed that it would soon be time to move on. Some of my older friends in the company had already done so, and a new, younger generation were coming up. I never discussed this with Mrs. G., but I felt she understood and accepted my decision. Although I continued to do theatre work after I left, she never inquired about it or came to see it. Nor did I expect her to. She had no interest in her actors going on to have professional theatrical careers; indeed she was rather opposed to the idea. Most of us ultimately chose other fields of endeavour: medicine, teaching, or architecture, for example.

Unlike her unacknowledged rival, Dora Mavor Moore, Mrs. G. had no interest in the theatre as a profession. I don't think I ever heard her use the word "professional," and even today it arouses my suspicion. I might paraphrase the words of George Bernard Shaw to say that in the theatre, professionalism is often the last refuge of the untalented. Dorothy Goulding was part of a generation of artists in Toronto who were highly cultivated and accomplished, but largely unconcerned with making money by pursuing the activities that dominated their interests and their lives. They were not all wealthy or influential, but they all seemed to know each other and many of them gathered at the Arts and Letters Club, the Heliconian Club, and Hart House. They lay the groundwork for the first generation of professionals who would come after and find their footing in the years immediately following the Second World War: the founders of the Canadian Opera Company and the National Ballet, the Crest Theatre and the Stratford Festival, Painters Eleven, Hart House and CBC Orchestras, and such writers as Robertson Davies and Margaret Laurence.

Like many of the other actors, I kept in touch with Mrs. G. after I left, and I went to see her productions. She was always happy to see me but she was preoccupied with her own work. A story told by Jack Medhurst rings true. He had been away, in New York I think, and on his return called Mrs. G., who said,

"Do come and see me on Saturday and we'll have a good old chat."

He arrived at Dentonia to find her preparing for an evening performance: "Thank heavens you've come. I need you to make a beard for Zeus. I've got some crepe hair."

She left him to go back to rehearsal, returning in an hour to say, "That's perfect. I do hope you can stay for the show." And back she went to her actors.

Although she appreciated the talent of her daughter Susan, she did not particularly support her when she decided to become a professional actress under the name Susan Fletcher. Susan went on to act in Hollywood, appearing in a film of *The Secret Garden* and later mounting her one-woman show, but at some point she gave up on the stage and went to Jamaica to live with her second husband. I remember Mrs. G. saying that Susan had a formidable talent but no ability to follow through. For Susan, a beard for Zeus did not come ahead of sitting down with old friends for a good old chat. She didn't have her mother's ability to organize and concentrate her efforts on the work. What she did have was an ability, vital in an actress, to seize and be in the moment.

In the late 1970s, I was mounting a professional production of *The Cherry Orchard* at Hart House Theatre. Susan arrived at my office and asked if she could audition for Ranevskaya, a role she had always felt she was destined to play. She had dressed the part with a splendid hat, furs, and gloves. She sat across from me and talked of her life in Jamaica: how she had scared off robbers with her husband's shotgun when she was alone in the big house, how she had put up with her husband's infidelities, how she had cried when they took away the horses. She asked if she might use my phone to call a friend. They spoke in German, and Susan promised to loan her friend some money for her rent. She reminisced about the good old days and told me what a handsome little boy I had been. She then asked the dates of the production, and when I told her, she said, "Oh darling, I'm so sorry, I can't do it. I have to visit a sick friend in Vienna." And she swept out. I had already cast the part but I was sorry; she might have been magnificent. But Susan did not need to play Ranevskaya. She had become Ranevskaya.

After I left the TCP in 1951, Mrs. G. continued to produce plays at Eaton Auditorium, but gradually the seasons became shorter with fewer plays, two a year and then only one. In 1958 she moved back to Hart House Theatre where she had started. The Kindergarten Association could no longer cope with selling tickets in all the Toronto schools as the city expanded. And no doubt the coming of television made entertainment more readily available to kids and changed their tastes. In 1959, Arthur Goulding had a severe stroke and she decided to devote herself to caring for him. Several of us visited her at Dentonia and she seemed much the same, though a bit diminished with the passing of time and the limitations she had placed on herself. When Arthur died she decided to move and took an apartment on Avenue Road. She was not happy there and it became apparent she was beginning to suffer from dementia. I called her and we had a number of lengthy telephone conversations. I offered to visit her and she said she would like that but not today. Others — Jack Medhurst, Charles Winter, and David Earle — arrived on her doorstep and sometimes took her for short walks, but her condition was deteriorating. She died in 1968. Many of the TCP actors went to her funeral at St. James the Less. It was a ceremony of simple dignity that she would have approved of, a chance for reminiscence and re-connection with old friends.

The years passed. In the summer of 2001, I was approached by Robert Morgan, an actor, writer, and director who had been asked to become artistic director of the Toronto Children's Peace Theatre, a group of kids who would participate in a summer program on the grounds of Dentonia. To help publicize this enterprise I conceived the idea of a reunion of TCP alumni. With the help of my sister-in-law, Alison Stein, I tracked down some of the hundreds of people who had acted in Mrs. G.'s plays over the years. On a sunny July afternoon we gathered at Dentonia. As forty people made their way across the lawn, many of whom I had not seen for fifty years, most were instantly recognizable in spite of their white hair, their glasses, their wrinkles. They came from Montreal, Halifax, New York, and Chicago, and there were greetings from London, Los Angeles, Vancouver, Bermuda, and New Mexico.

Memories, sometimes contradictory, were freely traded. Dorf, organized as always, provided food and drink with the help of a grandson. Her daughter Jane took us around the house and we revisited the basement where we used to make up, the big room that was used for receptions, the little rooms in the old servants' wing that used to contain costumes and props, the old nursery where Mrs. G. did her sewing and which she referred to as "The Chaos Room." Jimmy Armour, after forty years in a Presbyterian pulpit, gave a witty speech in which he confessed his teenage infatuation for Susan. I had been warned that Susan was suffering from a dementia similar to her mother's, but she responded with grace and vigour, invoking friendly ghosts and spirits of the past. More than Dorf, she seemed to have something of the eagle look of her mother. We talked together of Mrs. G. as the afternoon waned, and a great many of us said the same thing: "Dorothy Goulding changed my life."

THE BELLS OF HELL

My family didn't have a summer cottage. My father didn't take holidays; he liked work and preferred being at the office to being home with his family. My mother thought running a cottage was twice as much trouble as running a house; at a cottage there would be no conveniences and no maid. Neither of my parents had any interest in swimming, fishing, or paddling a canoe. They had no desire to commune with the great outdoors since they'd had quite enough of nature when they were kids on the farm. They did, however, think that my brother and I should swim, and paddle, and sail: these were things that middle-class kids were supposed to be able to do. And the best place to learn them was at summer camp. When I turned twelve, it was decided I should be sent off to the wilds to acquire these essential skills. I resisted the idea because I didn't want to be away from home. My parents countered by suggesting I should go with one of my friends, and then I wouldn't be homesick.

At this point in my life I had two best friends: Dick and Jimmy. I campaigned to go to camp with Dick, who the previous summer had learned how to swim the Australian crawl and inhale cigarette smoke. He had also learned the facts of life, which he imparted to me, with extravagant embellishments, some accurate, some fanciful. He produced a package of French safes and we tried them on. We had not yet started to develop, so the safes were too big and fell off, but Dick showed me how to manipulate my small penis so that I was able to get a hard-on. He also sang me several dirty songs he had learned. One I remember went like this:

> Away down in Blighty
> Where she wore her nightie
> And I wore my BVDS
> I kissed her, caressed her
> And then I undressed her
> And oh, what a form she showed to me.
> I tickled her boobies,
> Her lily-white boobies

And down where the short hair grows
Her lips they grew sweeter
I whipped out my peter
And whitewashed her red, red rose.

Needless to say I didn't try this song out on my parents, although I suspect my mother might have been quite entertained. But even without hearing the song, my parents believed Dick was a bad influence. They thought I'd do better to go to camp with my other friend, Jimmy.

Dick's parents were "artistic" and therefore suspect, but Jimmy's father was a Presbyterian minister. He was not dour but rather Dickensian in appearance, with a snub nose and a comical Irish accent. Twice a year as a guest preacher in our church, within two minutes of ascending the pulpit, he had the congregation laughing, something no other minister achieved or even attempted. Jimmy was like his father in both appearance and personality. He could make my mother laugh. The combination of respectability and humour clinched it.

But I suspected that Jimmy was wary of being too closely associated with me. I was nearly two years younger, and Jimmy moved in more advanced social circles. He had been to Mrs. van Valkenburg's dancing classes and he went to a lot more birthday parties than I did. (Though he was impressed that I'd been invited to a birthday party at Mickey Sifton's house, a vast mansion with a staff of six, even in wartime. I just happened to be in Mickey's class at school that year.) I thought Dick might be a genius but my parents thought he was crazy; Jimmy was a more appropriate companion in their eyes. I instinctively knew to keep the two apart. I sensed Jimmy was a bit jealous of Dick, and I used this. I told Jimmy that Dick wanted me to go to summer camp with him. Jimmy responded by saying I should go to his camp. He'd get his parents to talk to my parents.

My father was pleased to hear from Jimmy's father. My mother got a brochure from the camp and began sewing name tags in the required clothing: the two pairs of pyjamas, the three bathing suits, the windbreaker, the six coloured T-shirts and two white short-sleeved dress shirts for Sunday chapel, the four pairs of shorts, six pairs of underpants and six matching undershirts, the eight pairs of socks, and the tennis shoes and scampers and sandals and rubber boots. My mother hated sewing but was no doubt spurred on by the thought that she would have a whole month of the summer when I wasn't around to pester and plague her, as she might have put it. (In fact she had by this time perfected a triangular game in which she was the pivotal figure, a sort of suburban Mata Hari who acted as a double agent in the ongoing battle developing between my father and me; she alternately denounced me for some real or imagined misdemeanour, and then pleaded with him to mitigate my punishment. One would have thought that I should have been happy to escape from this endless farrago of conniving and treachery, but I couldn't imagine any other modus vivendi. Subterranean intrigue had become my idea of normal family behaviour.)

Eventually the name tags were all in place, my two suitcases packed, school over for the year, Sunday school and Cubs and my piano lessons suspended for the summer, and the day arrived to set off for camp. We boarded a train at Union Station. I sat next to Jimmy and he introduced me to his friends from last year. In no time at all he was surrounded by a group of laughing, joking boys who came up to him offering gum and chocolate bars. I basked in his glory, ignored by the others but happy enough until we arrived at our destination. Buses picked us up at the station at Gravenhurst and drove us down a narrow road under towering pines to the campsite on the edge of a sparkling lake. But the beauty of the scene was lost on me once I found out that Jimmy and I had been assigned to different cabins. I begged to be moved but was informed that Jimmy was in a senior age group, so that was that.

By the time I arrived in my cabin, the other seven boys had already settled in and were sitting around "shooting the breeze," to use an expression of the period. No one said hello or in any way acknowledged my arrival. There was one upper bunk left. I climbed up into it and lay on my belly. I felt left out and miserable. A great wave of homesickness washed over me. I wrote my parents the first of many letters telling them I wanted to go home. Then we were all summoned for evening prayers. These went on for about three quarters of an hour. As well as an appeal to the Almighty to guide every thought, word, and deed while at the camp, there were Bible readings from both Testaments and several hymns.

I began to realize something that I had not been prepared for: this camp was primarily a religious institution. It was run by clergymen and the wives and sons of clergymen. It was interdenominational and determinedly evangelical. As the prayers rolled on, we sought Divine guidance to be granted in the conduct of affairs by our King and Country and implored success for the

Allied forces fighting in Europe. But most fervently of all we prayed for the salvation of the soul of each and every boy present. That was the object of this whole operation: the saving of every camper's soul, nothing less. If possible, the camp sought to transform us all into Christian gentlemen, though if it came to a choice between manners and salvation, manners would be sacrificed.

It was further put to us that salvation could be fun. Christianity didn't have to be gloomy. God wanted us to have a good laugh once in awhile. He enjoyed seeing smiling faces; He liked to hear cheerful voices. Thus the hymns we sang were upbeat and jolly. The one that became my favourite was introduced to us at this first prayer service:

> The bells of hell ring ting-a-ling-a-ling
> For you, for you, not me
> The bells of heaven ring ling-a-ling-a-ling
> And that's where I shall be
> Oh death, where is thy sting-a-ling-a-ling
> Where, grave, thy victory?
> For it's ling-a-ling-a-ling, not ting-a-ling-a-ling
> Yes, it's ling-a-ling-a-ling for me.

Prayers were followed by supper, which featured greasy stew and corn syrup for dessert. I found both courses disgusting, little realizing that the quality of the food would gradually deteriorate as the month progressed. I had never imagined that corn flakes could be considered an adequate supper for a growing boy, but I was to plumb culinary depths as yet unimagined by my pampered palate. After supper came campfire. More evangelical songs were sung and two or three boys stood up and told us how they'd found Jesus Christ as their personal Saviour. One claimed to have seen Jesus walking toward him across the waves of Lake Minipiming as he paddled his canoe early one morning and realized he was being carried downstream by a strong current. The boy began to recount what Jesus had said to him: "Don't worry, kid, you ain't gonna be drownded . . ." at which point the campfire leader started up another song. Was he motivated by considerations of veracity or style? Jesus, I could imagine, wasn't supposed to make mistakes in grammar.

At this point Jimmy offered to sing a funny song he had learned from his father. He performed in a piercing soprano, with an expression of mock solemnity:

> While the organ peeled potatoes
> "Lard" was rendered by the choir
> As the voices rose to heaven
> Someone set the church on fire.
> "Holy smoke," the preacher shouted
> In the rush he lost his hair.
> Now his head resembles Heaven
> For there is no parting there.

The campfire leader's face was a study in conflicting emotions. Was this sacrilege? Surely not, if it came from the lips of the son of the general director of the British and Foreign Bible Society. Better to treat it as good clean fun, especially as the boys greeted it with giggles and a round of applause. And after all, he'd already told us that God liked a good laugh. So this song was accepted into the campfire repertoire and sung almost every night, and Jimmy's popularity grew rapidly. I determined to follow his example.

After campfire we went back to our cabin and our counsellor came in and sat on one of the lower bunks. He was a blond young man with wire-rimmed glasses and a serious expression. He had grown up in China where his parents were missionaries and been shipped home two weeks before the fall of Shanghai. Now he was in divinity school. (He was so short-sighted he was exempt from military service.) Because of the connection he was known as Lee Foo, though he couldn't have looked less Chinese. All the counsellors had assumed names, *noms de guerre* in their battle to control the kids. I never learned what Lee Foo's real name was, though I did ask him what Lee Foo meant. He gave me various answers, according to his mood: Wise Counsellor, Good Guy, and once, when I tried to wheedle my way out of something I didn't want to do, Tough Nut. I said it couldn't mean all those things but he told me that was the way Chinese worked. One word could mean many different things. It all depended on the way you said it.

Lee Foo talked to us rather intensely for half an hour, asking us what activities we were interested in and what sports we wanted to play. He himself taught canoeing and archery. I opted to take the latter. He was interested that

I had some acting experience and promised to take me to meet the dramatics counsellor. What about water sports? He was horrified to learn I didn't know how to swim.

"We'll do something about that right away. You'll be swimming by the end of the week or my name isn't Lee Foo. We'll start with skinny dip first thing tomorrow morning."

After lights out there was a lot of giggling and whispered dirty talk. The word "pecker" seemed to be favoured. One of the boys known as Little Red informed us that his friend Tommy had already started to grow hair around his pecker. Tommy was urged to display his equipment. Somebody produced a flashlight and without much urging Tommy obliged. Sure enough there was a little nest of dark hair around his penis, which started to swell slightly. "Make it real hard," Little Red urged him. "I can't," Tommy said and started to pull up his pyjama pants.

"Sure you can," I said. "Want me to show you?"

Instantly the beam of the flashlight shifted up to my bunk. I demonstrated the technique I'd learned from Dick. Tommy imitated my motions. His penis grew hard and firm. He leaned back against the wall of his bunk and started to gasp. After a moment a little spurt of white juice appeared out of the slit at the head of his penis.

"Wow," said Little Red. "How'd it feel, Tommy?"

"Terrific. You guys oughta try it."

They did try, several of them, but although their little penises became hard and upright, none of them could achieve orgasm. This automatically made Tommy the leader of the cabin. But I could tell my stock had also risen and in the days to come I would frequently be consulted about matters relating to sex. When I didn't have solid information, I usually made something up. I became something of an authority with a certain unique position in the hierarchy of my cabin. One I hoped Jimmy might envy.

I saw him next morning when we went down to the water for our skinny dip. He was naked except for his watch and his glasses, both of which he wore into the water. The watch was waterproof but Lee Foo warned him that if he lost his glasses he'd be in real trouble. Jimmy just grinned and swam away from him. Lee Foo told me to jump in and take them away from him. When I hesitated he threw me in off the dock. I spluttered, swallowed a mouthful of water and went under. The next thing I knew Lee Foo had dived in after me and dragged me to the surface. "You weren't kidding. You really can't swim at all."

"I told you."

"Okay, I'll hold you. Now relax." He put his hand under my belly and I tensed instantly. "Relax, I've got hold of you." His face was close to mine. Without his glasses his blue-grey eyes seemed bigger, the wet lashes making little points like stars. Gradually I let myself go, trusting his strong hands to save me from going down to the bottom. "Now kick. That's it. Okay, keep kicking for a couple minutes so you get the feel of it. Then we'll have to go up and get dressed. I'll meet you here at swim period and work with you some more. You're going to swim to the boat dock and back before the week's out."

And I did. In order to please Lee Foo, I would have done anything. I had a crush on him, though I didn't know it at the time. It was painful for me to realize that once I learned to swim he would no longer put his strong hands on my belly and I would no longer be able to get my face close to his and look directly into his beautiful, myopic blue-grey eyes. I stretched out the learning process as long as I dared. He never complained or called me stupid, but once he did say he couldn't devote his whole summer to teaching one kid to swim and I'd better catch on soon or he'd turn me over to one of the senior campers. That smartened me up, but in any case my wish to earn his good opinion triumphed over my lowdown desires. Did he have any notion of the carnal vibrations I was picking up from him? My sexual antennae were absolutely quivering in anticipation of picking up anything that seemed like an invitation to greater intimacy, but Lee Foo remained cool, even severe, in his manner toward me.

Then one day he asked me to go on a nature walk with him. He quizzed me on my knowledge of trees, birds, and insects, pointing out how each living creature had its appointed place as part of the wondrous design of Nature. I tried to seem suitably wonderstruck. I was thrilled when he took my hand and led me along into the woodland chapel. We kneeled together and Lee Foo asked me to pray with him. I realized that it was not my body that Lee Foo was after, but my immortal soul. I determined not to disappoint him. I prayed long and loud. Budding actor that I was, I gave him a virtuoso performance. The light glinting behind his wire-rimmed spectacles was better than applause. And I rightly assumed this would lead to further sessions of competitive prayer.

These became the highlight of my week, though they soon entailed hard physical labour. In his desire to be selfless in the service of his Lord and Master, who after all had made his living as a lowly carpenter, Lee Foo had placed himself even lower on the celestial totem pole and offered to dig a trench for our new KYBO (the word used for the camp's outdoor toilet: it was an acronym for Keep Your Bowels Open.) He asked me to help him with this labour of love, little realizing how apt the phrase was in my case. My reward was his tiny smile of approval and the bittersweet smell of his sweat as he swung his spade.

Lee Foo also set me up with my cabin mates, though I don't think this was his intention. Every night he would sit and talk with us. He asked us serious questions about how we were getting along in our classes, our athletic activities, and especially our struggle to come to Jesus and lead the good Christian life. These sessions were not exactly popular. Most of the boys did not share my idolatry of Lee Foo. They squirmed, sniggered, and gave evasive answers. One night when they were particularly unresponsive, Lee Foo abandoned his questions and indulged in a long prayer. The groans were audible. He finished and looked at his watch. Still eight minutes to lights out. He turned to me and suggested I tell the other kids a story.

I suppose he hoped I would come up with some moralistic fable, but I launched into an adventure story whose hero was a Chinese boy called Fee Loo who had a sort of split personality: by day he was a mild-mannered teller in the Hong Kong Bank, by night a high-kicking guerrilla warrior outsmarting criminals in the Forbidden City of Kowloon. The influence of Superman and Terry and the Pirates was obvious to me but not, apparently, to the others. When lights out sounded I left my hero in some impossible situation and promised to continue the next night, which I did. Soon my story became a nightly feature so popular that Lee Foo's question period was totally abandoned and his prayers cut down to three minutes to make way for Fee Loo's escapades.

As far as I could tell, Lee Foo enjoyed my stories as much as the boys. What he didn't know was that some nights after lights out, when he went down the path to visit other counsellors, I gave Fee Loo some rather more salacious adventures that owed less to the comic strips I'd read than to my thorough perusal of Thorne Smith. Fee Loo possessed not only advanced skills in kung fu and karate but also the biggest dick ever seen in the whole area of the South China Sea. He ran a brothel whose inmates practised sexual techniques of dazzling audacity. I wondered how long it would be before someone challenged the probability of some of my inventions, but no one ever did. I established myself as a sort of cross between Somerset Maugham and Mickey

Spillane, and my prestige in my cabin was enviable. I still lay in my narrow bunk and wrote frequent letters to my parents telling them I wanted to come home, but at least I wasn't totally despised, in spite of the fact that I couldn't catch a softball or master the J-stroke.

My prowess in Lee Foo's archery classes did not improve either. Here, try as I might, I could not gain his approval. He simply shook his head in sad disbelief as I shot arrow after arrow without ever hitting even the outer rim of the target. I have rarely been able to hit what I aim at. The harder I strain, the less successful I seem to be, whether I'm shooting at a dartboard or for political office. I eventually came to realize it's often better not to try too hard. Certainly I didn't make any particular effort in drama class, but here I was immediately successful. The dramatic counsellor was called Oscar (for Oscar Wilde, I realized years later when we met again and I learned his real name). Not many boys were interested in drama; there were in fact only five of us. Oscar decided the ideal play for us to present was Noël Coward's *Private Lives.* I had never heard of Noël Coward, but I took to the spare, acerbic dialogue like an egret skimming a lily pond. I was cast as Sybil, and Oscar was delighted with my first reading of the opening scene with Eliot, who was played by a handsome Argentine boy of sixteen. Angel was more like Ramón Navarro than Noël Coward, but Oscar didn't seem to mind. The boy playing Amanda was a striking but rather whiny redhead. He looked quite feminine but showed no acting talent whatsoever. Oscar began by coaching his every reading but soon decided it was better to demonstrate. This allowed him to roll around on a couch with Angel or sit next to him and trill "Someday I'll Find You" as he looked deep into the boy's limpid brown eyes. The rest of us were bored, but for me at least it beat playing netball or weaving raffia baskets.

In that first week at camp I didn't see much of Jimmy. He was a good swimmer, so it was understandable he didn't hang around with me during swim period. And he'd signed up for completely different activities. Anyway, he'd made a new friend called Budd. I never knew whether this was a first or last name or a pseudonym; he was simply Budd like one of those female movie stars: Valli, or Hildegarde, or later Cher. Budd's most obvious attribute was his size: he was already almost six feet tall and must have weighed nearly three hundred pounds. He moved slowly but with a peculiar, delicate grace and had a sudden mirthless high-pitched giggle. He loved to pray and sang out loudly at campfires, his piercing soprano soaring in an improvised descant above the other voices as we gave our all for Jesus in some rousing chorus such as:

> I will make you Fishers of Men
> Fishers of Men, Fishers of Men.
> I will make you Fishers of Men
> If you follow Me. Glory Hallelujah.

Budd also played sacred airs on the mouth organ and the Jew's harp, an instrument that he claimed was mentioned in the Apocrypha. It was difficult for me to take Budd seriously. I could not believe that his display of piety was not a mockery, but no one else seemed willing to call him on it. I questioned Jimmy about Budd's sincerity, but Jimmy merely smiled: "God works in a mysterious way his wonders to perform."

Then one day when we were standing in line in the tuck shop, Jimmy told me that he and Budd had decided to go into business together. They had observed that the camp laundry service was both slow and expensive. The boys had to pay for their laundry out of their tuck money and they resented the way this eroded the funds available for Orange Crush or Sweet Marie candy bars. They therefore decided to inaugurate the Jim/Budd Washing Service, which would offer lower rates and next-day delivery of clean clothes. They planned to invest in a supply of Sunlight soap, several hundred yards of clothesline, and a large quantity of wooden pegs, which they would buy in nearby Gravenhurst. I pointed out that they would also need a washboard and some scrubbing brushes. Jimmy then made me an offer: if I would buy these items I could come into the firm as a junior partner.

"Why me?" I asked.

"Many are called but few are chosen." His flattery won me and I accepted with alacrity.

I wondered how we would get permission to proceed with this project, but the camp leaders approved our enterprise and Jimmy and I were allowed to shop in Gravenhurst. The next day we assembled our capital on the dock and Budd unveiled a substantial raft, which he had apparently constructed in woodworking class. Actually, he confessed, he had supervised its construction, as his condition was somewhat too delicate to permit the wielding of a hammer. He stepped lightly from the dock onto the raft and commanded us to tow him out into the lake. This was a somewhat delicate operation, as it was necessary to keep Budd in the exact centre of the raft to avoid it tipping and pitching him into the drink. We sang "Fishers of Men" as we first waded and then swam pushing the raft before us.

When Budd was satisfied that we were out far enough, we turned our attention to washing the very considerable quantity of quite disgustingly dirty shorts, socks, and underwear we had collected from our fellow campers. As all the clothes were supposed to have name tags, we didn't worry about keeping track of which items belonged to whom. Rather, we were jubilant at the prospect of all the money that would be ours the following day when the clothes were reclaimed. Budd told us we should not let our minds dwell on filthy lucre but must contemplate higher things. It soon became apparent that neither Jimmy nor Budd had the slightest notion of how to wash clothes. I, on the other hand, had helped my mother do the laundry at home in periods when there was a hiatus between maids. My technique with a washboard was soon mastered by Jimmy but merely commended by Budd, who felt that he must preserve his hands for his musical activities. He would confine himself to sorting and supervising. He insisted that we should redeem this time spent in menial work by the introduction of some uplifting element. He would set the tone by quoting from scripture. He launched into a lengthy recitation of "begats" from Deuteronomy. As neither Jimmy nor I had even read the text we had no idea whether he was making up the names or had actually committed them to memory. When he was finished I offered up the Beatitudes, which I had learned under my father's tutelage. We then invented some Beatitudes of our own, only one of which sticks in my mind: "Blessed are the splendidly endowed, for they shall find bliss." But though we might be profane, we had to maintain a decorous seriousness. "We cannot countenance levity," Budd would say, pursing his rosebud lips and raising his non-existent eyebrows like some dowager empress. He even employed the royal "we."

We upset the raft going back to shore and insisted that Budd wade the rest of the way, which he did with affronted dignity, leaving us to collect the clothes that were gradually floating away or sinking to the bottom. Eventually we managed to get them all wrung out and hung up to dry. The next day Jimmy and I set up a little booth where our fellow campers could come to collect their clean linen. We managed to take in something like seven dollars. We got a dressing down from the dietician who discovered a hole in one of the nightdresses she had entrusted to our ministrations, and we also discovered at

THE BELLS OF HELL   101

the end of our free time that we still had a considerable quantity of unclaimed items, many of which lacked name tags. Jimmy stowed them under his bed and announced that we would reopen our booth in two days to take in more dirty clothes and also give people a second chance to get their clean laundry.

The following day there was a special event involving all the campers and none of the counsellors, who were going into a closed session of consultation and prayer. Meanwhile we would be engaged in a sort of war game. We were divided into two teams called Buccaneers and Desperadoes. The decision that assigned individuals to teams was both arbitrary and irrevocable. The Desperadoes were each given a secret message written on a small piece of paper. Each was told to hide it somewhere on his person. They were then trucked about ten miles down the road and told they must make their way back to home base (the dining tent) and turn in their message. Meanwhile the Buccaneers were to spread out around home base and intercept the Desperadoes. They had to try to get their hidden messages away from them. They could use any means short of physical mutilation to achieve this end.

Now I realize that the staff probably needed a day off so badly they would go to any lengths to get it, but it is hard to imagine such an exercise being tolerated today by any public institution. But in 1944 the whole world was at war. My friends and I played war games most days after school. We all had toy weapons, helmets, gasmasks, model airplanes, and soldiers. Nobody would have dreamed of confiscating our guns on the grounds that it aggravated our aggressive little natures. Water pistols, peashooters, and even cap guns were allowed at the camp, as long as they were not used in the middle of Divine Service. And we as young boys were being brought up to believe that the highest aspiration should be to go out and fight the good fight for God. Onward Christian Soldiers.

It turned out that both Jimmy and I were Buccaneers. We decided to work together and set out along one of the paths in the woods. We pursued and captured a boy called Brucie and then another, Eddie. We searched them assiduously, forcing them to strip, though as we all saw each other naked every morning when we went skinny-dipping, there were no surprises. It was sometime before I had the sudden inspiration of making Brucie, who was uncircumcised, pull back his foreskin, and sure enough out fell his message. Eddie was a tougher nut to crack. Two fingers stuck up his ass produced nothing, but eventually we took the back off his wristwatch and got his message too. The two of them went off together happily enough. They would be allowed to go out and mess about in a canoe, now they were out of the game.

Jimmy and I then proceeded triumphantly along the path till we reached an open field. There in the middle of it stood Budd. He did nothing to resist arrest, but produced from his pocket a small Bible and proceeded to read from the Book of Esther. We peeled off his clothes. For some reason I did not seem to have seen Budd naked before. He had rather large breasts and tiny genitalia almost hidden among folds of flesh. Then I noticed that he had messed his pants. Disgusted, I was prepared to abandon the search. Jimmy persevered while Budd sang "Rock of Ages" with throbbing intensity. Finally Jimmy managed to spot the paper in Budd's left ear. He tried to retrieve it but couldn't. Budd couldn't get it out either.

We forced him to get back into his smelly pants and marched him to home base. He had to go to the infirmary and have the paper removed with a pair of tweezers by the camp nurse. He remained in the infirmary for several days, claiming his inner ear was damaged and his balance affected. He convinced the nurse that he was running a fever; I suspect he faked a high temperature by plunging the thermometer in hot water when she wasn't looking. He asked that I be allowed to visit him every day and pray with him just before lights out. Delighted by this evidence of my developing spiritual growth, Lee Foo readily agreed. Jimmy was also given permission to be present at these sessions, I think because of his ability to come up with timely Biblical tags. Jimmy was adept at quoting scripture for his own purposes. And so it was that the Most Awful Order of the Solemn Sinners came into being.

I think this name must have been Jimmy's invention. Even as a fourteen-year-old he had a firm grasp of theology and knew that one of the basic tenets of Christianity was that we were all sinners who could only be saved by repentance and grace. The inspiring vision, however, came from Budd, who revealed to us that the Virgin Mary had appeared to him in a dream and insisted that he must conduct a high mass in her honour in the woodland chapel at midnight three days hence. We must be suitably robed for the occasion and drink real wine. And we must each make a suitable musical offering. These had been her commands before she vanished. Of course I didn't believe any of this. When I tried to get Jimmy to agree that the whole thing was just a joke, he looked very solemn: "Some of the saints were pretty odd characters. Think of Saint Francis preaching to the birds."

"Okay, but why would the Virgin appear to Budd of all people?"

"The wind bloweth where it listeth."

We became preoccupied with preparations for our midnight Mass. Jimmy undertook to obtain incense, which Budd deemed an essential element. My task was to get the wine. I couldn't imagine how I was going to do this and then remembered that Oscar had a bottle of gin and some vermouth stored in a dressing room. As part of what he called "period research" for *Private Lives* he had showed us how to mix the perfect martini. And we had all had a sip or two. When I suggested to Budd that the vermouth might be used for communion wine, he said he would consult the Virgin. She apparently felt vermouth as a fortified wine was completely acceptable. "She commanded that you also bring the gin," Budd informed me. So after rehearsal was over, while Oscar was explaining some fine point of characterization to Angel, I pinched both bottles and hid them in the pit Lee Foo and I had dug. It was not yet in use; the wooden housing over it was under construction but wouldn't be finished for several days. I returned to my cabin to write my daily letter home, detailing my discontent, my maltreatment at the hands of the counsellors, and the total inedibility of the food. This last complaint was justified, but otherwise I was really quite happy. But I couldn't do an about-face with my parents. And sadly I had become so used to lying to them, I no longer suffered the slightest qualm.

Jimmy and I did another major laundry on the actual day of the Mass. Budd remained in the infirmary, but as he wouldn't deign to defile his delicate hands anyway, we didn't miss him. We didn't talk for fear of being overheard; we knew voices carried clearly over the water. Instead we sang various evangelical songs as we scrubbed. We hung the clothes up to dry and had our supper and went to the campfire. After lights out and my nightly instalment of the Fee Loo story, I lay rigid in my upper bunk and listened to the usual smutty remarks and stifled giggles of the other boys.

Finally, when I was sure they were all asleep, I climbed down from my bunk. Naked under my grey wool blanket (the attire the Virgin Mary had decreed should be worn) I trotted down the path to the spot where I could see the new toilets would soon be operational. I retrieved the gin and vermouth bottles and carried them to the chapel. My fellow Solemn Sinners, Jimmy and Budd, were already there, wearing their blankets. Jimmy's was grey like mine but Budd was wearing a scarlet blanket from the infirmary. He informed me that the Virgin had created him a prince of the church and he would hence-forth be addressed as His Sublime Eminence Cardinal Budd. He insisted I kneel before him and kiss his ring. Jimmy lit a can of Sterno and the Mass began.

Budd said he could only speak in Latin. He began to drone loudly and I realized he was reciting the story of the Three Little Pigs in what was, I suppose appropriately, pig-Latin. Then we blended our voices in a rousing rendition of "The Bells of Hell." Budd produced a chamber pot and poured in the contents of the two liquor bottles. He raised the enamel potty high above his head and intoned: "Ithway isthay Upcay eway inkdray ootay Eethay, Ostmay Olyhay Irgenvay." The cup was passed around several times and we all took several healthy swigs. The gin was rough on our unaccustomed throats, but the warm sensation in our bellies was pleasant. We did a chorus or two of "Fishers of Men." Then Budd turned to me and commanded, "Ingsay."

"Make a joyful noise unto the Lord," said Jimmy.

I was determined to see if I could make Budd acknowledge this for the mockery it was. So I began Dick's song and got as far as:

> I tickled her boobies,
> her lily-white boobies
> And down where the short hair grows

Suddenly a blinding light shone in my eyes and a familiar voice commanded, "STOP THIS AT ONCE! Is there no limit to your depravity?" The voice was Lee Foo's. He stood a few feet away from me holding a flashlight in his right hand. "All of you back to your beds immediately. We'll deal with this in the morning." There was no point trying to explain. We stumbled in silence behind Lee Foo along the path. I could see he was shaking, I suppose with rage. At the door of our cabin I stopped and looked up into his face. His eyes were cold and condemning. I put out my hand. He slapped it down and turned away. I got into my bed and lay shivering. But the booze inside me was warm and comforting and even though I imagined I would lay awake till dawn, I was soon asleep.

The next morning I was told to stay in my cabin till I was sent for. I lay in my bunk and read. After about half an hour Budd appeared. He was dressed not in pyjamas and dressing gown but in his normal shorts and sweatshirt. He told me the delirium had finally passed; unfortunately he could remember nothing of the last week. His last clear recollection was standing in an open field reading from the Book of Esther. I couldn't believe he didn't remember the night before. "Surely your Serene Eminence hasn't forgotten the martinis . . ."

Budd's small eyes crinkled shrewdly: "I had a very strange dream. In it the Prophet Hezekiah, who, I think you are aware, is my closest confidant, came to me and said I must make a visitation unto you. He said you must take upon you the yoke of blame and the burden of reproof."

"What are you talking about?"

"I can hardly be accounted responsible for what has happened in my regrettable state of delirium. There is Jimmy, but think of the disgrace to his father. Whereas I believe your father is in trade . . ."

"You want me to take the rap?"

"It could be your finest moment. Can we count on you?"

"We?"

"Hezekiah and I."

I considered for a moment. I could see Budd had a point. If word got out that Jimmy had been involved in sacreligious rituals, it really wouldn't reflect well on his father, who probably knew and associated with most of the clergymen who ran the camp. Whereas my father was hardly likely to be disbarred as a chartered accountant because his son got caught dressed up in a sheet in the middle of the night singing bawdy songs in a chapel.

"Okay," I said. Budd smirked. His chins jiggled with satisfaction. He turned and left without a backward glance.

Soon after, I was summoned by the head, a balding, thin-lipped Baptist. Icily he asked for an explanation. I told him the whole thing was my idea. I thought getting Budd dressed up as a cardinal was funny. Jimmy had gone along reluctantly, though I was sure he'd thought better of it, once he sobered up. The head sighed deeply and said he didn't know how to begin to deal with my "manifold iniquities." (He actually used those words.) There was the question of strong drink; the camp was and always had been guided by Temperance principles. There was the profanation of the chapel, which was dedicated to the glory of God and was a living symbol of the beauty of Holiness. He was less concerned by the bawdy song — he knew what boys were — but the worst of all was the smell of popery that was implied by the appearance of Budd in the robes of a cardinal and his evocation of the Virgin. Was I acting as an agent of the Harlot of Rome? Did my family have ties with the Vatican? I confessed that my favourite aunt Effie was a Catholic. The head pondered for a moment. Then he announced that he had no choice but to send me home before I contaminated the rest of the boys with my pernicious influence. I could go back to my cabin and pack. I would be leaving first thing next morning.

Jimmy came to visit me as I stuffed socks and underpants into my suitcase. "I'm sorry," he said.

"I'm not. I've had enough of this place."

"We had some fun though. It was decent of you to say it was your fault. I don't care for myself but it would have been a bit sticky for my old man. I did try to tell them it wasn't fair and all that, but they didn't want to hear it. Look, about the laundry —"

"We split the take three ways last Monday. You're welcome to whatever you get from here on in."

"It's not that. There are more than two hundred unclaimed items with no name tags. What are we going to do with them?"

"Search me."

"Couldn't you take some home?"

"Are you kidding? I'm going to have enough to explain to my parents without having to account for a hundred pairs of somebody else's socks and undies."

"We've got to get rid of them."

"Get Budd to help you."

"Budd and I are no longer on speaking terms."

"You could have a sale."

"Not now. I can't go to the head and tell him I've got all this stuff."

"We could bury them."

"Where?"

"We better do it right now. I just hope we're not too late."

We got the bundles of clothes and took them to the new KYBO. The little wooden structures were finished. Inside the holes had been cut and the lids were neatly in place. But they were still not in use. They'd been painted, but the green enamel was still tacky. No doubt tomorrow would see their first day in operation. We lifted the lids and stuffed the clothes down the holes. The plop as they hit the liquid below was highly satisfying. Jimmy and I went to dinner together and afterwards said goodbye. I didn't go to campfire but went back to my cabin. Lee Foo was waiting for me.

He looked at me solemnly and took my hand in his. "I want you to come and pray with me," he said. We went outside and down the path to the chapel and knelt together. He began to address the Almighty. Fervently he pleaded for the sincere repentance that would assure my ultimate forgiveness. My problem was I had an overactive imagination. It was a God-given gift but it had been perverted by the powers of evil. He prayed that I might cleanse and purify my mind and heart and offer my gifts again to Jesus in all humility. He begged me to turn my back on the Devil who had tried to claim me for his own. I thought of Budd and saw in my mind's eye little horns sprouting out of his head and a long forked tail poking out from behind his obscenely jiggling rump.

I knew I was expected to pray but wasn't sure I could bring myself to do it. At last I opened my mouth to speak but Lee Foo stopped me, saying, "Pray in your heart." We knelt together in silence, and then he took my hand and led me back to the cabin. Outside he stopped, looked deep into my eyes through his glasses, and said, "I know you're going to make a new beginning. God bless you and keep you." There was actually a tear in his eye as he turned away. I felt somehow that this made the whole escapade worthwhile, redeemed it somehow and justified it.

Inside the cabin the other boys were waiting for the last instalment of my story. I decided to do them proud. After outsmarting the opium smugglers of Kowloon, Fee Loo spent the night in the arms of his favourite concubine, leaving her his accumulated savings in the Hong Kong Bank and appointing her grand madam of his brothel before he set out for Tibet to become a Buddhist monk.

Next morning I got on the train in Gravenhurst feeling light and buoyant. I was going home, and once I got there I was going to try to be a better person. I sat in the window seat looking out, when suddenly a voice said, "Hello there. I hear you put on quite a show the other night. I'm desolated I missed it." Oscar plumped down on the seat across from me. Angel sat beside him, glowering darkly. Soon after the train started, Oscar produced a flask and handed it to me.

"No thanks," I said as my nostrils caught the now familiar whiff of gin.

"Oh, come on, we all know this is *your* drink." He took a swig and rattled on. "Too bad about *Private Lives*. It could have been brilliant, though I suppose I might have known the project was doomed. Like so many of my brightest inspirations. I'm afraid I'm just ahead of my time."

Oscar kept up a stream of vivacious chatter, but offered no explanation as to why he and Angel were on the train. Presently Angel got up to go to the washroom. After a bit Oscar also got up and lurched down the aisle after him. They were gone a long time. Finally I made my own way to the washroom and opened the unlocked door. Oscar was standing facing me, his pants around his ankles. Angel was standing close behind him, gripping him around the waist. "Well, don't just stand there. Come in and join the fun."

I shook my head.

Oscar smirked. "We could do a rousing chorus of 'I Will Make You Fishers of Men' if you thought that would help you get into the swing."

I slammed the door shut and went back to my seat. Obviously Oscar had left the washroom door unlocked on purpose. I got my suitcase down from the rack and moved to another car. When we got to Union Station I stayed on board till I saw Oscar and Angel on the platform. Oscar kissed Angel on both cheeks and they went off in separate directions.

My father was waiting for me. We got into the car and drove toward his office. "I hope you're pleased with yourself," he said. "Well, you're not going to hang around and do nothing all the rest of the summer. You can come in to work with me and relieve the office boy while he has his holidays. You'll start on Monday." And that was all he said. I was dying to ask what the camp had told him but I didn't dare. Blessed are they who know when to keep their traps shut, for they shall get away with murder, as Jimmy might have said.

The year after we went to camp together, Jimmy and I began to hang out after school —when we weren't rehearsing for the TCP. I had just started grade nine at Lawrence Park, the local high school, and although I made a few friends in my own class I had more in common with Jimmy, even though he was two grades ahead of me. We not only shared an interest in theatre but soon began working on a script in verse, which of course contained roles for both of us. I was Stupid Prince Sidney of Serendip; Jimmy was a witty jester. We worked on this comic tale of royal hijinks at his house. We were both committed monarchists and Jimmy's family bore the stamp of aristocracy. His mother's father had been a knight and her mother the daughter of an Irish earl. Mrs. Armour had been presented at court, and in their living room there was a silver-framed photograph of her sporting a train and white ostrich feathers in her hair on this august occasion.

In fact Norah Armour, though she had the elevated diction and austere manner of a grande dame, a sort of Lady Bracknell washed up on the shores of Lake Ontario, was something of a rebel against her class. As a teenage girl she had nursed soldiers during the First World War, and when the armistice was signed announced her intention of working in a hospital. Her father, Colonel Sir Stuart Sankey, informed her that if she wished to associate herself with the medical profession she had better qualify as a doctor. She accepted this challenge and after graduation set up a clinic in Limehouse, where she ministered to the poor and indigent in London's East End. She had a number of suitors, including A. A. Milne, but chose to marry a Presbyterian clergyman and agreed to go with him to the wilds of Canada.

Initially I did not see much of Jimmy's father, who travelled a good deal, but I came to understand he was a widely admired raconteur and that Jimmy's ready wit was modelled on his father's. When he was at home, Dr. Armour was usually surrounded by congenial and appreciative friends and he dominated any gathering he attended. He quoted Shakespeare, impersonated characters from Dickens, and possessed a seemingly endless repertoire of funny anecdotes. It was said he never told the same story twice.

During that winter Dr. Armour became ill with a bronchial infection and the family acquired the services of a Scottish nurse/housekeeper, Jean Blackley, whom we all referred to as Miss B. A tiny woman with a beak of a nose and bright beady eyes, she hopped about like a blackbird and often gave us the sharp edge of her tongue. She adored Jimmy, who could give back as good as he got, and accepted me because of my Scottish ancestry. She quoted Robert Burns and sang Scottish songs, "Scots wha' hae" and "Wi a hundred pipers an' a'," in a wobbly contralto; I learned more about my Scottish heritage from her than from anyone in my own family. Miss B. added to what I had come to see as the eccentricity of the Armour ménage. I was delighted by the elegance of this household and the ready acceptance I found there. I spent as much time at the Armours' as possible.

It was a blow when I learned the family was going to England during the summer holidays. They wanted the children to visit their relatives for the first time since the war. I did not know it, but Dr. Armour realized he was dying and wanted to spend his last days back where he had come from in Northern Ireland. Indeed he did die during the course of the summer. After his death Mrs. Armour decided to stay on in Belfast. She put Jean and Jimmy in boarding schools while she dealt with the family's affairs. I remember getting this news from Miss B., whom I met by chance on the street, and feeling a pang of loss as I realized I might never see Jimmy again. He had become not only a friend but a role model; I had become inured to the sharp jabs with which he deflated my pretensions and pointed up my social inadequacies, and I realized that at the same time he had sharpened my wits. (I remember on one occasion he said of two plays we were planning to write, "Mine will be wildly applauded and yours will be laughed at." But he was delighted when I rejoined, "Mine will be a comedy.")

That summer I refused to go back to camp, so I was put to work as a messenger boy in my father's warehouse. I discovered I quite liked working for a living; not that I made a living wage: my pay was fifteen dollars a week and my father insisted I bank ten of it. I liked leaving the house at seven thirty in the morning with the paper bag of ham or tomato sandwiches that Mother had made the night before and riding downtown on the streetcar reading Noël Coward. (My first discovery of the work of this British sophisticate at camp had been strongly reinforced by seeing a still sexy and glamorous Tallulah Bankhead rolling around on a sofa in a production of *Private Lives* at the Royal Alex.)

I also liked the improbable mix of men who worked in the warehouse: half stern moralistic Bible-thumpers, half scatological storytellers. Somehow the sacred and profane coexisted under the command of the foreman, Bill Harpur, a former Irish policeman, now a Sunday school superintendent and pillar of the Boys' Brigade. He took a shine to me, exhorting me to read Defoe, Swift, and Butler, and lustily singing hymns such as "Fight the Good Fight." At lunchtime he challenged my skills as a chess player and tested my knowledge of scripture, encouraging me to think about the church as a calling. He eventually became an Anglican clergyman himself, and his son, Tom, would become a widely read theological journalist with radical views that would have scandalized his fundamentalist father.

When I was sent out to deliver samples, I nosed around the grotty streets at Spadina and Queen, then the centre of the garment and printing trades. In the old brick buildings, presses clattered, sewing machines hummed, and typewriters clacked. Bearded Jewish peddlers drove their dilapidated horse-drawn carts through back lanes collecting scrap iron. Girls from Weston's Bakery, their pink faces dusted with flour, jitterbugged during their morning coffee break to a jukebox playing songs like "Across the Alley from the Alamo" and "Five O'Clock Jump." Gypsy women sat in front of dirty bedspreads in Queen Street storefronts eyeing the men who passed. Once during this summer I went behind the bedspread with one of them. I held out my hand to be read, but it turned out she was more interested in another part of my anatomy. She grabbed my crotch, and in my excitement I pissed my pants. She laughed delightedly and turned me back out into the street in my stained cotton trousers. I sat in Grange Park with a newspaper spread over my knees till they dried.

Not that I was entirely innocent when it came to making a connection with the other sex. I had asked out girls in my high-school class, taking them to movies, buying them sodas at the drugstore, walking them home, getting a goodnight kiss on the doorstep. I had been taught to believe that nice girls didn't allow boys to go any farther, and indeed most of them didn't. We had been taught what was right and wrong, and before the pill we were all scared of the consequences. We had only a limited scope for amorous experiment, but we made the most of it. Some of us became pretty good kissers, and this skill would stand me in good stead later on.

I would work in my father's warehouse for the next four summers, travelling to Dentonia in the evenings and on Saturdays to go to Mrs. Goulding's classes. It provided a balance of two very different kinds of work and a respite from the more strained atmosphere of high school, with its inevitable competition — academic, athletic, and social. I was fairly successful in the first area and largely avoided the other two. I used my rehearsal commitments to avoid football games and tea dances. If I became too fractious, my father would threaten to send me to boarding school, but we made a bargain that I could stay in high school as long as I continued to get first-class marks. This I managed to do except in mathematics. I now realize that I didn't want to excel in this area because it was Father's specialty. But I managed to get passing grades and dropped the subject as soon as I could.

After two years in Ireland, the Armour family came back to Toronto and Jimmy and I picked up where we had left off. I was still charmed by his ready wit and fascinated by the veneer of civilized superiority that he had acquired at a British boarding school. I thought he was snobbish, but I was only too eager to measure up to his exacting new standards; in fact I was the snob while he viewed his recent experience with a certain healthy sense of mockery. The family now lived in a much smaller house, but Mrs. Armour continued to entertain. She frequently invited me to Sunday dinner after church, offering sherry in tiny eighteenth-century glasses. There was also overcooked beef, which she had taught Jimmy to carve with dispatch at the Georgian sideboard and hand round to the guests sitting at the table adorned with her Minton china and crested silver. The other guests were often widows of clergymen or retired missionaries from China or India, who spoke wistfully of the good old days in Shanghai or Bangalore. They existed in the afterglow of the Empire and their reminiscences fed by burgeoning Anglophilia.

Over the course of the next few years, Mrs. Armour instructed me in the rudiments and some of the finer points of manners as practised in good English society. I learned to stand when a woman came into the room, to shake hands and say, "How do you do?" not "Pleased to meetcha" when introduced to someone, to eat my meals without switching my fork from one hand to the other, to tip my soup plate away from me when spooning up the last two mouthfuls, to crumple my napkin after I finished a meal, to precede a lady going upstairs and follow her coming down, and a host of other niceties that the farmers in my own family knew nothing about. She did this with tact and humour, believing that these habits should be practised until they became second nature, so that one would never be at a loss in whatever society one found oneself. To this day I can dine with a duchess with perfect confidence, though unfortunately one doesn't meet many duchesses in Toronto anymore. Mrs. Armour believed that manners were allied to morals and rooted in religion. Religion for a young Presbyterian like me had meant learning the catechism and passages of scripture, and being lectured on the virtues of truth-telling and temperance, though not of tolerance. Most of the good Christians I knew were unashamedly anti-Semitic, a prejudice often displayed in supposedly humorous guise, as in an oft-quoted little verse:

> How odd
> Of God
> To choose
> The Jews.

The Christians I knew were also deeply suspicious of and antagonistic toward Roman Catholics. My father's company was run by Scots and Ulstermen who never hired Catholics or foreigners, or for that matter Englishmen. They did business with Jewish customers, and — as I had learned on the New York trip — my father quite liked some of them but this did not prevent him from calling them "kikes" or "Hebes," and he certainly never thought of asking them to his home. He was similarly abusive of "dogans" or "left-footers" (Roman Catholics). When my mother's favourite sister Effie married a Catholic, my mother cried for a week. "We won't see Effie in Heaven," she sobbed. And she meant it.

The person best able to console her was Jimmy: "The Lord moves in mysterious ways."

"Poor Effie. We used to sing together at Sunday school. 'Shall We Gather by the River?' She was a pretty little thing and she had such a sweet little voice."

Jimmy sat down at the piano and thumped the tune out vigorously. And in a few minutes he had Mother singing along. "You have a very nice voice yourself, Mrs. H."

"Who are you trying to kid?" But she kept singing.

"You shouldn't hide your light under a bushel. You should be in the choir at Glenview. Singing right along with Mrs. Smythe." This was an ample contralto whose bosoms heaved mightily as tears coursed down her rouged cheeks while she sobbed her way through "Oh, for the Wings of a Dove."

"I'd be ashamed to make such a spectacle of myself."

Jimmy chuckled appreciatively. I was always surprised by the easy connection between Jimmy and Mother. She distrusted most of my friends, but Jimmy instinctively knew how to jolly her along. They shared a relish of the peculiarities of various members of the congregation at Glenview Presbyterian and lampooned them for each other's amusement: Mrs. Fowler, who peered short-sightedly at her hymnbook through a gold-handled lorgnette and sang in a throaty baritone; Mrs. McRae, an ample motherly woman whose perpetual mourning for some distant relative included loops of black beads and dangling black earrings; Professor Ainsley, who had just missed being a dwarf and wore a cutaway coat so old it had turned green. This shared satiric streak was at once liberating, making them feel superior to the pomposities and pretensions of hypocritical or merely foolish churchgoers, but it could also be somewhat mean-spirited, allowing their uncharitable instincts an outlet. I soon learned I was not exempt from their ridicule. It sharpened my self-awareness but also encouraged me to be secretive. I learned to afford them as few opportunities as possible to poke fun at me and became determined to keep my own counsel.

Listening to Mother and Jimmy trade barbs, I came to appreciate the art of gossip, muted malice tempered by a certain acceptance of human folly, quite different from the crudely savage and scourging satire my friend Dick practised. I understood that Dick and Jimmy belonged to different worlds and that they would probably not hit it off. So I made no effort to bring them together but learned to manoeuvre in their separate milieux, switching tactics and shaping my personality to suit my companions. I would continue this practice throughout much of my life, aided by the anonymity afforded by living in a large city, as opposed to the more exposed situation of dwellers in small rural communities, like those where my parents had grown up. They were secretive too, but they didn't live double lives. Their contradictions were internal.

During our late teens Jimmy and I began to frequent various churches on Sunday nights. Our parents were persuaded that this was a healthy interest in religion. Initially my father was suspicious of the idea; he didn't see why we weren't satisfied with the church we had been born and baptized into. But one of the senior partners of his company was a great believer in shopping around among the preachers of the day, some of whom had deserved fame as orators, and so Father accepted this idea.

The preacher who left the most lasting impression on me was a visiting American evangelist, Sister Fern Hofsteader. She came to town for a week and we went to hear her as one of our regular Sunday-night outings. She preached for more than an hour, quoting scripture fluently and illuminating it with colourful anecdotes, many of them highly personal. She confessed freely and openly that she had experienced sin on a monumental scale: lying, drunkenness, adultery. But Jesus had spoken to her as He would speak to each one of us, if we would only open our hearts to him. She led us in hymns, backed up by a large choir:

"Sweetly and tenderly, Jesus is calling. . . ."

The singers included a considerable number of blacks, an uncommon sight in white Toronto churches at the time. They sang gospel hymns and spirituals: "One more river and that's the river of Jordan . . ."

Other musical interludes included people playing banjos and xylophones and even a series of musical bottles, as Sister Fern built her act and reiterated her call for people to come to Jesus.

And come they did. Someone would stand and shout: "Hallelujah."

And "Hallelujah," Sister Fern responded, upping the volume. And before long the whole place was shouting, "Hallelujah, Hallelujah, Hallelujah."

Then one or two people started down the aisle as if drawn by the force of some gigantic invisible magnet. Sister Fern ran to meet them, forcing them to their knees and clasping their foreheads. This, she told us, was "the laying on of hands" and it elicited shrieks of ecstasy and a voluble stream of gibberish. "They're speaking in tongues," Sister Fern bellowed, "praise be to Jesus' sweet name. Hallelujah." By the end of the evening at least thirty people had come up to the front and accepted Jesus as their personal Saviour. Sister Fern made a plea for everyone to come back the next evening, and we closed with a rousing rendition of "I Am So Glad That Jesus Loves Me . . ."

We did come back the next night, and several other nights that week. Sister Fern never flagged in her efforts to bring people to God, and more answered her call every evening. She was a wonderful performer and I was impressed by her sheer virtuosity. Jimmy may have been motivated by a more professional curiosity. I was aware that even then he was considering the ministry as a profession. It was after all the family trade, with three generations of Presbyterian clerics looking down on him, as well as the unspoken but palpable expectations of his strong-willed and dedicated mother. To me it seemed a waste of his comic gifts, but I knew my opinion would not carry much weight, for all Jimmy was amused and perhaps a bit flattered by my admiration.

In mid-August of the fourth summer I spent working in his warehouse, my father surprised me by announcing he thought I should have a little holiday before I went back to school. I was surprised because my father was not keen on holidays himself; he preferred "talking business" (gossiping with his colleagues about the foibles of his customers or about the pecking order of "the big boys on Bay Street") to trying to make conversation about schools and sports with his sons. He was most at ease when he had some clearly defined managerial goal to achieve: a sales target, a fundraising objective, a membership drive. But he did believe in rewarding accomplishment. I had worked hard for him that summer and I think in his typically indirect, unspoken style he wanted me to know he appreciated it.

I had taken over the running of the sample room when André, the regular sample man became ill. It meant giving up the easy freedom of roaming the streets, but Bill Harpur took me into his confidence and I began to get some understanding of how the business worked, who the important customers were, and how I could influence them with my sample presentations. I began to enjoy my own efficiency. I told my father I had been thinking I should go straight into the business instead of "wasting four years at university." I thought this was sure to win his favour, but I was wrong.

"Of course you'll go to university. I haven't worked hard all these years in order to give you a chance at something I missed out on, so you can just throw it away. Now about your holiday. You've got a good two weeks before school starts." My mind filled with images of Boston, New York, Los Angeles. "It occurred to me you and your mother might like to visit Effie and Bessie. You've always said they're your favourite aunts. And your mother could use a change." I quickly understood that Father's proposal had less to do with my needs than Mother's. She'd been at home alone all summer while I was working downtown and my brother was on the farm with our cousin Willis Montgomery. Mother spent her good afternoons playing bridge; on bad afternoons she turned to the rye bottle. "I thought the idea might appeal to her if you suggested it."

I was supposedly my mother's favourite. I didn't much want to spend a week with Mother but I supposed I owed her this. I agreed to sound her out.

"What do you want to go away with a back number like me for? Wouldn't you rather hang around with those society girls?"

"Society girls?"

"Those actresses."

"You mean Anne and Judy?" These were two girls in the Toronto Children Players that I occasionally took to a movie.

"Stuck-up things. Why can't they act natural for a change? Well, at least they're girls. That's something."

"Come on, Ma. We could both use a change."

"I don't get it. Why do you want to cosy up to me all of a sudden? You've been giving me the air all summer."

"I'm sorry. Okay, I'd like to make it up to you."

"Who do you think you're kidding?"

"Look, how about this? Why don't we ask Jimmy to go with us? Maybe he and I could go on to Ottawa. It's something we've talked about doing anyway." Mother cocked her head with interest. "If you can talk Jimmy into it, you can count me in." Talking Jimmy into it was surprisingly easy. He genuinely enjoyed Mother's company and was curious to meet her sisters. And he did want to visit Ottawa, where he had a distant relative we could stay with. So it was agreed we'd spend a few days with Effie and then proceed to Ottawa by bus.

Looking back I regret I was not more sympathetic to my mother at this time. I no longer depended on her to encourage my attempts to act out my artistic ambitions. I did not entirely trust her to understand them. I feared her sharp tongue and her tendency to go to my father and betray what I had told her in confidence. As my brother and I became more and more involved outside our home, she found herself trying to please us by cooking special treats and imparting an occasional juicy morsel of gossip or smart crack, but it wasn't enough to hold our loyalty, just as doing petit point and trying new recipes wasn't enough to satisfy her need for an outlet for her emotions and abilities. Though largely uneducated, she was intelligent and perceptive, and my father's unwillingness to let her find meaningful work outside the house gradually curdled her enjoyment of life.

None of us drove, so Mother decided to round out the party with Jane Jarrell, a relative by marriage and one of her bridge partners. Jane was a tiny woman, less than five feet tall. She had to sit on two cushions to get an adequate view of the road. She wore dozens of silver bangles on each wrist, which jingled as she lit one cigarette from the butt of the last. She had a throaty laugh and quickly responded to Jimmy's sallies. He and Mother did their imitations of various church worthies, and when that began to pall we sang camp songs:

> Be kind to your web-footed friends
> For a duck may be somebody's mother . . .

Jane encouraged Mother to do imitations of our country cousins. She had already heard all Mother's routines, but many of them were new to Jimmy. He and Jane laughed heartily at each repetition and they even got Mother to sing along with us in a reedy falsetto. By the time we reached Ogdensburg, Mother seemed less sour than she'd been in months, maybe years.

Ogdensburg was a small but prosperous city on the American side of the St. Lawrence where Mother and her two younger sisters, Bessie and Effie, had trained as nurses under the sharp eyes and sharper tongues of the Grey Nuns. (Mother told me one nun assessed her as "zero from the neck up." Her own verbal style verged on the brutal, the rough tongue of the Irish farm girl having been further honed by the nuns' example.) Mother returned to Canada when she married, but her sisters stayed in the States. Bessie married Howard, a Presbyterian whose family had an established position in the small town of Gouverneur. Effie married Glenn, a Catholic, and stared down her family's opposition. Effie was a redhead, tart of tongue and a bit raucous; she had been delicate as a child but had put on weight and now spoke of herself as "a dainty little thing" with a self-deprecating snort. She was fond of saying she was "fading away to a cartload." When I was twelve I'd stayed with Effie for a week in her little apartment on State Street. Glenn was away in the army, so Effie and I shared their double bed and a lot of laughs connected with bodily functions. She took me to adult movies and a party celebrating vj day, where a marine major persuaded me to drink champagne. But Effie drew the line at taking me to Mass with her; she knew better than to open up that can of worms.

Jane, Mother, Jimmy, and I arrived at the little house where Effie and Glenn now lived. Within five minutes a bottle of rye was brought out. There were the usual jokes about Uncle Herbert's stinginess, Effie's weight, and Aunt Annie Holmes' blindness. My own tolerance for these familiar tales was limited; such rustic hijinks didn't quite measure up to the sophisticated elegance of Noël

Coward or the formal decorum of the Armour household, but Jimmy seemed delighted with them. I sat listening with a pained expression, which prompted Effie to offer me a drink. I declined: "I don't need to drink to have a good time."

"Okay, it's your loss, kiddo."

Jimmy, who had reached the legal drinking age of eighteen, accepted a mild rye and ginger. The women were on their third glass by the time Glenn came home. He greeted Mother and Jane with hugs and chuckles but there were no kisses for Effie. She challenged him head on.

"Well, if it isn't old sourpuss."

"That's a pretty nice way to greet your tired hubby after a hard day at the bank."

"I hope you brought home a few samples. Those slot machines are waiting for us down at the Elks."

"I thought you were making dinner here, Effie."

"Yeah, I might, if I can find the stove." Effie staggered to her feet, and made her way to the kitchen, banging into the furniture.

"Look at that. Isn't that awful? Not six thirty yet and already she's got a load on." Effie blew him a raspberry and clattered some pots and pans. "Never mind, Effie, I'll be glad to take you to the Elks. Save you the embarrassment of burning the Swiss steak."

"You think I'm too loaded to cook, eh? We'll see about that. Go get yourself a drink and get that sour look off your puss." She poured herself a refill. They sparred back and forth for half an hour, during which time Effie managed to peel two potatoes and down two more glasses of rye. Then we drove three blocks to the Elks, a social club where Glenn ordered steaks and at Effie's insistence shrimp cocktails. (Effie called it "shimp.") Effie and Mother got fresh drinks, then headed to the slot machines, which they continued to visit intermittently between courses. By the time coffee arrived, Effie had lost thirty bucks and Mother had won twenty-three.

At nine the next morning we set out to drive to Gouverneur where Bessie lived. It was about an hour's drive. Glenn, who was still fairly sober, insisted he drive us in his car. I sat beside him while Effie and Mother were in the back with Jimmy, who revived the duck song while Effie made swipes at the back of Glenn's head, calling him "Baldy," "Sourpuss," and "Spoilsport." It started to rain, at first lightly, then quite heavily. Even in the dark I could see that Glenn's face was red and his temper rising as he tried to concentrate on the road. Finally he reached around and grabbed Effie's wrist. The tail lights of the cars ahead of us suddenly flared bright red. "Look out!" I yelled, and Glenn managed to brake inches away from the car ahead of us. I got out, looked up ahead, and called back, "There's been an accident."

"Come on, kid, we better go see what's cooking." Effie managed to get herself out of the back seat and was peering short-sightedly down the road. "Glenn, you better call an ambulance."

I took her arm and she tottered down the highway through the rain on her high heels. Already there was a ring of people around the two cars. A dark green Buick had been side-swiped when a pickup truck skidded over the white line onto the wrong side of the road. The driver of the truck, a chunky middle-aged man, was dazed but unhurt. The driver of the Buick was a middle-aged woman; she was slumped over the wheel.

"Stand back, I'm a nurse," ordered Effie. She surveyed the scene a moment, wiped the rain off her glasses and turned to me. "Get that door open." I couldn't even turn the handle, but the driver of the pickup truck smashed the window, reached inside and tugged the door towards him till it gave way. Effie moved in to take the woman's pulse. She crouched beside her, making comforting sounds.

Effie stayed holding the woman in her arms until the ambulance arrived. She helped the driver get the woman out of the car and onto a stretcher, then climbed in with her and the ambulance took off with its siren wailing. I went back to the car. We turned around and headed back to Ogdensburg through the rain. When we got to the hospital, Effie was waiting for us. "She's gonna be all right. Just some bruises and abrasions." She climbed into the front seat and we drove in silence back to Effie and Glenn's house. "You better have a drink, Effie. You earned it," was all Glenn said. He got out a fresh bottle of rye and everybody had a shot. We watched the news on television and finally bedded down, Mother and Jane in the guest room, Jimmy on the sofa, and me in a hammock on the porch. I lay listening to the rain and thinking about the upcoming week. I couldn't wait to get away from Ogdensburg.

The next morning the four of us drove to Gouverneur in Jane's car. Bessie's house was a tall Victorian mansion with gingerbread trim and a square tower crowned by iron spikes. The living room was the envy of my mother, who loved Victoriana. It had ornately carved chairs and sofas covered with needlepoint, tasselled velvet curtains, converted oil lamps with painted glass shades, and a grand piano. The only drawback was that Howard, who was an undertaker, sometimes used it as a funeral parlour. Bessie ran her house and her life efficiently, needled Howard into staying sober till dinnertime, maintained a sort of armed truce in her ongoing battle with Howard's overbearing mother and two spoiled sisters, and gave her two sons enough support for them to develop their own very different temperaments.

Bessie expected us to stay to dinner. At five o'clock Howard arrived with his assistant. They set up a platform and draped it with velvet, then set the coffin on it. "You wanna have a look?" Howard asked me. "We did a pretty good job on this one, if I do say so myself." He opened the rosewood lid and revealed a man of about seventy with a beaky nose and an expression that looked as if he was trying to smile but couldn't quite manage it. "Pretty lifelike, huh?" I'd never seen anyone look so dead. I escaped into the kitchen while Howard's assistant set up baskets of gladioli around the coffin.

The next day Mother decided we should drive back to Ogdensburg. This time Effie had managed to get dinner organized and we ate at home. Once again the rye bottle was passed around and everyone partook freely. Glenn said the meal was overcooked and Effie burst into tears.

"You think Helen's a better cook than I am."

"Now, Effie, you know I didn't mean . . ." Glenn tried to put his arm around her.

"Stay away from me. It's not my fault we don't have kids," said Effie and headed out onto the porch. Mother rolled her eyes at Glenn, who suggested we go down to the Elks, but Effie wouldn't go with us. Jimmy offered to stay with her and the rest of us set off. Once again Mother stepped up to the slot machine, and once again she won, $36 this time, while Jane won twelve. We got home at eleven to discover Effie and Jimmy sitting in front of the television. They were holding hands and Effie seemed content — a bit sodden but content.

The next morning, Jimmy and I were going to cross on the ferry and take the bus for Ottawa. Jane and Mother drove us down to the dock. While Jimmy was buying our tickets, Mother suddenly took my hand. "You're lucky to have Jimmy for a friend," she said. "He's so human." It was one of the very few times I heard her speak a word of unconditional praise for anyone.

We found the house of Jimmy's cousin in Sandy Hill. He was a retired schoolmaster who still did occasional supply work at a boys' private school. He offered us sherry, of which he had already partaken a generous sampling, and fed us with a lamb stew that he had kept simmering on the stove for some months, if not years, adding ingredients from time to time. It was surprisingly tasty. He then quizzed us on our political views. Mine were ill-formed, though basically left-wing in a primitive sort of way. I had read Bernard Shaw and some Co-operative Commonwealth Federation pamphlets and had an instinctive belief in equality and distrust of privilege, in spite of being dazzled by the glamour of royalty. Jimmy, on the other hand, had a fairly sophisticated grasp of the workings of practical politics, gained from long hours debating with his father. He and his relative discussed the foibles of Mackenzie King and Louis St. Laurent till almost midnight, while I retired to my bed with a book.

The next day we visited the Parliament buildings and were assaulted by their neo-Gothic splendour, this in spite of my prejudice against everything Victorian, from Tennyson's *Lady of Shalott* to Sullivan's *The Lost Chord*. It would be another five or six years before Robertson Davies would open my eyes and ears to the richness and variety of the late nineteenth century. For me, Ottawa's spires and weathered bronze roofs were like an extension of my grandparents' "golden oak" parlour, and I was not about to be impressed.

Even more suspect was the ornately faux marble interior of the basilica where we attended high mass on Sunday morning. In our ecclesiastical shopping expeditions we had not yet ventured into a Roman Catholic sanctuary, but Jimmy said it was high time we did. Without warning he headed up the aisle to take communion. I knew that this was forbidden to non-Catholics, so I sat in my seat wavering for a bit before deciding to follow his example. I aped the rituals of the devout around me, bowing to the high altar and ostentatiously crossing myself. The wafer stuck to the roof of my mouth, and I thought I could discern the taste of blood as the voices of the choir rose above me and echoed through the vaulted ceiling. Afterwards we went and sat at the foot of Champlain's statue, looking out over the wide waters of the Ottawa.

"I think I experienced transubstantiation."

"Nonsense. The combination of plainchant and incense went to your head. Get a grip on yourself, boy."

"You weren't affected?"

"I love all the pageantry, sure. I can really see myself in a cope and mitre with people kissing my ring. But it's all just a show."

"I sometimes think that shows are the realest things in my life. I mean when I'm in a show, I'm free to be myself, even when I'm pretending to be somebody else."

"You're trying to find yourself by getting outside yourself. Like when you were playing the lame boy and you told me you felt you were stealing people's sympathy."

"You think that's phony?"

"No. You're sensitive to other people. That's good, as far as it goes . . ."

"I'm not good with other people like you. When we came back to the house the other night and you'd got Effie calmed down. That's a gift."

"I like your aunt. And your mother. They're very emotional. Very human."

"I don't find them easy to deal with."

"You're too much like them."

"I hope not."

"It's good to be in touch with your emotions."

"I find it scary."

"It doesn't do any good to be scared."

"I feel something for you . . . admiration." It was as much as I dared venture.

"Let's go for a walk."

We crossed the clattery iron bridge over to Hull and walked through the little town with its brightly painted wooden houses and storefronts dwarfed by the huge piles of lumber and the smoking chimneys of the paper mills. I suggested we have a real French meal, but the restaurants looked either expensive or rundown and Jimmy persuaded me it would be safer to go back and eat a good roast-beef dinner at Murray's in the Lord Elgin. We finished up with coffee, which was unusual for me.

"I wish you weren't going off to university," I told him. "I'll miss after-school tea with your mother. I guess we'll see each other at rehearsals."

"I'm not going back to the TCP."

"Why not?"

"When I was a child, I spake as a child, I understood as a child, I thought as a child, but when I became a man, I put away childish things."

"This child's going to miss you."

"You don't need me on your back. You're ready to stand on your own two feet."

It turned out Jimmy was right. When I went back to school that fall I soon became involved in a whole new range of activities. I stepped out of the shadows cast by Dick and Jimmy and started to become something of a personality in my own right. It was time.

In my last year in high school I began to redefine myself. In that era schools believed in streaming, and I found myself in "the smart form." Academic competition was keener, and I took it in my stride. I knew I had to get good marks or I would be sent off to boarding school. I did well in English, history, languages, and science, and got rid of mathematics, though I trailed in chemistry. The teacher, a hard-boiled ex-military Scot, referred to me as "Number two, but not in my form." Number one was a fresh-faced girl called Jane Farquharson, whose seemingly jolly exterior hid an inner tension. We became friendly rivals. I didn't mind being number two; it made me less conspicuous. After the first term, I dropped chemistry so I was able to maintain first-class marks across the board. My father objected but didn't act on it. Perhaps he decided to leave well enough alone.

The smart form was divided, both sexually and socially. The boys fell into two groups: the jocks, who were considered sexy or cute by the more attractive girls, who dressed in tight sweaters or sheer blouses and gave parties on the weekends; and the eggheads, who were physically odd or sometimes just unkempt and would today be classified as "nerds" but were then called "jerks," or "drips," or maybe "goofs." There was a corresponding gaggle of girls who were plain, or shy, or just uninterested in making the most of their appearance, and there was very little interaction between the two sexes in this group. I didn't really have the qualifications or the interest to belong to the first group, but I was damned if I was going to be classified as part of the second one. Instead I became friends with two girls, Jean Robb and Stephanie Parker. Jean was nervy, angular, and striking, with honey-blond hair, a strong aquiline nose, and flashing green eyes. Stephanie was rounder and softer but had a sharp eye and a tart tongue. We amused ourselves in class by writing doggerel verses and parodies of every author that was served up to us, from Shakespeare to Katherine Mansfield. We drew caricatures of our teachers. The primary butt of our satire was Miss South, who taught us French and then German. She often sang to us, and I remember particularly her renditions of "La Vie en Rose" and "Lili Marlene." Piaf or Dietrich she wasn't, but she had a certain ridiculous pathos that I still remember, and many years later when I won an award she wrote a letter saying how much she'd enjoyed having us in her class. I felt a tiny twinge remembering our heartless teenage mockery of her.

We hung out together after school, sometimes at Stephanie's house in Lawrence Park and occasionally at the local drugstore, which had a soda fountain where the smart set gathered to gossip and giggle. We kept to ourselves, but we were observed and achieved a certain offbeat notoriety. There was apparently some speculation about the romantic underpinnings of our ménage à trois, but in truth, although there were some unspoken sexual vibrations, nothing overt ever happened between us. Both Jean and Stephanie dated other guys, and I occasionally went out with one of my fellow TCP actors, two of whom had become special friends.

Powell Jones, a boy my own age, had a gentle and amiable manner underlaid by a sharply observant eye and a wicked sense of humour. Powell was at Lawrence, so we often travelled back and forth to rehearsals together. The other was Judy Cunningham, a tall, rather coltish girl with straight brown hair and extremely long arms and legs, which she used onstage to good comic effect. Judy claims to remember the first time she saw me, but I think I only gradually tuned into her. The three of us became the nucleus of a group that began to hang out together after Saturday-afternoon performances, taking a table at the Honey Dew at the corner of Carlton and Yonge Streets, where we would order Red Hots (hot dogs), French fries, and the rather sickly sweet orange liquid that gave the restaurant its name. We would gossip and show off, trying to be funny or outrageous, provoking but pretending to ignore amused or disapproving glances from middle-aged ladies at the neighbouring tables.

Gradually our social activities expanded as we got to know each other better. We went to movies together: the revival of *Gone with the Wind*, British costume epics like *Caesar and Cleopatra* and *Black Narcissus*, Olivier's *Hamlet*, Jean-Louis Barrault's *Les Enfants du paradis*. Mrs. G. did not go to these films with us, but we sometimes discussed them with her after rehearsal. I remember particularly that when someone asked if she thought that Lermontov, the Diaghilev figure in *The Red Shoes*, was in love with the ballerina played by Moira Shearer, she replied rather icily, "I don't expect you could understand what that man felt towards the artist he had created." I didn't get it then, though some fifty years later I think I know what she meant. We also went to the Royal Alex to see plays that Mrs. G. recommended: *Macbeth* with Michael Redgrave and Flora Robson, Donald Wolfit's *King Lear*, Julie Harris and Ethel Waters in *Member of the*

Wedding, Gratien Gélinas in *Ti-Coq*, and the initial Toronto season of the Sadler's Wells ballet with Margot Fonteyn in *Swan Lake* and Robert Helpmann in his own ballets of *Hamlet* and *Miracle in the Gorbals*.

We went to see each other's high school plays. Many of the boys in the group attended UTS, which presented an annual Shakespeare production. I recall Bobbie Jackson stealing the show in *Henry IV, Part I* in a tiny part, and Billy Ballyn being eerily sexy as Lady Macbeth. A number of us went to hear Rupert Brook (named for the English poet by an overly aspiring mother who taught elocution) give a poetry recital at the Heliconian Club; during his rendition of *The Highwayman* we got the giggles and bit our cheeks raw trying to suppress our mirth. We all got into costumes that were meant to suggest the title of a book or play for Denise Pears' Hallowe'en party. My ploy of painting a large grinning mouth on a sheet was fairly easily identified as *Blithe Spirit*, but Billy Ballyn stumped us when he showed up in his Lady Macbeth outfit adorned with silver bells. He rather huffily announced he was impersonating *Death Takes a Holiday*. The evening involved games and food but no dancing and certainly no booze. Occasionally one of the boys in our little group would ask one of the girls to a school dance, but there was no serious dating. We were friendly companions and quite satisfied with that more or less platonic arrangement.

The most hospitable of our little circle was Judy Cunningham. We went to her parents' house in Rosedale after films for cinnamon toast and milk served by her mother, a small but pretty woman with a welcoming smile and easy manner. Judy's father Frank was tall, skinny, and bald, with the comic elegance of a Ronald Searle cartoon. Like many lawyers he was highly confrontational, challenging every opinion we advanced, arguing now on one side of a question, now on the other, and laughing delightedly when his inconsistency was exposed. He enjoyed company and, unlike my parents, encouraged his children to bring people home. He was inquisitive, sharp-tongued, and subject to sudden rages, which could dissolve in a moment into peals of mocking laughter. He kept us all guessing, off-balance, on our toes. Both of the Cunningham parents seemed infinitely more sophisticated than my own. They drank martinis, sang Cole Porter and Gershwin songs, and went supper dancing. They had been to the Savoy, the *Tour d'Argent*, and the Stork Club, and had taken it all in their stride.

Judy's younger brother, Jamie, and sister, Alison, were much in evidence.

They were both active in the TCP and ambitious to keep up with Judy. Alison was darker than her siblings and had an earthier, more emotional quality, combined with a considerable dollop of her mother's ready charm. Though different in temperament, she and Jamie were only a year apart in age and enjoyed a close emotional and intellectual connection. The two of them took for granted they would be treated as equals by Judy's friends, and so they were. In my last years in high school I often called Judy in the evenings for a chat during a break in doing homework. Sometimes her father announced in forbidding tones that she had already gone to bed, but when she did come on the line we would talk about upcoming plays we wanted to see or stories and poems we were reading. Frequently Jamie and Alison picked up the upstairs extension and chimed in on the line. Judy pretended to be annoyed, but I was charmed by their bright, saucy banter.

Gradually Judy and I began going out together. We walked a lot, from her house to Massey Hall for concerts or to movie houses: the Towne Cinema, the Uptown, the Carlton, the Imperial, and Loew's. We walked through the streets of Rosedale with her Great Dane, Bach, and sat in Osler Park. We strolled down Philosopher's Walk and down to Hart House to go to student plays. We walked along University Avenue to the old conservatory for concerts given by precocious friends. We didn't go to restaurants, but I was an occasional dinner guest at the Cunninghams'. Jean, Judy's mother, was an excellent cook who produced traditional meals: roasted chicken, shepherd's pie, deep-dish casseroles, creamed vegetables, and desserts like floating island and crème caramel. Her table was set with real silver and good china. At the end of the table Frank presided imperiously, complaining if the plates hadn't been properly heated or the meat was overdone, and firing off loaded questions that I tried to field in a style matching his own. He was delighted at my more outrageous sallies, but often feigned shock or horror, putting his napkin over his head or pretending to fly into a rage. Jamie would later say he was terrified of his father's sudden outbursts of temper, though he admitted Frank taught his children to question everything and encouraged them to think for themselves. I was hugely stimulated by my contact with the Cunninghams. I think at this time I fell in love with the family, rather than specifically with Judy. Even the tension was exciting, and I was impressed by their combination of solidarity and individuality.

In our second-last year at Lawrence Park, Stephanie and I had submitted some of our comic literary efforts to the school magazine. We were both published and asked to join the masthead, which led to my appointment as editor in my final year. This position involved trips to the printer's, and I soon discovered that I could come and go from school as I pleased. I abused this privilege, cutting classes I didn't like, especially phys. ed. class. At the end of the year my gym teacher summoned me into his office and said, "You know, Hunter, I should fail you, but I respect your nerve and audacity. If you weren't so poorly coordinated you could have been a darn good football player."

That same year, a new teacher arrived who decided to produce a school play for the first time in several years. He selected *Arsenic and Old Lace*. Although I was initially contemptuous of his choice, we all went out for auditions. Stephanie and Jean were cast as the two old sisters, and when the teacher realized I knew more about theatre than he did, he apparently panicked. His solution was to let me direct in his place. The play was popular with the students, and Jean, Stephanie, and I briefly became minor celebrities.

The editorship of the school magazine carried with it a seat on the Student Council, and so, in spite of my lack of ability or even desire to compete socially and athletically, I gained a certain acceptance, perhaps notoriety. When I stood up to give a speech in assembly, I could get the whole school laughing. I was recognized as a character, not quite an eccentric but close to it. I had profited from Dick's outrageous antics and Jimmy's sharp-tongued challenges more than I knew. I had also taken a very cavalier attitude to my studies. In those days everything depended on writing the provincially set final exams in June. About mid-May I realized I would have to cram like mad. Luckily my parents went away on one of their rare holiday trips. I stayed home and swotted feverishly. The principal called me after about a week and asked where I had been. I explained that the only way I was going to pass my exams was to stay home and follow my own rigorous plan of study. There was a pause, and then he said, "Very well, Hunter. And good luck." When the results came in I had achieved eight firsts and four seconds. I left Lawrence Park confident in my ability to go out and conquer new worlds.

That summer Jean went to work as an apprentice in summer stock in Peterborough. She played a number of small roles and did backstage work. Stephanie and I went to visit her for a weekend and stayed in a private house run by an elderly widow. She was horrified to learn we had come to consort with theatre people, and we were afraid she might turn us away. We assured

her we didn't smoke or drink. "Well, that's a mercy," she said, but we knew she
was not totally reassured. We set out to find Jean, who turned out to be painting next week's set in a shed. She introduced us to her friend and roommate,
who rejoiced in the name of June Lane-Drury, as blatant a stage name as I had
ever heard. Both of them were wearing evening dresses or, as they were called
at the time, "formals." They explained they had dirtied all their other clothes
and hadn't had time to do laundry. They splashed paint around and swore like
troopers, using words like "cocksucker" and "cunt," which were not part of a
teenager's vocabulary in that era. They also used a number of English theatrical terms such as "Too utterly twee" or "You're going for a burton," and greeted
every other remark with the exclamation, "My dear, I'm fainting."

Stephanie and I retired to a tea room for supper and rolled our eyes at each
other. Then we went to the evening show. The play was a slight little comedy
and the performances utterly pedestrian, except for a wonderfully fresh, nervy
girl with red hair who brought a vibrant immediacy to every scene she was in.
We found her name in the program: Kate Reid. After the show Jean and June
took us to a party, which turned out to be in a rather elegant house owned by
an enthusiastic supporter of the theatre whom everybody called "dear
Ronnie." There was a plentiful supply of liquor, and Jean didn't hesitate when
offered a manhattan on the rocks. Stephanie and I declined, remembering our
landlady at home, who was probably sitting by the window waiting. June
began to play the piano and Jean danced with two actors and then Tony, the
prop boy, a lean gangly kid with a prominent lower lip. I asked if the red-haired
girl would be coming to the party. "She's just married the director, my dear,
and they spend all their time snogging. Too sick-making."

Our host came over, grinned at me, and asked if I'd like to go upstairs with
him. The grin was altogether too voracious and I declined. Later I noticed him
putting the arm on Tony. "Dear Ronnie is too utterly incorrigible, but I guess
Tony's used to it. He comes from a theatrical family in New York. His father's
quite well known. Osgood Perkins. Ever heard of him?" I hadn't.

June struck up a series of chords based on Tchaikovsky's *Marche Slave*, and
Jean launched into an interpretive dance solo. At the end she fell dramatically
to the floor. There was a bit of applause and somebody helped her get up. She
swayed slightly and was led away. Stephanie and I returned to our boarding
house and tiptoed up the stairs to our separate rooms as the clock struck two.

The next morning we were served breakfast in silence, paid our bill, and got on the bus for Toronto.

"Looks like Jean's taken to the theatre with a vengeance," I said.

"And how," said Stephanie, without looking up from her paperback.

Jean returned from her summer theatre in possession of an old green Ford roadster that she had christened Bessie. We had all enrolled as students at Trinity College and we drove down to the campus many mornings in Bessie. She had a leaky gas tank and Jean calculated how much gas was needed to get us down to the campus, filling the tank from a large tin can. Her calculations were not always accurate and stops were frequent. We did not go unnoticed. I had chosen Trinity on Jimmy's recommendation; he claimed the college had the best Dramatic Society on the campus, and he was its vice-president. In the first month of term he decided to direct a short play by Mazo de la Roche that was set in an old people's home. Jimmy cast all three of us: Jean and Stephanie more or less reprised their roles from *Arsenic and Old Lace*, and I played a cranky old codger in a wheelchair. Our performances were nothing if not broad: cracked voices, hobbling walks, and a great quantity of cornstarch in our hair. But we got our laughs.

A few days later Jean announced that she wanted to go to audition for Robert Gill, the artistic director of Hart House Theatre. Gill was greatly revered, on campus and off. He had arrived in Toronto shortly after the war and established a level of production that surpassed most other local theatre work at the time. His annual season of four plays was attended not only by students but by Toronto's theatre aficionados. I had already seen two memorable productions: *Medea*, starring an electric young actress Helen Ormesto, who would later become a nun, and *Crime and Punishment*, which was made remarkable by the performance of a waiflike triangular-faced young woman of great intensity. (This again was Kate Reid.)

Jean asked me to go to Gill's office with her for moral support. We set off, making our way down the stone steps and along a damp corridor to the crowded backstage office of the theatre. A pleasant young woman took Jean's name, and suggested we have a coffee and come back in fifteen minutes. As we turned to leave, she asked, "Aren't you going to audition?"

"I don't think so."

"You aren't interested in the theatre?"

"Yes, but I don't know if I'm ready . . ."

"You might as well audition now you're here. You can see Mr. Gill after Miss Robb."

Jean and I sat with our coffees and I confessed I didn't even know what plays were on the bill. She didn't know either. There was no time to prepare. We'd just have to wing it. When I think of the kind of preparation young actors do for auditions nowadays, our youthful arrogance appalls me, but that was the way it was.

Half an hour later I found myself sitting across the desk from a man with intense blue eyes, a furrowed brow topped by closely waved brown hair, and a face like an Indian mask. His accent was mid-Atlantic, featuring elongated vowels, crisp consonants, and softened Rs. He took in the fact that I'd had experience in children's theatre and in high school. "Now, Mahhtin, I want you to read something for me." Mr. Gill handed me a speech of some twenty lines in blank verse. I had no idea what it was, but I knew it was not Shakespeare. I swallowed hard and read. I had no idea what it meant, but I knew I was reading it not too badly. So it was not a total surprise when the woman in the office, who identified herself as Marian Walker, called a few days later and asked me to come back and read again. I had no time to get the play and study it, so I approached the second reading as I had the first, simply trying to make sense of the words. Gill watched me closely, the blue eyes glittering in the mask. He thanked me and I left. Marian Walker said they would be posting a cast list at the end of the week. On Friday, fortified by several cups of black coffee, Jean and I went to Hart House to look at the list. I had been cast as Cuthman in *The Boy with a Cart* by Christopher Fry. Rehearsals would begin a week later.

Even by the more demanding standards of that time Robert Gill ran a tight ship. His rehearsals were conducted according to a rigorous schedule. If you were called from 7:30 to 9:15, you could count on being through at 9:15 and also on being kicked out of the show if you weren't in the theatre by 7:25. He blocked according to a carefully prepared plan, and rarely changed his original instructions. He demanded absolute clarity of diction, corrected our pronunciation, and gave us very specific instruction on breathing and inflection. He instructed us in the correct way to sit, to kneel, to turn. It was important to gesture with the upstage hand, to pivot on the upstage foot when turning on a staircase or ramp. He used a highly technical vocabulary, peppered with "you mustn't upstage the lead," or "cheat that line out more." He was more concerned with making effective stage pictures than subtle characterization or emotional nuance.

I was playing a boy saint in Saxon England, a role I would never have dreamed I could tackle. Why Gill cast me was a mystery to me.

After two weeks of rehearsal I went to his office and said, "Mr. Gill, I really don't know what I'm doing. I need help." He suggested we go onstage. We ran through all my scenes. He didn't comment except to say, "It's fine. Just carry on with what you're doing."

I was not reassured. I remembered that I had cracked the role of the lame boy in *The Christmas Star* by using a crutch in normal life. About a week before the opening of *The Boy with a Cart* I began going to the tiny chapel of St. Thomas Aquinas on Hoskin Avenue half an hour before I went to theatre. It was dark except for a few candles burning in their red glass holders. I would kneel and cross myself the way Robert Gill had instructed me and try to empty my mind of all the trivia that normally occupied it. I would arrive at the theatre and speak to no one till I went onstage. I had my own dressing room, so this was easy.

I remember the opening performance. Partway through I had a strong feeling of rapport with the audience. I sensed they were with me, that they believed in me. And perhaps because of that I began to believe in myself. When the show was finished, we took a company call. Robert Gill had offered me a solo call, but somehow it didn't seem appropriate. When the curtains closed, the set had to be changed for the other half of the double bill, another Fry play, *A Phoenix Too Frequent*. Gill had worked out the change in precise detail using the actors from the first play. I was exempted from this lowly chore, but, I suppose drawing on my backstage experience with the TCP, I told Gill I would like to be part of the scene change. He didn't comment but gave me a couple of flats to shift. Did he admire my company spirit? If so, he never voiced it. But he had grown up with the star system. In this show I was the star, and perhaps he thought I was demeaning myself.

I remember only one incident during the performance. I arrived at the theatre one night half an hour before performance to find the entire cast onstage. Gill was in the audience livid with anger. He had posted a photocall and I had failed to see it. I was included in only one or two shots and Gill kept me after the others were sent to their dressing rooms.

"You have behaved in a manner which is completely unprofessional. I will not cast you again for at least a year." And he didn't, though at the cast party, held at the home of Morley Callaghan, whose son Michael was in the cast, Gill melted somewhat and said, "Why don't you call me Bob?" Which I did from then on.

The Boy with a Cart was a tremendous break for me. Bob Gill kept up with the latest trends in New York and London. Previous to our performance Christopher Fry had become an overnight sensation with the production of *The Lady's Not for Burning*, starring John Gielgud and Pamela Brown. Gill had not been able to get the rights for this play but did snap up *A Phoenix Too Frequent* and the Fry one-act I was in to go with it. They made an interesting duo: one a story of simple sanctity, the other a profane love story. I have to believe that somehow I was right for Cuthman: young, untried, awkward but intense. This last quality is something I was completely unaware of, but others have commented on it, so I must have projected it. Although I thought of myself as an inexperienced novice, I had in fact already appeared in some forty productions and I suppose this weighed in.

The whole of the Toronto theatre world turned out to see these two plays. It was the first chance they had had to experience the work of Fry, who was being hailed as the most important playwright of the century, the man who, along with T. S. Eliot, had restored to the British stage the glories of poetic drama not experienced since the Elizabethans. And I was playing the leading role in one of them, and apparently playing it with integrity and conviction.

I had established myself as an actor to watch, a likely successor to the Davis brothers, William Hutt, and Kate Reid, who had all recently appeared on the Hart House Theatre stage under Gill's direction. I was acknowledged by the campus theatre community and greeted as an equal by the other actors on campus who had made their mark: David Gardner, George McCowan, Michael Tait. It also set me up with people who knew or cared little about the theatre, but who acknowledged ability in any field. The dominance of athletic prowess, which had been overriding in high school, gave way at university to a wider-based appreciation of a variety of talents and interests.

Not that it went to my head. I knew that more than anything I had simply been lucky. I did not have the temperament or training to capitalize on this, and my friend Jimmy, though pleased at my success, pointed out that I shouldn't imagine that my run of luck would continue. I was, after all, only a beginner, and in the larger picture of university drama I couldn't expect to cut a wide swath. This marked the beginning of a slight strain in our relationship; though it would not prove to be permanently damaging, it subtly altered the colour of our friendship. Another casualty of my success at Hart House Theatre was my close relationship with Jean and Stephanie. Jean, having failed to be cast by Robert Gill, began to look for and find theatre work off-campus. Stephanie decided to pursue other interests. Perhaps I should have made more strenuous efforts to preserve the connection, but I didn't.

By the end of my first year, Jean had left university and joined a travelling company playing in *Tobacco Road.* I went to see her in Vancouver that summer when I got a weekend leave from my stint with the navy. She was completely convincing as a white-trash slut, her green eyes flashing daredevil defiance, her red lips alternately pouting and smirking. We met for a drink afterwards and I saw her in a new light; she seemed more driven, more exposed, always on the edge of slightly hysterical laughter, more obviously exploiting her physical charms. She told me she had become engaged to a policeman; she intended to break it off, but crossing over on the ferry she had lost the diamond ring he had given her. What should she do? She saw the funny side of this situation but her shrill giggle had an edge of desperation. I could already see the outline of the performer she would become as Jean Templeton: smart, sexy, sharp, and vulnerable. Bridging the gap between Jane Mallett and Sandra Shamas, she would have a brief career as a stand-up comic, marry three times, suffer from epilepsy, and have a child before her early death in the 1960s.

In spite of Bob Gill's warning that he would not cast me again for a year, I went to his next set of auditions and read for the lead in *Liliom.* I was not cast; he was looking for someone plausible as a burly stevedore, and that wasn't me. This time I saw Bob in a different light: not encouraging, but calculating, chilly-eyed, remote. It was my first glimpse of him as a cool and lonely manipulator. I would come to understand later how isolated a director can be — indeed often *has* to be.

Bob Gill was an outsider in Toronto. As an American he stood outside the cozy self-absorbed British enclave that considered the arts, and particularly the art of theatre, their preserve. He did not fraternize with the members of the Arts and Letters Club or hobnob with academics at the Faculty Club. This latter group was suspicious of, not to say hostile to, the practice of the arts. Some of them, like Wilson Knight and Edgar Stone, had staged plays at Hart

House Theatre before the war, but their attitude was that of the gentleman amateur. Bob had also beat out Mavor Moore for the job at Hart House Theatre. Consequently he reaped the antagonism of the formidable Dora Mavor Moore, who ran the New Play Society and would hold a major role in the early stages of the founding of the Stratford Festival. Whether Gill had any ambitions to direct there is not clear, but as so many of his students and protegés were part of the company in the opening seasons, it seems strange that Bob was never considered as a Stratford director. Did Dora or Mavor disparage Bob's talents to Tyrone Guthrie? Perhaps. Certainly Bob found himself shut out of the CBC, where Mavor was a major player, even though Bob had had considerable experience in radio drama in the United States.

Bob Gill saw himself as a consummate professional. He chose and directed four productions each season, cast them, supervised the design, worked out his rehearsal schedules, and designed the lighting. He had two trusted assistants: general manager Jimmy Hozack, who managed the money and organized publicity, ticket sales, and front-of-house arrangements; and Marian Walker, who acted as secretary, receptionist, design coordinator, and production manager. There were also two union men: stage manager Roy Befus and electrician Billy Dineen. When I first encountered them, they were a compatible and indeed chummy little family. The highlight of their day was afternoon tea, served in Bob's office. They sometimes included students in this ceremony, and I was occasionally a participant. At the end of every season, the student actors were given tea on the stage and shown slides of the shows from that and previous years. Apart from this annual event and cast parties on the closing night of every show, I never saw Bob outside the theatre. He had little time for socializing and not much taste for it.

He was, however, very close to his staff members. Jimmy Hozack was a large man who squeezed his bulk into a tiny office. He had gone through the war as a non-commissioned officer managing troop shows and had obviously had a good time, junketing through France and Italy, trading military rations for cases of champagne, and lining up gigs and digs for his performers. He was not stage-struck and would rather watch a hockey game than a theatrical performance, but he and Bob had a rapport grounded in a shared sense of humour. Bob was a frequent visitor at the Hozack cottage at Lake Simcoe, where he exercised his penchant for word games and verbal contests by insisting that everyone speak in rhyming couplets only.

Bob had a very different kind of relationship with Marian Walker, a sensitive and elegant young woman with a sharp eye and sardonic wit. She had a considerable knowledge of art history and learned much about design working with Bob, who followed in the tradition of the American designer Robert Edmond Jones. Bob's stagings were never less than visually arresting; he made effective use of a cyclorama, which he understood how to light to stunning effect, often employing a minimal amount of scenery. But he depended on Marian to pull together the costumes for his shows. I remember Marian working backstage with pinking shears or curling irons, squeezing out the maximum value from very limited resources. She had an active social life, gave cocktail parties for theatrical friends in her family home in Forest Hill, and was an accomplished golfer, scoring in the '80s even at an advanced age.

Marian was utterly devoted to Bob; indeed, it was evident to me from the first shows we did together that she was deeply in love with him, and her total dedication never wavered throughout the years. When he died alone in his apartment and was not discovered till three or four days later, Marian blamed herself for not being with him. She had apparently gone to visit him on the last day of his life, but when she rang the buzzer he said, "Marian, I can't see you today. Please, go away." She felt guilty about this but turned her back on the theatre, becoming an art historian with a particular interest in the Italian baroque.

In contrast, Bob seemed to have no personal life. He enjoyed the company of women but from an emotional distance. He spoke sometimes of Judy, whom he usually referred to as "my father's wife," and it was apparent his stepmother had been a strong influence on him when he was growing up in Baltimore. He had also been engaged to a young woman named Lisa, who died shortly before they were to be married. He carried their two wedding rings in his pocket and continued to grieve over this loss, occasionally saying, "Lisa is with me today." Lisa's death was a strong motivation for him to leave Pittsburgh, where he had been teaching at Carnegie Tech, and begin a new life in Toronto.

His first show at Hart House Theatre was *Saint Joan* and it set the tone for everything that he would do in the next twenty years: clear, well-spoken, a splendid visual pageant. Bob had a considerable knowledge of classical painting. As a student at Carnegie he had been required to analyze the composition of the Italian masters as a means of devising effective stage pictures. He continued to use this pictorial approach even when directing modern comedies. Gill's shows were always a delight to the eye, and his most effective work was in that which lent itself to spectacle, from Shakespeare's *Richard II* and *Romeo and Juliet* to Tennessee Williams's *Camino Real* or Thornton Wilder's *The Skin of Our Teeth*.

Gill had a deep love and understanding of music, though he never included musical comedies in his season, believing that this was better left to student-directed shows and revues. He disdained Gilbert and Sullivan but had a passion for Italian opera, particularly Puccini. He adored Callas and Tebaldi and went to New York to see them perform at the old Met. He directed opera productions on the West Coast in the summer and later staged several works, most notably *La Bohème* for the Canadian Opera Company at the Royal Alexandra in Toronto, and was a valued teacher at the university's opera school.

Bob also directed professional shows in the summers, initially in Woodstock, New York, where he took various actors from *Saint Joan* to try their professional wings. Later he would direct summer stock in Peterborough and Gravenhurst, working with the Straw Hat Players that the Davis family had founded. He also directed for them when they established the Crest Theatre in Toronto, but he always used a pseudonym, apparently from fear that the university would resent his moonlighting and take punitive action. His relationship with the university establishment was always a bit shaky. Now that he's gone, a small theatre has been named in his honour and he is spoken of in reverential tones, but throughout his tenure there was an ongoing undertow of antagonism.

Bob's natural hauteur no doubt played a part in the students' perception of him. When William Hutt auditioned for *Saint Joan*, he came across as something of a smart aleck and Bob decided not to cast him. Hutt was crushed, but he went to see Gill and explained that he intended to be a professional actor.

"You should have told me that in the first place. I'll let you carry a spear in this show and we'll see what happens." Hutt was soon playing leads for Gill, who early on saw his comic potential.

On another occasion, Bob was attacked by a young actress who said, "Some of us think you're just running a closed clique here."

Gill replied with asperity, "Yes, I am, and the entrée is *talent*."

In the first few years Gill was closer to the students who worked with him than with most of those who came later. He had not yet established himself in Toronto and was probably more open. Many of the early students were returning servicemen like Hutt and Murray Davis. They had some maturity and were closer in age to Bob. Their experience in summer stock invited greater intimacy and they quickly assumed the stance of professionals, so Bob felt he could deal with them as colleagues. After a few years the majority of his actors were kids like me straight out of high school. There was less formality in rehearsals than in the classroom, but we didn't expect to be treated as equals and we often didn't behave in a very mature or responsible manner. Bob became more isolated, and like many people who spend a lot of time alone, he began to take to the bottle and also to indulge his natural tendency to hypochondria.

The last show I did for Bob was Ibsen's *Wild Duck*. Bob encouraged me to play up the comedy in early rehearsals, but after he blocked the show he seemed to lose interest. For the last two weeks of rehearsal he was absent, supposedly because he had the flu, and Marian supervised the rehearsals. She allowed the cast, which included Stan Daniels, Molly Golby, Hal Jackman, and Aline Kamins, a fair amount of freedom to make changes. Bob reappeared on opening night and came backstage afterwards. "It's certainly different," was all he said. He didn't show up at the cast party in Hal Jackman's Rosedale house, which featured a collection of Group of Seven paintings that rivalled those at Hart House itself. I was pleased to have the opportunity to play Hjalmar Ekdal, but by that time I had succumbed to the blandishments of another director.

In addition to Bob Gill's four-play season, several of the colleges produced a production of their own every year at Hart House Theatre. Trinity College's productions were directed by Herbert Whittaker, who was at the time the drama critic for the *Globe and Mail*. He was also a freelance director who had directed productions for the University Women's Alumnae in the annual Central Ontario Drama League competition at Hart House Theatre and Jupiter Theatre at the Museum. This latter organization was a loose collection of professional actors who worked mainly for CBC radio drama and included such up-and-coming talents as Lloyd Bochner, Robert Christie, Lorne Greene, and Donald Harron.

Whittaker was a very different personality. He was very much tuned into the Anglo artistic and social scene in Toronto, having been born in England (he could remember seeing German bombs dropped on London as a small boy at the end of the First World War). He had grown up and begun his career in Montreal, which in the 1950s afforded him a certain cachet as it was still seen as Canada's premier city. Whittaker had cut his theatrical teeth at the Montreal Repertory Theatre working with the likes of Martha Allan, Robert Goodier, Joy Lafleur, and Eleanor Stewart. There he functioned as designer for productions directed by his good friend Charles Rittenhouse. In Montreal Whittaker experienced a wide range of theatrical events, including many more plays by French and other European writers than he would have seen in Toronto in the same period, including productions directed by such luminaries as Jacques Copeau and Theodore Komisarjevsky. In his last years in Montreal Whittaker himself began to direct as well as write criticism for the *Gazette*. He witnessed the emergence of a clutch of promising young actors that included John Colicos, Richard Easton, and Christopher Plummer.

Whittaker was highly gregarious; he enjoyed hobnobbing with the overlapping artistic and social worlds in Toronto. He had a sharp, sly wit, a huge store of anecdotes about personalities in the theatre in London and New York, and a relish for gossip. He trod a fine line between professional reserve and indiscretion, hinting that he knew more than he could tell, as indeed he did. He was happy to sit for an hour or two trading stories until the small hours at Diana Sweets or Chez Paree, two hangouts on Bloor Street frequented by professional and student actors. He attended private parties in Rosedale and Forest Hill, often arriving early for a drink and then showing up again at midnight and demanding supper after he had seen a show and turned in the copy for his *Globe* review. His slightly raffish appearance gave him an air of sensitivity, almost distinction. He was certainly not handsome, but he had style. He was almost universally known as "Herbie," which suggested an endearing accessibility. But this could be misleading.

I learned from Jimmy Armour that Whittaker was to direct a production of Molière's *Tartuffe* for the Trinity College Dramatic Society at Hart House Theatre in January of my first year. I met Herbie before the auditions, and he was affable and charming. He had seen me in *The Boy with a Cart* and was looking forward to working with me. I don't remember much about the auditions except that they were very informal in comparison to Gill's. To my surprise I was cast in the title role of the religious hypocrite.

This put a further wedge between me and Jimmy, who had set his heart on this role and had probably used his influence with other members of the

Dramatic Society to support Herbert's choice of the play, which was not the sort of British piece they would normally have chosen. But Herbert had had a considerable success with Giraudoux's *The Enchanted* in the previous year and was bent on opening up the repertoire in Toronto. (He did the first productions of Brecht's *Life of Galileo* and Chekhov's *Uncle Vanya* in Toronto and also introduced Andre Obey's *Noah*.) Herbert decided to cast Jimmy as Orgon, the deceived husband in *Tartuffe*. It's a larger role and Jimmy was well suited to it. He went to bat to see if he couldn't get Herbert to switch our roles, but Whittaker was immovable. Like Gill, he was confident in his own perceptions, although his methods of getting what he wanted were quite different.

Herbie's rehearsals were also completely different from Bob's. They rarely began on time and depended much more on improvisation, not to say whim. Herbert collaborated with his actors, taking them into his confidence, sharing his insights with them, encouraging them to voice their ideas and feelings. He discussed the effects he was trying to achieve, occasionally demonstrating what he had in mind, but rarely in a definitive manner. Where Bob had been a professional actor (and on the evidence of his performances in class and rehearsal, a highly effective one), Herbie made no pretence of being an actor and never to my knowledge appeared on any stage. Both men could dig in their heels to get what they wanted: Bob, when frustrated by an actor's inability or intransigence, resorted to a flare of temper; Herbie was more likely to walk out in a fit of pique.

Whittaker's approach was intuitive: he used his sharp wits and shrewd insights to draw performances out of his actors rather than imposing his ideas on them. Trained as a designer, he had a strong and original visual sense and the sets he devised were fanciful and light-hearted improvisations on period styles, rather than the often splendid reconstructions that Bob was able to manage. Both men were skillful in achieving a strong impact with highly limited resources, but their methods differed radically. Years later Bob confided to me that a student once said to him, "Mr. Gill, you are amazingly organized. You come to rehearsals with everything planned. Mr. Whittaker makes everything up as he goes along. But, of course, Mr. Whittaker is a genius."

As might be imagined there was a fair amount of underlying animosity between the two men, although they didn't allow it to show, at least not in this period. Bob was openly appreciative of Herbie's wit and inventiveness; Herbie admired Bob's skill and authority. They once went on a vacation together, but the experiment was never repeated. Bob later commented, "It didn't work out very well, I'm afraid. We're not exactly cut from the same bolt of cloth."

Both men were great promoters of young talent. Bob was perhaps the more adventurous in giving unknown actors an opportunity to show what they could do, as he did when he cast me as Cuthman. Herbie was more inclined to pick up on and advance talent that someone else had discovered. I doubt if he would have cast me as Tartuffe if Bob hadn't given me that first opportunity, but it was typical of Herbie that he saw something else in me and gave me an opportunity to do something seemingly unrelated. I had a considerable success in the role, though it took me awhile to find it. Of course I eventually tapped into the comic vein, which I had already learned to mine with the TCP and before that as a sidekick of Dick's. The two roles, being so different and coming within a few months of each other, established me as an actor of considerable versatility and I was able to coast on this throughout the rest of my time at the University of Toronto. Arguably I never did anything as good again. Fifty years later, I still get compliments from people who remember one of these two performances.

Both Bob and Herbie would continue to give me advice and opportunities during my undergraduate career and for a long time afterwards. I was a protegé, in whom they took some pride, though in Herbie's case I was given the impression that I never quite lived up to his expectations. Bob, on the other hand, welcomed me when I stepped into his shoes as artistic director of Hart House Theatre twenty years later. I think he was by nature more generous than Herbie. He was not uncritical, but he was not a professional critic. Both men had their favourites; they liked certain actors and disliked others, but Herbie wrote critically about them and this made his friendships with actors tricky, particularly if they went on to become professionals. You gradually come to realize that you cannot really be a friend of someone who savages you in print. Herbie tried to play on both sides of the fence and in the end it soured some of his relationships.

In the long run Herbie chose to be a critic first and foremost. When Tyrone Guthrie came to Canada to set up the Stratford Festival, he spoke to Herbie about becoming a director, suggesting that he go to England and work with some established practitioners for a year or two and then come back and work at Stratford. Herbie declined, saying that he needed to support his mother, and no doubt there was truth in this. However it seems likely that given his previous experience as a director he felt he really did not need to go back to school. He enjoyed the position he had carved out for himself, on the one hand encouraging and helping to shape the careers of ambitious young Canadians, on the other judging their work from on high and socializing with major theatrical personalities, not only in Canada but in London and New York. He maintained close ties not only with Richard Easton and Christopher Plummer, but with Sir Alec Guinness and Sir John Gielgud, Brooks Atkinson, and Christopher Fry.

Herbie preferred to live at the centre of the web, a crafty and sometimes conniving spider. He dispensed advice and opinions, made connections, set up situations, and then sat back and watched to see if the players acted out his intentions. What he had no gift for was personal commitment. His commitment was to the theatre and his own vision of it. He had many friends and depended on them for food and drink, holidays, and transportation. In return he offered wit, charm, and the glamour of his theatrical associations. Throughout much of his life his close companion was Helen Ignatieff, the attractive and gracious widow of the second warden of Hart House. They had a strong, sympathetic understanding. Helen was happy to offer her social connections and managerial skills in return for the pleasure of his company. There is no doubt that she was very fond of him, and perhaps she saw a softer side that was not visible to the rest of us. After her death, there would be a number of other women who ministered to Herbie's needs, but none who shared in his life to the same degree.

As an undergraduate I did two more shows for Herbie, playing Valentine in *You Never Can Tell*, a rather slight comedy by George Bernard Shaw, in which I wore a red beard and wig to assume the persona of the playwright; and playing Don John in *Much Ado About Nothing*, offering a rather camp performance as the villain, though of course that term was not yet in use. The latter was a production that involved the combined resources of Trinity and Victoria Colleges. I was by now the president of Trinity's Dramatic Society and my main role as a producer was trying to realize the vision that the whimsical imagination of Whittaker devised. I was ambitious to play Benedick and my friend Molly Golby aspired to the role of Beatrice. I still think we would have given more accomplished performances than the actors who were cast, and I began to question Herbie's intuitive but sometimes capricious choices.

Perhaps as a reaction to this experience, I decided that it would be good for Trinity to look for a new director for its next annual production, the first Canadian performance of Arthur Miller's *The Crucible*. The director we chose, Leonard Crainford, did not cast me as John Proctor but instead chose a young actor fresh from England, John Saxton, and opposite him my old TCP team-mate Judy Cunningham as his wife Elizabeth. I was instead tipped to play Danforth, the irascible and unrelenting governor of Massachusetts, in a strong cast that included Paul Bacon, Tony Grey (son of Earle), Meg Hogarth, Rex Southgate, and Judith Teague. Having assembled what proved to be a rather formidable cast by the standard of student productions of the day, Crainford decided we weren't up to it and jumped ship. In desperation I turned to Jimmy Hozack for help, and he suggested we engage an actor who had recently grad-uated from Trinity. And so the direction was taken over by a young William Hutt.

Bill Hutt, or "Slutsie" as we boldly came to call him, was a rather outrageous figure: tall and willowy with a full head of dyed blond hair, left over from a recent portrayal of Hamlet. He directed with panache and verve, demonstrat-ing how to make an entrance, a dramatic pause, a double take, or to phrase a line to get a laugh or kill it. He was keen, witty, and pungent in his comments, unsparing in his mimicry of our stagiest effects, yet encouraging when we did something he considered fresh and original. He treated us as colleagues, never condescending to us and yet never taking advantage of our inexperience. I had one big speech, which I was inclined to rush through. After I'd whipped it off a couple of times, he said, "Darling, that was utterly boring. If you expect anyone to listen to this, you will have to think your way though it and invent it for us every night. Otherwise you might as well phone it in from the nearest telephone booth."

I heeded his advice and was rewarded by a strong sense that I was connect-ing with the audience who really wanted to know what verdict I would deliver. Our production of *The Crucible* was much admired and a fitting conclusion to my career as a producer of student drama. Without really meaning to, I had abandoned my promising start as an actor. I see now that I didn't want it badly enough.

There were perhaps eight or ten of us who were fairly active in university theatre, playing major roles and trying our hands at directing, including John Douglas, Hal Jackman, George McCowan, John Saxton, and Ivan Thornley-

Hall, but I doubt if anyone would have picked a gangly goof named Donald Sutherland as the guy who would end up having a high-profile movie career — though he claims one review of Herbie's was crucial to his decision to go to England and try his luck on the stage.

Bob certainly supported and encouraged Leon Major, realizing that although he wasn't going to be an actor he was destined to spend a lifetime in the theatre. I think Bob understood I was not seriously committed to being a theatre professional and left me to go my own dilettantish way. When the Edgar Stone Prize for the outstanding contribution to theatre by an undergraduate went to Leon, I thought it was only fair. Douglas and McCowan made places for themselves in radio and television; the rest of us moved into other areas.

When I recently asked Hal Jackman whether he ever regretted not becoming a Canadian actor, he grinned and said, "Oh no. You see, I wanted to be a success."

Perhaps that says it all.

MAKING THE DEBS' LIST

I had been an outsider at Lawrence Park, at least partly by choice. I didn't connect with the slangy, sock-hopping, sports-sodden social world of high school and also I wanted freedom to manoeuvre. Trinity College presented another scene, at once smaller, more inclusive, and infinitely more colourful. It was immediately apparent to me that here originality was valued, eccentricity cultivated and encouraged. I was up for the challenge.

In my first weeks at Trinity I felt isolated from most of the guys I met. I was on the lookout for acquaintances who might become friends, but I was aware that most of my year-mates had been at private schools: Ridley, TCS, St. Andrew's, Upper Canada, or UTS. They already had a circle of school friends and established roles: jock, joker, lady's man, brain, or whatever. It was also clear to me that some of them were outsiders in their own group, considered "weedy," "limp," too "cocky," or just plain jerks. These guys were available for easy cultivation, but a close association with them didn't seem like a good idea.

I trod a careful path, having coffee with whoever was available but not hanging out too obviously with anyone. I spent several hours a day in the Buttery, the basement coffee shop that was the hub of the Trinity social scene, and gradually developed an ever-widening network. I had my friends Jean and Stephanie, and I was fairly quickly accepted by Jimmy's circle, now in their third year. Perhaps this gave me a certain cachet; at least I didn't appear to be a complete loner.

Within a month or so, it began to be apparent who would turn out to be the leaders in our year. As people settled on their courses, class representatives were elected, and the more popular guys were pledged by fraternities. Some joined teams: football, soccer, or hockey. Others debated for the "Lit" or wrote for the college magazine. In the first few weeks of term there was a round of social events: "smokers," at which the freshmen, or "worms" as we were called by the seniors, were encouraged to consume as much alcohol and tobacco as possible. Within a month I was going through half a pack of Players a day and downing several pints of beer many an evening.

Trinity was the only college on campus that allowed alcohol on its premises, and this was the cause of a certain amount of attention from the local press, which gleefully reported incidents of booze-fuelled pranks by Trinity men. It was not uncommon to come down to breakfast in Strachan Hall to find a scarlet MG perched on the high table, or for the chaplain to approach the high altar in chapel for the elevation of the Host and loose a couple of pigeons that had been placed in the tabernacle by some wag. The great perpetrator of these shenanigans was a red-haired math student named Donald Ross. Whenever some highly outrageous stunt took place, the dean of residence would immediately set up a search for Ross, who would most likely be found in the showers, naked and singing a hymn.

We would then be addressed by the provost, Reginald Seeley, himself no stranger to the bottle. He preached moderation but covertly encouraged prankishness. In a plummy baritone that bordered on a growl, he would drawl, "Gentlemen, we must endeavour to coexist with the yellow press and the LCBO." He never disciplined Ross, or indeed anyone else, as far as I can remember. On one occasion later on, when my friends and I were editing the weekly college newspaper, *Salterrae*, and had published some particularly scabrous piece, I was summoned to the phone and told that the provost wanted to see me in his office. I sat waiting with some trepidation until he came in and greeted me with, "Good morning, Mr. Hunter. Beautiful day."

"Yes, sir, I believe you wanted to see me."

"Did I? I can't think why. Good issue of *Salterrae* this week. Most amusing. Keep up the good work." And he shambled into his office followed by his pet bulldog, the two of them snuffling and wheezing, and shut the door.

I later learned he frequently received calls from outraged parents who demanded, "Mr. Provost, what *are* you going to do about *Salterrae*?" To which he would reply, "I really don't know. I haven't finished reading it yet," and hang up the receiver. By that time I was under his protection, having established myself in his eyes as a Trinity character.

In my first year, however, I was an unknown quantity although I did have the advantage of starting with a clean slate. The fact that I liked a drink was duly noted, but this hardly made me stand out in the crowd. I made smart remarks that sometimes garnered a laugh and quickly mastered a number of ribald drinking songs with lyrics like:

Our house has a dismal aspect
It is rather like a tomb:

Father has a swollen rectum,
Mother has a fallen womb.
Sister Sue has been aborted
For the forty-second time.
Brother Bill has been deported
For a homosexual crime.

I would not have deigned to besmirch myself with such low rubbish a year or two earlier, but I now had decided to pursue a more active social life than I enjoyed at high school and I was prepared to explore any and all possibilities.

Decidedly more civilized than the "smokers" were the receptions organized by Mossie Mae Kirkwood, the dean of women at St. Hilda's, the sister college of Trinity. Mossie Mae was every bit as much a character as Provost Seeley. She presented herself as a sort of flirtatious bluestocking, although by the time I knew her she was already in her late sixties. She had snow-white hair and favoured afternoon dresses in oyster-coloured satin, cut in a style reminiscent of the early '30s and featuring a startling décolletage that exposed her almost concave bosom. She was fond of making outrageous double entendres, the most celebrated being "I have just spent an hour having *fertile intercourse* with the provost in the quadrangle."

Although married for over forty years and the mother of three children, she remained an incurable romantic and did whatever she could to foster the amours of the young ladies of St. Hilda's. She decreed that they might entertain young gentlemen in their rooms up to a certain hour, and when she discovered that the college matron had insisted that unless the doors remained open beds must be dragged out into the hall, Mossie Mae Kirkwood frowned and said, "My dears, how *inconvenient.*" Although there was a curfew of eleven o'clock for the girls who went out on dates with young men, they soon learned they could come in at any hour. When Mrs. Kirkwood appeared in her nightgown to answer the bell, they had only to say, "Oh, Mrs. Kirkwood, I'm in *love,*" and she would clasp their hands and say, "Of course, my dear. I'm so happy for you. But you should have asked your young man to come inside where you could enjoy *fruitful congress* in warmth and comfort."

Mossie Mae eagerly received the new crop of young men and questioned them about their antecedents, keen to establish a connection between them and her wide-ranging acquaintance: "You would be the grandson of old

Professor Hunter, the distinguished botanist. But no, what a goose I am, he was a lifelong bachelor. You remember him, of course? No? Now that I think of it, if he were alive today he would be a hundred and thirty-seven."

These receptions involved dancing, and the young ladies of St. Hilda's clustered in groups around the walls of the room. The young men were thus more or less obligated to ask them to dance, and although I had a very limited repertoire of steps I felt that I could cover my inadequacies with a steady stream of witty banter. This worked well enough in some cases when the young women would rather have their toes trodden on than be seen as wallflowers, and as long as I kept talking, their own limited conversational resources were not over-taxed. But occasionally one of them would respond with a few spirited jibes of her own and a spark of mutual interest would be ignited. It was at one of these receptions that I first met Gillian, who said at the end of our rather uninspired first outing on the parquet, "Let's sit this one out, shall we? You're obviously much quicker with your tongue than your toes."

Gillian was impressed when I told her that I had been cast by Gill in his next production. She herself wrote short stories and had submitted one to the *Review*, the college literary magazine. She was a rather plain girl, with an overly large mouth that she made no attempt to disguise but emphasized with bright scarlet lipstick. Her hair was frizzy, her bosom flat and skimpy, and she was exceptionally tall for the time, just under six feet. Here too she made no concession but wore three-inch spike heels. We chatted amiably for a bit and agreed to meet two days later in the Buttery.

At the appointed hour she swooped over to my table and held out her long bony hand for a cigarette. I lit it and she took a quick puff then came right to the point.

"I've been thinking about you."

"I'm flattered."

"So you should be. I've decided to ask you to be my escort at the Artillery Ball. Not, as you might imagine, because of your skills on the dance floor, but you're the only boy I know who's tall enough. If I wear flat slippers, you should do nicely, but for God's sake, don't slouch. You have evening clothes, I assume? White tie. If necessary you can hire them, though it's a bit sordid."

"In fact I've got the complete kit."

"Good. We'll have to waltz. I'll arrange for you to take lessons from Mrs. van Valkenburg. Well, what about it?"

"Charmed, my dear Gillian."

The Artillery Ball was an annual event at which the city's debutantes were presented to the Lieutenant-Governor. There were nearly a hundred carefully selected young ladies, though I had no idea how they were chosen. A little research revealed that each of the girls would acquire a new white formal evening gown for the occasion and each of them would be escorted by a young man who was considered suitable. Thus not only Gillian would be launched into Toronto society but so would I, hanging onto, as it were, her billowing bouffant skirts. The debutante season involved a round of parties, as each of the young women hosted an affair for all the other debutantes: a cocktail party or a dance. And of course suitable young men would be invited to these gatherings as well, as their purpose was to introduce the young women to likely future partners in matrimony, which was assumed to be the ambition of every sensible girl in the group and was certainly the goal of their mothers, who planned the parties, and their fathers, who footed the bills.

Making the Debs' List assured a young man a round of social engagements and introductions to a highly select group of the city's acknowledged leaders. I was never quite sure whether Gillian had any difficulty selling my credentials to her family. In fact her parents were divorced, and the expenses of her "coming out" were paid by a doting spinster aunt, whom I met on only one occasion. Thus I found myself invited to a good many parties that season. I think that some of the mothers probably did a bit of research and discovered that my father was the president of an old, established company, and that my family were respectable Anglo-Saxon Protestants. I quickly learned that when questioned about my antecedents, the best answer was to say that my family had been farmers in the St. Lawrence Valley for 150 years. This had the advantage of being true and showed I was not trying to pass myself off as something grander than I was. Modesty was still considered a becoming quality in those days.

I would come to understand that in the early days of Upper Canada, no one looked down on the farmer, although the merchant class was regarded with some suspicion. At the turn of the century, there were people like the Jarvises, the Powells, the Ridouts, and the Baldwins who wouldn't invite the Pellatts, the Eatons, the Flavelles, or even the Masseys to their houses because they were "in trade," but this snobbery soon gave way as the wealthier tradesmen became the mainstay of institutions like the hospitals and the university, and also equipped regiments to fight in the First World War. The members of the Family Compact may have constituted an elite, but they weren't exactly aristocrats tracing their descent to Charlemagne or William the Conqueror. They were doctors, lawyers, and accountants, and they too had come to Canada to better themselves financially. A social order based essentially on money has a very positive aspect: it is accessible to the enterprising.

The Artillery Ball itself was both impressive and boring. The receiving line of matrons in their elbow-length kid gloves; the wheezy colonels and brigadiers in their bemedalled dress uniforms; the young subalterns in kilts, or scarlet or navy bumfreezer jackets; the parade of girls, some pretty and charming, many plain and frumpish (they had not after all been chosen for their looks — this was no vulgar beauty pageant); the antiquated dances (waltzes, polkas, and such ethnic novelties as the Gay Gordons) — all of these combined to suggest a social order more stratified and ritualistic than it actually was.

Gillian proved an amusing companion: she thought the whole thing ridiculous and provided me with tidbits of gossip about some of the grandees on display. Afterwards we went back to her aunt's place and drank brandy. I offered to kiss her but she declined. This had been a purely practical arrangement as far as she was concerned. We continued to meet at parties, but no romance blossomed.

Of course I didn't go to all the parties, but I found myself going out once or twice a week during "the season," which lasted more or less from the beginning of November till the start of Lent in late February. The parties varied enormously, from Judy Bongard's splendid supper dance at the Royal York, where champagne flowed like water, to Julian Armstrong's drinks party in her parents' slightly decayed house on Elgin Street, where a single uniformed maid served canapés and her father played tunes from the '20s on the piano. The Armstrongs were to become good friends, and I remember on this occasion being questioned by Polly, the mother, about my father's business. I told her it was located downtown on a street she had probably never heard of, Peter Street, to which she replied, "My dear boy, I was *born* on Peter Street."

Polly Armstrong was a member of the Wrong family; at that time her brother Hume was our ambassador in Washington. She was on intimate terms with the Pearsons and the Masseys, and through her grandfather Edward Blake, the first leader of the Liberal Party in Canada, she was related to just about everybody of any social consequence in Ontario or Anglo Quebec. (The

Blakes summered at Murray Bay on the north shore of the St. Lawrence.)
Several years later, when her daughter Jo married Laurier LaPierre and moved
to Montreal, a female relative gave a party for her. When Jo asked her, "Who
are all these people?" her hostess replied, "I don't think there's anyone here
who isn't at least your fourth cousin."

The Armstrongs were great talkers and combined a characteristic drawl
with a sharp wit. I apparently endeared myself to Mrs. Armstrong at our first
meeting by announcing I was allergic to weather: any weather. She laughed
throatily and said, "I do hope you're not allergic to gin."

I said I thought not.

"Good," she said, "Then get us both a refill."

"Gin and what?"

"Oh, it doesn't matter. After you've been an ambulance driver in the war,
you can drink gin and anything."

I realized she must have been talking of the First World War, in which I
would later learn she had lost two brothers, both close friends of Vincent
Massey. Her father, the historian George Wrong, had set up a small bequest to
Hart House in their memory, which was to be used to buy pictures. It financed
the purchase of the Group of Seven canvases that formed the first major collec-
tion of their work and influenced Vincent Massey in his acquisition of the
Group's paintings. This in turn would provide the foundation of the National
Gallery's Canadian collection.

It was this sort of connection that I began to discover underlay the brittle
chatter at the cocktail parties, which were at the heart of Toronto's social life
in this period. These people never went to bars or hotels; they entertained
each other either at their clubs (the York Club, the Toronto Club, the B&R, and
in the summer the Toronto Golf Club) or in their own houses, almost always in
Rosedale, the Annex, or Lower Forest Hill. I recall one matron telling me she
didn't think she had ever been north of St. Clair, though I think that was a bit
of an affectation. Most of these people had country houses in Caledon or the
area north of Cobourg and Port Hope, as well as summer houses at Roche's
Point, Muskoka, or Georgian Bay. They valued the ability to paddle a canoe
more highly than ownership of a Maserati, a taste for hiking and skiing in the
Laurentians above vacations in Gstaad or Cap Ferrat. They were provincial and
proud of it.

I would also learn parties were not given merely so that people could have a good time. There must be a purpose: if not the launching of a daughter into society, then a christening, a wedding, the going away or coming home of a family member, the promotion of some worthy or needy individual, an Argentinian or Hungarian academic looking for a position, the child of a friend beginning a career as a pianist or a political journalist. (The exception was Christmas when it was permissible to be merely festive.)

Back at Trinity I was starting to make a mark. I had established myself as an actor and that was to be my entrée. I was careful to dress correctly: grey flannels and a tweed sports jacket or blue blazer, a suit for church and informal dinner parties, a meagre collection of striped ties, always black oxfords. As my reputation as a "character" grew, I adopted a few colourful touches of my own. I began to wear knee-high riding boots that I'd borrowed for a one-act play and whose owner said he had no further use for them, and a long scarf thrown over one shoulder in the manner of Aristide Bruant. We were required to wear academic gowns in the dining hall, chapel, and college lectures. Somewhere I found a gown that was green with age and added that to my costume. If the college prized eccentricity, I would endeavour to supply it.

There were a number of college dances during the year, some of them formal. The biggest event of the season was the Conversazione in January. I asked Juliana Gianelli, a tall and striking actress who was to play opposite me in *Tartuffe*. She had a strong and vigorous personality and studded her conversation with bits of French learned during a prolonged stay in France, telling people they were *"vachement soigné"* or *"affreusement louche"* and greeting us with a delighted cry of, *"Salut, mes anges."* She too had been a debutante and wore her gown to the dance. Her bouffant skirt was so extended that she occupied the entire back of the taxi and I had to sit in the front with the driver. The evening began with a dinner party given by a classmate whose parents employed a houseman who served us from silver entrée dishes. I was unfazed by this unaccustomed grandeur and managed to acquit myself honourably, thanks to Mrs. Armour's tutelage.

The music at the Conversat was more contemporary than at the Artillery Ball and featured a number of tunes from the '20s, which were just then being revived. I had learned to do the Charleston for some skit I had been involved in, and I boldly launched into it when the band struck up "Five Foot Two." Gianelli kept pace with me; her voluminous skirts hid her footwork, but her gestures and facial expressions were extravagant as we egged each other on. A space cleared in the middle of the floor as we put on a show that gained a round of applause. I have no doubt some of our classmates considered us vulgarly exhibitionistic, but we were actors after all. We would reprise this performance from time to time in the next few years, adding to our repertoire an eccentric version of the tango. Gianelli and I became good friends, a relationship based on genuine affection that neither of us ever wanted to cloud or complicate with physical passion.

In my first year at Trinity I became friendly with Tony Bourne, a graceful and easygoing fellow whose light-hearted approach to life I found congenial. Tony was the younger son of a British career officer who had been colonel of the Shanghai Police before the Second World War. The family visited Canada on long leave in the summer of 1939 and stayed on when war broke out, the boys being boarded at Ridley College. Tony arrived at Trinity buoyed up by the traditions of Edwardian England and lived by an outmoded code of a world he had never seen (and as it turned out never would see). He had exquisite manners, a wardrobe of Savile Row suits and evening clothes inherited from his godfather, the last colonel of the Gurkhas. He also had an endearing giggle. He too was on the Debs' List and valued for his skills on the dance floor and his amiable disposition. Like me, Tony had a very cavalier attitude to his studies. He often rose too late for breakfast, then went back to bed and slept through lunch. Consequently he was always hungry and I often bought him snacks in the Buttery. He had vaguely artistic leanings and wrote light verse, which he would recite on the slightest encouragement.

Tony was a Kap, a member of the Kappa Alpha Society, one of the big four fraternities, the others being the Zets, who tended to be wheeler-dealers or "big men on campus," the Dekes, who were mostly jocks, and the ADs, who were on the whole more intellectual. The Kaps were the most aristocratic, the oldest Greek-letter society in America, and boasted many distinguished alumni including Mackenzie King, Hume Wrong, and Raymond Massey. Tony and another friend — Alastair Grant, a Trinidadian who wore elegant waistcoats, studied architecture, and played the bagpipes — put me up for their fraternity and in my second year I was duly rushed, pledged, and initiated into the mysteries of this secret society.

The Kap House was a dilapidated old mansion on St. George Street with a spacious front room that featured a large bay window overlooking the street. Here each day at noon, the brothers gathered before and after lunch to play

Liars' Dice, a gambling game in which I rarely participated, though when I did, apparently I showed a certain aptitude. Based on my performance in this game, one of the brothers taught me the rudiments of poker. He told me I could be quite good, if I could just learn to take fewer chances. I didn't see myself as a gambler, so this comment surprised me, but I would remember it later on when I went into business and realized there were other games in which one could take chances and sometimes win big.

Most days at lunchtime Bill Dafoe played the piano: his repertoire was limited to two Fats Waller songs: "I've Got a Feeling I'm Falling" and "I'm Gonna Sit Right Down and Write Myself a Letter." Bill was the son of a distinguished doctor and the nephew of a famous journalist, and he seemed determined to make up for their overachievement by a life of complete indolence. He was one of a number of the brothers whose charm and amiability were their great assets. Another was Roddy Brinckman, a member of the Southam family who eventually inherited a baronetcy. Bright, elegant, and highly entertaining, Roddy would have an extremely amusing life but had no inducement to accomplish anything of substance. There were other brothers who were highly ambitious (and I knew I belonged in this camp) but I soon saw that an aggressive attitude would not be tolerated and so took up a stance as a dilettante. As I was already skipping classes to loiter over coffee or go to afternoon movies, this pose was convincing. I was following a model I had encountered back in high school when I first read Evelyn Waugh's *Brideshead Revisited*. It would continue to colour and indeed inspire my performance during my undergraduate years.

Every Monday night all the Kaps turned up in dinner jackets for the weekly meeting, a ritual shrouded in secrecy. I will only reveal that although there were lots of smart remarks, the meetings had considerable intellectual content and were taken surprisingly seriously. The rest of the Kap activities consisted of parties, from formal dances to informal Saturday night get-togethers that usually involved a lot of singing around the piano, beer bottles in hand, and visiting the other houses up and down the street. The rivalry between the houses was good-humoured. I had several friends who were Zets or ADs, and these houses became almost as familiar to me as the Kap house. Many of the brothers had permanent girlfriends, but I played the field and rather enjoyed keeping them guessing about whom I would show up with next. I managed to date a number of real beauties: my secret was that I never made any real demands emotionally or sexually. And they seemed to be happy to enjoy a good time without serious involvement.

Many older Kaps were frequent visitors at the house. Charlie Armstrong wrote a grace for us to sing before our Monday dinners and Laddie Cassels always turned out for alumni events. He and his wife Nan (the daughter of a former headmaster of Ridley College) took it for granted that anyone associated with one of the institutions they valued must be associated with the others: Ridley, Havergal, Onondaga camp, the Kap house, and St. Andrew's Church. At a reunion of any one of these, Nan could be found thumping away at a piano, while Laddie, often rigged out in Nan's old Havergal tunic, sang "Braw Ben Whorple, Hielan' Man" in a lusty baritone.

A highly trusted lawyer, a spirited prankster, an aggressive but gentlemanly hockey player, even at the age of eighty, Laddie Cassels was a good exemplar of that elusive animal, the Toronto man of society. And yet the phrase doesn't ring quite true, probably because most Toronto men wouldn't admit to being part of "society." If asked, Pearce Bunting, Jim Elder, Jim McCutcheon, Donald Ross, or Hugh Smythe would probably shrug and say they don't know anything about it. Just because they jump horses or sail boats doesn't mean they are "social." Reserve has been bred into them by Scottish nannies and private schools, though they can be quite frolicsome when partying with their cronies. My inclusion in the world of the Kaps was an education into the ways and mores of what was at the time the ruling elite of Toronto, and even though their day is past, an aftertrace of their values lingers.

The other main Kap activity consisted of annual visits to sister houses in Canada or the United States. Several of the brothers would pile into a car and drive to Montreal, Pittsburgh, or Williamstown to spend a weekend that consisted of a serious meeting for one evening and a lot of hijinks on the road there and back, when, for example, someone would get out to pee and the others would drive off and leave him to hitchhike the rest of the way. These and similar pranks seemed hilarious at the time.

One memorable trip involved a weekend in Ithaca, New York. The car was driven by Bill Spragge, a medical student with the face of a friendly pug dog and a keen sense of fun. Bill was a jazz freak with a collection of Billie Holiday records, and we sang "Them There Eyes" and "That Old Black Magic" with improvised lyrics, the theme of which seemed to be "we're going to get Hunter laid this weekend." We arrived in time for the cocktail hour.

The Cornell brothers were an amiable bunch in their neat blue shirts with buttoned-down collars and spotless chinos. There were already three or four girls standing around. They mostly wore sweaters and skirts with knee socks and loafers and projected a sort of sophisticated sportiness. Someone brought in a teapot full of whisky sours and started pouring them into china mugs. A mug was put in my fist. A Cornell Kap named Royce Burton IV came over to greet us. He was tall and blond with intense blue eyes set very close together. With him were two girls, one dark with a petulant mouth, the other tall and willowy with deliciously uneven teeth. Royce peered at me shortsightedly and extended a long bony hand. His grip was steely. "You're Canadian. Knew another Canadian once. Didn't like him at all."

"You're English."

"No, just went to decent school where they taught me to speak properly. This is Vanessa. She *is* English. Perhaps the two of you can exchange a bit of gossip. Ness knows all about the Queen. Her uncle is a lord-in-waiting or something."

"An equerry. H.M.'s a silly cow, actually. All she cares about is practical jokes. She runs wires across the drawing room at Buck House and when Philip trips over them she laughs like a drain. *Too* banal. But I came here to get away from all that."

"I suspect our Canadian friend is an ardent monarchist. Shaw says somewhere there are no more enthusiastic imperialists than the colonials, doesn't he?"

"In fact I'm an anarchist," I said.

"Really? What sort of anarchy do you engage in?"

"I put bombs in postboxes. Mail Molotov cocktails to bank presidents. That kind of thing."

"Really, I had no idea there was political unrest in Canada. How *amusing*."

"Aren't you afraid of being put in jail?"

"No. I'm a master of disguise."

"Really?"

"Yes. For instance at the moment I'm posing as a university jock. Actually I'm a delivery boy."

"What sort of things do you deliver?"

"Come upstairs and I'll show you."

"Well, I must say you are cheeky. *Too* hilarious. Is it typically Canadian, would you say, to make a pass at a girl exactly one and a half minutes after you're introduced?"

"Don't ask me," said Royce Burton IV. "I don't know anything about Canada. These whisky sours are disgusting. We should go to Zinck's. They make wonderful whisky sours. And the waiters sing."

"How *entrancing.*"

"You want to go upstairs and change?" asked Burton, eyeing my grubby flannels.

"No, no, don't *ever* change," declaimed Vanessa. "Your sweaty bags are the perfect badge of your anarchy."

"Well then, shall we quit this friendly retreat?"

"Indeed. I hate oak panelling. Reminds me of everything I thought I'd left behind. *Too* depressing."

We piled into Royce's Jaguar and drove at ninety miles an hour up and down the hilly streets. The screeching of tires alternated with shrill giggles and warlike whoops all the way to Zinck's, which turned out to be a roadhouse on the outskirts of the city. Eventually there were seven of us sitting around the table, including Bill and a rather hatchet-faced girl he'd hooked up with. (I remembered him saying, "If you want to get laid, go for the plain girls. They appreciate you. You can always put a pillow over their heads. Or turn out the lights.")

Royce ordered four pitchers of whisky sours. The waiter was a handsome black guy and sang for us in a high tenor, almost a falsetto: "Sugar Blues" and "Melancholy Baby" and an imitation of the Ink Spots' hit "If I Didn't Care." After four whisky sours I asked him if he knew any Bessie Smith songs. He didn't but suggested I sing one of them. This idea appealed to Royce and Bill, and at their urging I stood up on a table and sang "Gimme a Pigfoot" to such thunderous acclaim that I went straight on to "Nobody Knows You When You're Down and Out." By the end of it my voice was gone, but I was the centre of attention and far too drunk to care how I'd attracted it.

I don't remember how we got back to the house. But I do remember waking up in the middle of the night. I was unbelievably thirsty. I was in bed but fully dressed. And I was not alone.

"Three in a bed. *Too* decadent." Vanessa's voice. I rolled over and found her face beside mine. Beyond her I could make out the profile of Royce Burton, snoring audibly. Vanessa disengaged herself and moved towards me. Our lips met and I put my arms around her. She was wearing a satin slip. I felt her hands on my body, stroking me through the thin cotton of my shirt and shorts. I pressed against her and felt her tongue in my mouth. A short spasm of intense pleasure, then slackness, a feeling somewhere between guilt and shame and the discomfort of damp underpants.

"My word, that *was* brief." She continued to stroke me till I took her hand and moved it away. I squeezed her fingers. "Never mind. We can always have another go in the morning." She grinned with her charmingly crooked teeth. We lay holding hands until she fell asleep.

I got up and made my way down the hall and found the bathroom. I drank about a gallon of water and then had a shower. I didn't feel like sleeping, so I set out on a long walk through the quiet streets of Ithaca, down to the lake and along the shore. Eventually I headed back into town and had a substantial breakfast at a diner. I walked around the campus, admiring the monumental stone buildings, Victorian Gothic softened by ivy. Eventually I ran into one of the brothers who greeted me cheerily. "I hear you were the life of the party."

"Oh, yeah?"

"You gotta perform for us tonight after dinner."

The prospect didn't exactly thrill me. We went back to the house together. Bill was in the kitchen drinking coffee and looking a bit green. "You're quite the entertainer, huh? Hell, am I hungover. What about you?"

"I woke up with this terrible thirst but I'm okay now."

"Yeah, I didn't have any problem the first few times I got loaded. Just wait, that's all."

"What's happened to our friend Royce?"

"He took off this morning with his two Smithies. Couple of snobs. All English broads are colder than a snowman's dick."

I said nothing.

"That Vanessa liked you though. Too bad you got loaded."

"I didn't get that loaded."

"No? We had to carry you upstairs. You were out like a light. That's why we put you in Royce's room. We figured you were dead to the world. You wouldn't know what was going on."

"Oh, yeah?"

"Don't tell me you came to life in the middle of the night and scored with old Vanessa?"

I shrugged, but couldn't suppress a small smirk.

"You sly bastard. Well, good for you, kid."

That night there was a barbecue and the brothers sang "Far Above Cayuga's Waters," "Shenandoah," and "When the Saints Go Marching In." Nobody asked me to sing, which was just fine by me. I had two beers, felt relaxed and happy, and went to bed early. The next day we drove back to Toronto and several times Bill started to hum "Gimme a Pigfoot" but I didn't rise to the bait.

"You're a sly devil, Hunter, and smart. Full marks on this weekend. You going to run for office in the house next year? You'd make a great secretary. I'll nominate you, if you like."

"I don't think so."

"Got better things to do, huh?"

I did have better things to do. I enjoyed being a member of the Kaps, but my real ambitions lay elsewhere. I would be president of the Trinity Dramatic Society in my next year and that would give me a seat on the college Board of Stewards and a place on the Hart House theatre committee. I didn't really aspire to be a "big man on campus," but I was prepared to bask in the glow of a little recognition from my peers.

I moved into residence, which freed me up considerably. My father opposed it as a waste of money, but I was able to pay for it out of my summer earnings. It eased our relationship as I no longer came home at two in the morning and broke a cellar window to get into the locked house. He feared it would allow me to turn night into day, and he was right. I would often go out drinking after a rehearsal, performance, or dance and arrive back at the college at three in the morning, or even later. Because I had made friends with the porter, he would let me in and I would weave my way into the quad to see flames rising up in one of the windows of Body House. Investigation revealed that Donald Ross had set up a barbecue in the third floor washroom and was cooking steaks. These would be eaten by whoever was still up, probably Peter Russell, or Crickey Ketchum, myself, and Ian Vorres, a highly civilized Greek who lived in residence while finishing a graduate degree in philosophy and writing columns for the *Hamilton Spectator*.

I would then go to my desk and work on an essay till dawn, sleep till eleven, then begin my day with coffee and a cigarette in the Buttery. There was always someone to hang out with there: members of the British Empire Club, a gang of malcontents who in the words of one of my classmates seemed to "misfit together," or members of Jimmy's group, which circled around two very bright, animated women, Joan Densem and Liz Somerville, and a long, lean guy with a slow drawl and nimble fingers which he employed to pound out forgotten '20s songs that he had somehow uncovered. One that I remember went like this:

> Ever since Rebecca
> Got back from Mecca
> She sits around and chews her Turkish tobacco
> With a smile upon her face
> She goes dancing 'round the place
> The other night her father found her
> With just a Turkish towel around her
> Oh, oh,
> Everybody's worried so.
> They think she's crazy in the dome;
> Nobody home.
> She's as bare as Theda Bara
> Theda's bare but Rebecca's barer
> Ever since Rebecca got back home.

There were house parties involving scavenger hunts and charades, and theatre parties, the most memorable of which took place at the farm of Rex Southgate's parents after the closing night of Herbie Whittaker's production of *Much Ado About Nothing.* There was square dancing, singing, and as usual a good deal of alcohol consumed. I backed into a stove, and in order to save myself from falling put my hand on a red-hot stove lid. I went upstairs to run cold water over it and discovered that one of the actresses had passed out in the bathroom. We eventually were able to get in through a window, clean her up, and wrap her in a blanket. We stuffed her into the back seat of Gianelli's father's car and drove her home. We carried her up the front steps and were greeted at the front door by her father, a huge Swede, whose face when presented with his comatose daughter, smelling of vomit and wrapped only in a blanket, was a study in outrage. Why he didn't knock my block off I don't know.

Gianelli drove me home to her house, where her mother bedded me down with an ice pack for my hand. The next morning she greeted me with strong black coffee but no judgmental comments. As a world commissioner for the Girl Guides and the wife of the colonel of Lord Strathcona's Horse, she had dealt with much more demanding situations and taken them in her stride. She nursed me for two days and sent me back to college.

Other theatrical parties took place at the house of Grania Mortimer, a stunningly beautiful girl who stage-managed shows for Trinity and then for the professional theatre. The Mortimers were Irish, and anyone who happened to be visiting from the Emerald Isle was a welcome guest in their living room at any hour of the day or night. It would be occupied by twenty or thirty people standing around with drinks in hand.

The four Mortimer daughters all had colourful personalities. Maureen, the youngest, became a good buddy, and we often went for a drink at Chez Paree to hobnob with the likes of Andrew Allan and John Drainie, and to listen to the pianist, who specialized in lesser-known Rogers and Hart tunes and introduced us to "My Funny Valentine." Mr. Mortimer was a lawyer and a horseman who rode several times a week. In his older age he developed an allergy to horses and could be seen astride his mount, sporting his First World War gas mask. His wife, Flora, was a woman of great charm and vivacity, the daughter of an Indian princess who also lived with them, a tiny wizened woman who sat on a sofa, smiling benignly, dripping with pearls, rubies, and sapphires, and pronouncing on the suitability of any young men present as possible husbands for her granddaughters. Many of the guests who dropped in for a drink at sundown stayed on to dinner; twenty or more regularly sat down to dinner and some stayed on for days.

Grania was not much of a student, but she was a particular favourite of Trinity's registrar, R. K. Hicks, a man in his mid-seventies who was hopelessly stage-struck. I met him when I went into his office to register for my first-year courses. He admitted he had not looked at the university calendar for twenty years, but upon discovering my interest in theatre sat me down and talked for three-quarters of an hour about his recollections of Ellen Terry and Johnston Forbes-Robertson while a lineup formed outside his office and down the hall. His secretary, Mrs. White, eventually broke in and freed me, but he implored me to visit him again soon. He would often call to me when I passed his door, and I would look in. Mrs. White would tell me he was much too busy to see me, but he would shoo her away and drag me into the inner office, shutting the door and saying, "Poor Mrs. White, she's a bit past it, you know. I only keep her on because she's the sole support of her deranged sister."

In my third year, when I was president of the Dramatic Society, I persuaded R. K. to take to the stage one more time in a one-act comedy about a drunken poacher. He didn't know his lines, but it didn't really matter as he improvised in an impenetrable Lancashire accent and had fortified himself with a few good belts of whiskey. About fifteen minutes into the piece he had a heart attack and the curtain had to be rung down as he was taken away to hospital. He recovered but was finally persuaded to retire at the age of seventy-eight. A widower, he had a good many children and they arranged to keep an eye on him.

He invited me to lunch not long after along with one or two Trinity actresses. He was very partial to pretty young women and had what were referred to as "roaming hands." I suspect he included me as a sort of permissive male chaperone. He suggested we come a bit early, and we discovered he had laid in a good supply of alcohol but not much food. One of the actresses pulled together a passable salad while I whipped over to a neighbouring store and bought some cold cuts. The lunch party was a roaring success, and every Saturday thereafter I would get a call from R. K. saying he had asked a few friends to drop in for lunch and could we come a little early? Each week the number of friends increased, until finally I felt forced to call R. K.'s daughter, Maud, who moved in and rang down the curtain on these theatrical lunches. R. K. lived on into his nineties, and the funeral at which several of his protegés paid him tribute was one of the most satisfying I have ever attended. I felt the many Trinity colleagues who had gone on before really were standing on the further shore holding out their hands in welcome.

In my final year I settled into residence life and had a room on the third floor of Whittaker House, traditionally the privilege of the college's "movers and shakers." I was on friendly terms with Crickey Ketchum, the head of Arts, Douglas Hill, the editor of the *Trinity Review*, and Peter Russell, the brightest of us all, who would be the Rhodes scholar in our year. We busied ourselves with committee meetings and enjoyed many informal bull sessions. I still went to Monday meetings at the Kap House and a fair number of parties, as well as directing and acting in plays and editing *Salterrae,* the weekly college rag which I took to new levels of scurrility. For the Conversat, the big dance of the year, I decided not to invite a girl but merely to entertain in my room, wearing a splendid dressing gown I had borrowed from the wardrobe of Hart House

Theatre. I eventually made it onto the dance floor and gave my final Charleston performance.

We wrote our exams, and then we third-floor residents decided to give a party for our graduating year. It was a warm spring afternoon and we planted a tree in the quad. Then we served drinks in our room. Tom Symons, the dean of residence, was present and was making a particularly pompous speech when I had the drunken inspiration of throwing my glass at him. It crashed against the wall over his head. This was followed by other crashes, and the party ended in an orgy of glass-smashing.

The guests dispersed, and Ketchum, Russell, and I made our way to a Bloor Street restaurant where we had dinner with Professor Emil Fackenheim, the eminent philosopher. He talked of the Holocaust, but I can't remember much of what was said and I doubt I contributed much to the dialogue. We then made our way back to the campus and ran into the warden of Hart House, Joe McCulley, who invited us to his rooms for a nightcap. Joe expounded on Canada's peace-keeping role in the world, the evils of McCarthyism, and other political topics of the day, all the time plying us with whisky. He would sit in his armchair, toss his glass to one of us and say, "Crickey, darlin', will you touch me up?" his brogue becoming thicker with every sip. Somehow we found our way back to Trinity and headed for our beds. Even in our drunken state we were aware there seemed to be a lot of broken glass on the floor.

Next morning we rose late and surveyed the wreckage. We felt we should return the glasses we had borrowed from Strachan Hall, but although we remembered having received some 200, we could find only eleven that were intact. We wondered whether we should phone Tom Symons and apologize, but there was no answer from his rooms. We decided to polish off the one remaining bottle of gin.

While we were sitting in Crickey's window sipping martinis and looking out over the quad, the porter arrived and knocked on the door. "Gentlemen," he said, "I bring a message from the provost's office. You are to pack your bags and be out of your rooms by five o'clock and there'll be no more said about it." We packed our bags and left. So ended my days at Trinity College. I had spent a great deal of my time socializing and partying when I might have been more profitably employed from an academic point of view in the libraries and lecture halls. But I had no regrets then and I have none now. I may not have reached my full intellectual potential, but I had a whacking good time.

The summer I turned nineteen, I was so keen to get away from home, I joined the navy. This was a surprise to my friends and family. I was about as unmilitary as anybody could be. I had an ungainly slouch, long unruly hair, and an aversion to any kind of physical exercise. While the Second World War was tugging at the heartstrings of most Canadians, I had never collected lead soldiers or built model airplanes. I didn't even get excited by war movies.

Nevertheless when I applied in 1950 I was immediately accepted into the UNTD, an officer-training program. This was the time of the Korean War. Our political leaders thought we would be fighting small wars against the Communists for the foreseeable future and that it would be a good thing if we had a cadre of trained young professional soldiers. I had good eyes, good marks on my senior matric, and knew enough to call an officer "sir," so I must have seemed like a reasonable prospect. (I was also quick-witted, energetic, and even, I guess, attractive in a gangly sort of way, but I wasn't aware of that.) I was as skeptical of my ability to turn myself into an effective fighting man as I was about most of my ambitions, but I kept my reservations to myself. "The navy may be making a big mistake," I thought, "but that's their lookout."

I didn't really expect to learn anything valuable from military life, but I suppose in some primordial way I thought the navy might "make a man of me," as they used to say. I hadn't yet heard the word *macho*, but in the '50s the notion of manliness was pretty clearly defined in everyone's minds, including mine. It involved being clean-cut, decisive, and courageous. I knew I could use a little more of these qualities. I was also responding to the recruiting slogan, "Join the navy and see the world." So far the only world I'd seen was a bit of eastern Canada and the United States. The navy was prepared to send me to the West Coast, which seemed like a good beginning.

We started with preliminary exercises at HMCS York down on Queen's Quay, but these were makeshift efforts. The real adventure began when we embarked for the three-day train trip to Victoria from Toronto's Union Station at about 11:00 on a Sunday night in early May. Forty cadets in dark-blue uniforms, each sporting the gold crown-and-anchor badge of the RCN above the peak of their caps and shouldering huge canvas duffle bags crammed with official gear — boarded their own private car at the back of the train and immediately staked out their territory.

About a dozen were experienced veterans of a previous summer. They quickly commandeered the lower bunks and almost before we left the station broke out bottles of rye and decks of cards. Poker games were started that would last until we pulled into the station in Vancouver. In the next three days, hundreds of dollars would change hands. Some of these guys would lose or win more money during that train ride than I'd earned working as a messenger boy in the whole of the previous summer. Others just sat back and drank. Of course I'd already experienced total intoxication, but it had never occurred to me that it was possible to stay completely, deliriously sozzled for three whole days.

Initially I remained an observer. I hadn't thought to stock up on whisky, which I was still too young to legally buy. And I was too cautious to gamble. I was, after all, the son of a Presbyterian accountant. I didn't really know any of the other guys very well. There was Harry Hazelton, a former child actor like myself, but this was an area of accomplishment I was not anxious to advertise. Harry looked terrific in his uniform, slim and graceful with jet black hair, and the green eyes of a voracious pussycat. The trouble was he looked too good and he knew it. He had a sort of doomed arrogance that I could admire but would not have dared to share. Then there was a high-school acquaintance, Bruce, a sad-eyed, pug-nosed little guy with a quietly understated sense of humour. He seemed a better bet, and indeed, as it turned out, we hung around together throughout much of the summer, comparing verbal notes on the absurdities of the system and lending each other moral support and the occasional five-spot. There were a couple of other first-year types who looked interesting, but I figured it would be smart to wait and see what patterns emerged, before I formed any firm alliances. I'd learned in my first year at university to be wary in matters of friendship.

The second day out, while Bruce was in the washroom, I was surprised to be accosted by a tall, slightly overweight guy with a big nose, prominent yellow teeth, and a forced chuckle in his voice.

"You're Hunter, aren't you? Have a smash."

I knew he was a second-year guy and so I accepted the amiable condescension with which he proffered a silver flask engraved with a baronial coat of arms. He explained that it contained not rye but Scotch, "The only really acceptable drink for someone who considers himself both an officer and a gentleman." He introduced himself and graciously suggested I call him Sandy. "It seems our fathers are professional acquaintances. I saw you act at Hart House Theatre with my cousin. Damn fine thing to do if you have the gift for it. Nothing quite like the words of the Bard."

I wondered if these somewhat tenuous family connections really promoted in him a sense of obligation or whether he simply enjoyed talking down to younger guys. It was possible he didn't realize how pompous he sounded. Sandy quizzed me a bit about the technical business of learning lines. He was training his own memory and committed both a chapter of scripture and a major English poem to memory every night before turning in. He already had most of Shakespeare's soliloquies by heart and favoured me with a rendition of "There is a tide in the affairs of men."

He then moved on to a more delicate but equally compelling question: "That guy who directs, is he all right? I've seen him wandering around the campus late at night a couple of times. I thought he might just be looking for a nice clean boy." He brayed suggestively. I pointed out that rehearsals often finished fairly late at night and assured Sandy that our director had never made a pass at me, or any of the other students, as far as I knew. Reassured though clearly disappointed, Sandy returned to more serious matters, imparting to me some vital aspects of navy lore, or in his phrase, "a few scraps of *pusser bumpf*." I was too intimidated to ask for a translation.

Sandy was my introduction to a type I was to encounter with some frequency in naval circles: the glory-starved colonial clinging with a certain desperation to the tattered remnants of British imperial splendour in an effort to reinforce a sense of his own superiority. "A fellow has to have some standards, some ideals," Sandy said. "The navy provides that. Gives him a context in which to exercise and develop the more forceful aspects of his personality."

Sandy saw himself as a leader in the making. His attempt to facilitate my initiation into the mysteries of naval life provided him with both an opportunity to demonstrate his ability to command attention and at the same time display his keen judgment of character. The onus would be on me to live up to his example and vindicate his choice of me as a likely candidate for advancement. He intimated that he was likely to be a cadet captain, which I realized was some sort of superior rank, and that if I proved an apt military acolyte he could see that it worked to my advantage. I too could become not only an officer but a gentleman. The idea had a certain appeal for me. For the moment I was prepared to buy the package Sandy was peddling. I was enjoying the attention he was giving me and also the whisky. If Scotch was the drink of a gentleman, I was happy to swig it down.

Sandy next turned his attention to clothes, evidently a matter of even greater importance than what one drank. He was concerned not with the expression of personal taste but with adherence to a code: I was informed that "highly polished black oxfords are the only acceptable footwear with a blue blazer"; that "a white shirt, preferably with a detachable starched collar, is the correct wear for evening"; and that "a tie is really *de rigueur* at all times and in all weathers unless one's engaged in some form of sporting activity." Thus Sandy prepared me for the sartorial demands of naval life. At Royal Roads, I learned, we would change our clothes five times a day: work clothes at 5:00 a.m. when we took out the boats; blues at seven for "colours" and morning classes; white gaiters and webbing for drill after lunch; gym clothes at four for games; back into blues with bowties and wing collars for dinner at seven thirty. In midsummer we would wear khakis instead of blues. At sea in the tropics, "pusser work rig" would be baggy shorts worn with sandals, and in the evening we would change into dress whites. It sounded as if there would be little time for anything besides costume changes. My theatrical training was obviously going to be an asset.

Sandy then moved on to another area of vital importance: "the proper use of nautical terminology to promote absolute clarity of communication between officers and men." I learned that the navy had virtually developed its own language, which seemed to be only tangentially related to English as I spoke it. There were different words for practically everything: the floor was the deck; the wall became the bulkhead; the kitchen was the galley; the toilet, the head. Directions were expressed by words like port, starboard, fore and aft, aloft, below, amidships, and my favourite, abaft the beam. These were official terms, but there was also a slang made up of words like "pusser," apparently a contraction of "purser," which was used to denote anything that was officially correct; "gash" meaning garbage, a generally derogatory term; and "tickety-boo," a humorous term of approval. The apparent object was to render one's speech totally incomprehensible to anyone outside the naval fraternity.

All of this indispensable information was imparted to me in a series of sessions spread out over the next few days. Meanwhile outside the train

windows the scenery of Canada sped by: the endless boring miles of impenetrable bush that cover northern Ontario eventually gave way to the vast
flatness and open skies of the Prairies, astonishing in their power even though
I'd heard about them all my life. Finally, on the third day, the mountains
loomed and even the poker games were briefly interrupted as we marvelled at
the splendid snow-capped peaks towering above us.

Three times each day we ate elaborate four-course meals in the dining car,
served by obliging elderly waiters who treated us with kindly indulgence
when we slopped soup and spilled wine on their starched linen cloths and
napkins. Sandy instructed me in the fine points of handling cutlery.
Fortunately for our developing relationship I already knew better than to
switch my fork back and forth between hands, but I was ignorant that dessert
should be eaten with both a spoon and a fork used as a pusher. "One should be
able to eat wearing white kid gloves and never get a spot on them. Though of
course that went out in the last century. Pity." This sort of comment was delivered with a braying laugh at the end in order to disarm ridicule; it was nevertheless evident that Sandy's preoccupation with etiquette was a serious
matter.

Every day we drank wine with both lunch and dinner, so by the end of the
latter meal we were fairly sloshed. On the third evening Sandy and I stopped
and sat down in a darkened compartment partway back to our own car. Sandy
had already interspersed his lectures with a wealth of observations on
Canadian and British politics. "It's going to be vital for us all in the years ahead
to have passionate and committed political leadership," he stated. It seemed
that his personal gods were Sir John A. Macdonald and Sir Winston Churchill.
"Both were men of forceful opinions with a cultivated taste for splendid
oratory and fine whisky. But who is to carry on the great tradition? Who will
pick up the torch and hold it high, flaming brightly above us like a beacon as
the storms of the century swirl around us?"

"Who better than you?" I shamelessly picked up my cue. But after all, I'd
been an actor. I'd also drunk a lot of his whisky.

Sandy admitted that his deepest ambition was to be Prime Minister of
Canada. He grasped my hand and squeezed it firmly as he confided his secret
to me. He explained that he was already gathering a few bright spirits around
him, igniting sparks wherever he found they would take. There was a bright
future ahead of us when the sparks joined together and formed a compelling

political blaze that would consume the hearts and minds of our countrymen. Perhaps I could see myself as a part of this upcoming conflagration. He could put me in touch with other like-minded spirits whom he had already enkindled with anticipation and desire.

As Sandy continued to hold my hand, I was relieved to hear him speak in glowing terms of his girlfriend. Whatever might be his own shortcomings, she was the perfect helpmate for a political leader, a sort of latter-day Canadian cross between Lady Laurier and Clementine Churchill. With her at his side, Sandy was confident he could shine strong and claim a place in the hearts of his countrymen. At this point we ran out of Scotch. We staggered drunkenly back to our own car. Sandy very decently gave me a boost into my upper berth before he lunged off to his own, a lower one as befitted a future leader of the nation.

Sandy was indeed made a cadet captain and continued to be friendly to me in his affably patronizing way. But at Royal Roads I came face to face with the Real Thing. The precepts to which Sandy had introduced me with his self-conscious imitation of British elitism were embodied in the very person of our gunnery officer, Commander Hornsby, who sported a lace-edged hanky tucked into one of his starched shirt-cuffs, carried a telescope under his arm even when off-duty, and spoke in an elegant English accent that had gone out of fashion about the end of the Edwardian era. He had once met Admiral Jellicoe and knew more about Admiral Nelson than Lady Hamilton.

He not only set the tone, he commanded time itself. He made up the intricate and ever-changing schedules by which our daily lives were governed. And he demonstrated his temporal power to us every morning when we would be lined up on the parade square waiting for one of the petty officers to bellow, "Eight bells, sir." The commander would bellow back, "Make it so." The look of smug satisfaction on his face as he heard the bell being struck eight times at his command in front of the assembled flowers of our colonial dominion — us in our trim blue uniforms and gleaming black boots — told us that all was well with the world as long as there were men like himself to take charge of it. In the glory-swollen imagination of Commander Hornsby, the British Empire would endure forever, whatever a few hundred million Americans and Russians might think to the contrary.

I have to admit I bought into this idea to some extent. I became a royalist at the age of six in 1939, the year of the first royal visit to Canada, and I loved the pageantry and pomp of military ceremony just as I loved the processional ritual of the Anglo-Catholic Church. It was a world I did not belong to but aspired to become part of. I looked forward to the moment of the day when I stood rigidly at attention on the parade deck at Royal Roads and listened to the band play "Hearts of Oak" and "Rule Britannia." I felt a tingle of the scalp even though my critical little brain couldn't quite buy into this display of imperial tomfoolery. The truth was: it was splendid, it was stirring, and it was also deeply silly. I've always had a soft spot for silliness, and this was high silliness, what would later be called "high camp." One day I would look back on all this and imagine Lindsay Kemp or Peter Sellers standing alongside Commander Hornsby and commenting, "*C'est magnifique, mon brave, mais c'est n'est pas la vie.*"

Of course I was not the only cadet whose appreciation of the ridiculous was nourished and honed by the proud posturings of naval martinets like Commander Hornsby. I was surrounded by a group of skeptics that included some fairly keen intelligences: Peter Russell, Ian Scott, and the embryonically outrageous Scott Symons, who every night after lights out used to vocalize elaborate sessions of mutual masturbation and simulated intercourse with various figures from our daily lives: the hugely burly chief who ran the boating exercises; the stingy dietician who believed too much red meat would increase our sexual appetites and was said to sprinkle saltpetre on our morning cereal; Commander Hornsby, whose lace hanky was put to good use; and inevitably Sandy, whose braying laugh Scott reproduced with stunning accuracy. Scott was a person nobody wanted to become too closely identified with, but his nocturnal performances made me realize I should probably keep my distance from Sandy. The next time he asked me to join him and his cronies for a rubber of bridge, I declined on the grounds that I couldn't afford it. In fact I wasn't skillful enough to play for two cents a point.

Effective as Scott was as a social critic, the guy who really put Royal Roads in perspective for us was an easygoing, soft-spoken cadet called Ronnie Newell. About a week after we arrived at Royal Roads, Ronnie simply decided he was not going to any more parades, inspections, classes, exercise periods, or mess dinners. Instead he hung out in various spots on the huge property that formed the grounds of the naval college and read Mickey Spillane paperbacks. For a day or two, no one noticed that he was missing, then the PA system began carrying messages: "Cadet Newell, to the quarterdeck," or "Cadet Newell, report immediately to the senior cadet captain's office." Over the next few days the messages became more frequent and more frantic. "Anyone knowing the whereabouts of Cadet Newell, report at once to the commander's office." Of course we all knew where he was; we were supplying him with food from the dining hall. But no one gave him away. We were proud of Ronnie and his utter disregard for naval routine. He confirmed and somehow validated our basic disbelief in the archaic postures and precepts that were being pushed at us in daily lectures and pep talks. We didn't so much mind the marching and drilling, but Ronnie's passive revolt left no doubt in our minds that all this parading up and down was, when it came right down to it, fundamentally bull-shit.

Eventually they caught Ronnie Newell and we expected a big showdown. But in fact, one afternoon while we were being shown either Noël Coward's *In Which We Serve* or Nicholas Monserrat's *The Cruel Sea* for about the tenth time, they simply took back his cap and uniforms and put him on a plane to Toronto. This was final proof, if we needed it, that the people running this absurd show didn't take it seriously either. Yet none of us followed Ronnie Newell's example. We all hated getting up at five in the morning to strain our muscles pulling heavy eighteen-foot cutters across the choppy waters of the bay, or standing for three-quarters of an hour at attention in the blazing sun waiting for some pompous old fart of a commodore or admiral to arrive and address us on the continuing power of the Nelson Tradition. Most of all we loathed lying in our beds at attention at ten o'clock at night while the commander, resplendent in gold-braided mess dress paraded through the dormitories with a drummer and two buglers to make a final inspection of us before "lights out." Often we then got dressed, slid down the drainpipes, and hitchhiked into Victoria to down as much beer as we could before closing time. But we always got back to our beds somehow and got up the next morning, doubled down to the boats, and manned our oars. I realize now that in this we were being very Canadian: withholding belief, reserving judgment, but nevertheless going along with the gag.

And there were definitely things that were positive about our time at Royal Roads. I particularly enjoyed the classes in navigation, which were conducted by Commander Craven, an owl-eyed man in a stained and crumpled uniform who had been King's Navigator of the British Fleet at Singapore when it was captured by the Japanese, who tortured him horribly. He was discharged as technically blind at the end of the war and retired to Victoria. He worked at

Royal Roads as a gardener until someone discovered he knew more about navigation than anyone on the staff, including the commandant, so they put him in charge of the training school. He could do calculations in his head in thirty seconds that took most of us twenty minutes to work out on paper. He called us not by our surnames but by nicknames he invented for us and, on the grounds that he couldn't see, never returned a salute. We took a shine to each other and he called me Cantab, because he said I had a Cambridge accent. I was flattered: the fact was I had admired the accent of one of my philosophy professors and incorporated, I suppose, some of his idiosyncrasies into my own speech.

I had abandoned maths at the first possible opportunity in high school, a reaction against my father's vaunted arithmetical skills and his scorn for anybody whose mind did not have a mathematical bent. Navigation was largely based on trigonometry, which I had never studied, but I enjoyed trying to solve the problems Commander Craven set us to sharpen our wits and I was pleased when I managed to score the second highest marks on the navigation exams. I also found, to my great surprise, that I enjoyed the challenge of mastering complicated drill manoeuvres. I'd always had poor posture and been poorly coordinated, but I somehow managed to make a reasonable showing on the parade square. The day Commander Hornsby paused in front of me and commented, "Well turned out, Hunter," I confess I was rather pleased with myself.

Physical training, on the other hand, was something I had always strenuously avoided, and I was not about to demonstrate my inadequacies on the football field or the baseball diamond. Instead along with Bruce I joined the band. I played the piano and Bruce had once taken cello lessons, but neither of us had any martial musical experience. This didn't bother the bandmaster. He assigned us to the percussion section and sent us to band stores to draw our instruments. Bruce wound up with a triangle; I was issued a pair of cymbals. I was happy enough banging them together until we were involved in a major parade on Canada Day. After two hours of marching and a tattoo that didn't end until we played the retreat at sundown, my ears were ringing. For the next few days I thought I was going deaf. I decided to get out of the band before I suffered permanent hearing loss.

My next ploy was to join the admiral's cricket team. The other players were private-school boys who had learned this game at Upper Canada, Bishop's, or

Ridley. Because the officer who was supposed to supervise our practices was away on some sort of special training course, we spent our afternoons sprawled on the grass playing liar's dice and talking about girls. Then one day a British cruiser came into port and challenged us to a game. My teammates told me not to worry; they'd put me in the outfield, where nothing much would happen.

They were right: the game was excruciatingly boring, but at least I wasn't making a fool of myself. Eventually I had to go up to bat, where I didn't exactly cover myself with glory, but cricket is a gentleman's game and nobody seemed to mind. Then back to the outfield where the wanderings of my mind were suddenly interrupted by a ball coming straight at my head. If I hadn't caught it, it would have knocked me out. As it happened my catch meant the end of the game. We'd won. The onlookers clapped politely as we trooped across the lawn to the refreshment tent. "Well done, Hunter," said the admiral, who then stood us all to champagne.

Curiously enough this incident consolidated my new friendship with the other most curious member of the admiral's cricket team, Syl Laflamme. There were probably about twenty-five French-Canadian cadets in our year. They came mostly from Montreal, Quebec City, and Windsor. They all spoke English of course, some with a bit of an accent, but they spoke French among themselves. The glories of Nelson and Jellicoe meant nothing to them: I wondered what had induced them to sign up. Laflamme, who was their self-appointed spokesman and leader, explained. "The answer, she's simple, eh? The navy pay me good bucks and it's not so 'ard as to work in the paper mill or the lumber camp."

Although we didn't spend a lot of time together, there was no animosity between us and "the frogs," as we unashamedly called them in the days before political correctness. We played bridge; they sang songs: "*Alouette*" and "*Les Chevaliers de la Table Ronde*," and some others that were obviously less conventional. Laflamme taught us the words to one dirty ditty, which went, as far as I can remember, something like this:

> *Quand je bande sur toi*
> *O quelle joyeuse spectacle*
> *J'ai perdu ma capotte*
> *Dans ta calice de plotte*

Jeanne d'Arc
Ma tabernacle.

(Decency forbids a translation to those unacquainted with Québécois argot!)

When we were sufficiently fortified with champagne, at my suggestion, the whole cricket team sang it for the benefit of the admiral and his guests, who apparently found it charming. Of course in those days none of them understood more than a few words of French and they certainly didn't have any kind of a grasp of Montreal street slang. Syl Laflamme was delighted and said afterwards to me, "Hunter, you good guy. We make you honorable *habitant*." I understood he meant honorary. I was flattered.

I'd come to really like Laflamme, this cocky little guy with his bow legs and a *beau-laid* face, who belted out his songs in the manner of a great singing star: Maurice Chevalier imitating Edith Piaf. He called himself Le Grand Syl, to distinguish himself from another cadet of the same name who was easily eight inches taller. This was a characteristic Laflamme conceit: provocative and outrageous. His determination to be on the cricket team, that emblem of Anglo exclusivity, and then to send it up was typical.

My very first memory of him dates from our second or third morning in the dormitory. As usual the bosun's pipe shrilled out of the loud-hailer at five thirty, followed by a fatuous voice intoning, "Wakey-wakey, rise and shine." Laflamme leapt from his bunk stark naked with an obvious hard-on, shinnied up to the speaker and yelled into it, "*Mange-moi, mon commandant.*" Then he hauled his blanket out the window, jumped onto the roof, and bedded down while the rest of us stumbled to the showers.

Laflamme was sexy as hell and totally unashamed of it. In fact he proclaimed it, talked about it, boasted about it. In our second week at Royal Roads we discovered "the frogs" spent their free Sunday afternoons sunning themselves completely naked on the roof. They passed around a flask of rum, smoked incessantly, and discussed the size of their dicks and how long they could hold an erection. The champion on both counts was René, an astonishingly beautiful guy who lolled in the middle of the group languidly soaking up their admiration. They seemed perfectly content to have us "*maudits anglais*" join them and immediately began to comment on our sexual equipment. There was a heated discussion on the advantages and disadvantages of possessing a foreskin. Le Grand Syl then showed us how to sustain an erection with the help of a bootlace. It should be understood that this was a purely technical demonstration: there was no suggestion that Le Grand Syl was coming onto us.

In fact, although the air at Royal Roads was sexually charged, as was inevitable where a couple of hundred healthy young guys between the ages of eighteen and twenty-one were housed under one roof, there was a strong unspoken understanding that overt sexual activity would not be tolerated. There was a fine line between what was acceptable and what was not, and not surprisingly Harry Hazelton got on the wrong side of it. We were awakened one night at two in the morning, told to get into our boots and muster as we were on the quarterdeck. Most of us wore our pyjamas or underwear but Harry elected to go on parade wearing nothing but his boots. Had Le Grand Syl done this it would have been just one more exploit in his colourful career. But the other cadets sensed somehow that Harry was showing off his body as an object of desire to them, and they turned on him. From that night on he was always referred to as Hazelnuts in a tone of derision, and nobody wanted to be his bridge partner. He stuck it out for about a week, and then one day he went to the commandant's office. Nobody knew what was said, but that night he was on a train back to Toronto.

Although we all talked about sex incessantly, there never seemed to be any real activity, at least none that I twigged to. Except once. We used to stand watch in the middle of the night to prepare us for life at sea. One night I was on watch between midnight and 4 a.m. when I thought I heard a noise in the head. I investigated and found René having a shower with Scott Symons. I should have reported them, but I didn't. I intended to ask Scott about this incident, but never got around to it. I can't help wondering if this just might have been the beginning of the fascination with French Canada that was to colour and indeed define his future career as a writer.

Our days at Royal Roads went by quickly enough, filled with the minutiae of military life: polishing our boots till they shone like black glass; sanding the bottoms of whalers and cutters; learning how to take apart and reassemble a field-gun, a piece of military equipment that hadn't been used since the Crimean war, but which we were to know about in case ever required to participate in a military funeral. We waved semaphore flags at each other and measured the course of the sun with sextants. We learned to fire rifles and read radar screens. We marched and hollered commands at each other. We rode around the surrounding countryside in the back of transport trucks singing "I've Got Sixpence" and "The North Atlantic Squadron":

> The cabin-boy, the cabin-boy,
> The dirty little nipper,
> He stuffed his ass with broken glass
> And circumcised the skipper
> Away, away with fife and drum
> Here we come, full of rum
> Looking for women to peddle their bum
> To the North Atlantic Squadron.

None of this was meant be taken very seriously, and none of it was. The military training provided by the Canadian Navy was absurd, yet it provided a framework in which we all got to meet other young guys from all over the country: mannerly East Coast guys, shy Prairie farmboys, easy-osey West Coast kids, and of course the irrepressible French Canadians. It did more to give me a sense of my country than anything I've done before or since and makes me wonder whether some form of national service, not necessarily of a military nature, might not still have some value as a way of holding our fragile nation together.

Two other incidents that happened while I was at Royal Roads stick in my memory. The British cruiser that had challenged us to a cricket match invited us to attend a court martial. Whether this was our reward for winning or not was not clear, but it was certainly an impressive affair. Two chief petty officers wearing more medals than the combined members of the royal family stood by with drawn cutlasses. The presiding commodore was ablaze with gold lace; two midshipmen armed with telescopes followed him everywhere. The men being tried were tough-looking young ratings who had been ordered by one of their officers as a punishment for smoking on watch to paint the head with red lead. Instead they'd hauled the officer into the head, debagged him and painted him with red lead from the waist down. This seemed quite witty to us, the sort of prank Laflamme might mastermind. The commodore thought otherwise and gave them five years in the brig. We remembered Ronnie Newell and understood that the Brits took all this disciplinary stuff a little more seriously than we did. Maybe that's why they ruled the waves and we didn't. At least they did for a while.

The second incident happened about a week later. We had been asked to go aboard a destroyer that had just returned from training manoeuvres in order to be lectured by a lieutenant-commander who was an acknowledged expert in weaponry. He announced he had prepared a special treat for us. He talked at some length about his particular area of expertise, mine-sweeping, and as the climax to his talk produced an actual Japanese mine that he had retrieved the week before somewhere off the coast of Alaska. He informed us that the mine was probably still active and passed it around. It travelled from hand to hand rather quickly. He scoffed at our queasiness and announced that he was now going to show us how to dismantle it. Perhaps just to be on the safe side, we'd better stand back. As we retreated, my friend Bruce made a comic face so I was looking away when the actual explosion occurred. I looked around. Where the commander had been standing was a sickening mess.

We were moved ashore and into our transport truck as quickly as possible. We didn't sing on the way home. We talked in subdued tones at dinner and went to our beds quietly. That was as close to the horrors of real war as we were to come that summer. Two days later the navy gave the commander a splendid funeral. We slow-marched for an hour and a half in the blazing sun and stood at attention while the last post was played over his grave. Then we quick-marched home to the strains of "Colonel Bogey." It didn't make us feel better, but the ritual served some purpose: it underlined the basic if unstated philosophy on which all military life is based. Whatever happens, you have to get up and get on with it.

After six weeks playing toy sailors at Royal Roads, the day arrived when we actually packed our gear into duffle bags and went to sea. I was lucky enough to be assigned not to one of the little frigates that were the usual training ships for cadets, but to a destroyer that had just come back from a tour of duty in Korea. It was an elegant ship, sleek and well-run by a seasoned captain who set a very distinctive tone. He was a smallish man in his forties, but very handsome in a sort of square-jawed, flaring-nostril fashion. He was soft-spoken, extremely mannerly, and had yellow-green eyes as bright and glittering as a sparrow hawk's.

He also had a formidable personal mythology. It was rumoured he was an illegitimate son of George v, and in fact he did look uncannily like the Duke of Windsor. It was also said that during the war he had been in command of a small ship doing escort duty and that halfway across the North Atlantic he suddenly decided he wanted to see his mistress; he turned his ship around and sailed back to Halifax. The story went that he was pardoned for this outrageous piece of misconduct because of who he was, but that he was permanently frozen at the rank of commander and as a punishment always required to do sea duty. If so, it was an ideal arrangement from his point of view.

He arrived a mere fifteen minutes before we were scheduled to sail, wearing an impeccable blazer and white flannels. He was driven to the foot of the gangplank in a red MG convertible by his wife, a sleekly handsome brunette about ten years his junior. He kissed her goodbye, came aboard, and went straight to the bridge where he took command. We slid smoothly away from the jetty and out into the choppy waters of the Strait of Juan de Fuca. Having set a course and satisfied himself that the two frigates were following in our wake, he went to his cabin to change. He was a superb shiphandler and we were to learn that he could take his destroyer into any harbour in the middle of the night without the aid of tugs or pilots. He would sail straight ahead, cut his engines, swerve neatly into position and stop: no bumping up against the jetty or missing his berth by several hundred yards and having to take another run at it. This skill, and his absolutely unflappable certainty that he knew exactly what to do at all times and in any circumstances, had earned him the unquestioning loyalty and respect of his crew. He ran the ship with calm authority, easy grace, and a certain puckish humour.

The standard of dress, he set by example. He was an expert in coming up with new and amusing combinations of the various uniforms available: for instance, khaki trousers with a blues jacket, a white silk scarf, and brown wellingtons. He encouraged his officers to emulate his sartorial ingenuity, and this was ultimately to be a source of friction between the commander and Sandy, who as senior cadet captain on this cruise deplored any deviation from the rigorous dress code so dear to his own heart. But the commander thrived on friction, although smoothness and good humour were hallmarks of his own style. He regarded Sandy with amused tolerance, returning his quivering salute with raised eyebrows and a wryly mocking twist of the wrist as his own arm snapped upwards.

As he strolled about on the upper decks, the commander often chatted amiably with us cadets. I remember brief conversations about chess: he recounted in detail a strategy developed by a noted Russian master. Poetry: he admired Byron and accurately quoted three or four stanzas of *Don Juan*. Indian religion: he explained the various attributes of Krishna, Brahma, and Shiva, and made a plausible case for the adoption of Hinduism as a more suitable religion for a fighting man than Christianity. Indeed he once went so far as to read a brief passage from the Upanishads at morning prayers. He also offered to introduce me to his wine merchant in Bond Street and his tailor in Savile Row, should I ever get to London.

The commander exemplified order, precision, and assurance. There could be no doubt that he was in command as he pitted his style and wit against the raw, elemental power of the sea. I had experienced the mystery of woods, the majesty of mountains. But the sea was new and strange. Never still, it moved in ever-changing patterns, surged, and then subsided. It was potent, unpredictable, impervious to human needs or wishes. And here we were in the middle of it: surrounded, contained, at its mercy. We adapted to its moods, rolled with its rhythms, but we couldn't change or control it. We could survive or perish; it wouldn't care, or even be aware.

I used to stand on watch and drink in its power. I think we all did, especially for the first few days. We experienced wonder, awe, and a fair amount of fear. We got into little boats called whalers that were lowered over the side, and we tried to establish a course using ten-foot oars that often broke like matchsticks as our boats were tossed on the twenty-foot waves. We watched enormous breakers sweep across the quarterdeck carrying away everything that wasn't battened down. And once when I let go of a signal halyard, I had to clamber up the mast to the crow's nest. I hung onto the rigging as we lurched through the raging waves. I looked out over plunging breakers that spread below me as far as my eye could see. I was rigid with sheer terror. I thought I would never summon up the guts to scramble back down the mast, but somehow I did. Once back with my feet on the deck, I stood grasping the railing of a ladder watching the luminous spray dance in the gathering darkness, thinking I was alone when a voice spoke out. It was Laflamme. "The ocean, she is alive, Hunter, and we are inside her belly, like unborn brats, *hein*?"

Laflamme had somehow got separated from his Montreal comrades who had been assigned to the frigates, just as I'd got separated from Bruce. Laflamme decided we should be buddies, inspired I suppose by the unexpected success of the performance I had initiated of his song at the end of the cricket match. He signalled his desire to establish a rapport with me by deciding to rig his hammock alongside mine in the crowded mess deck. Every night we swung beside each other in the eerie darkness after lights out as the ship pitched and tossed through the green-black water of the Pacific. Every morning, after the boatswain's pipe sounded at six bells and a squeaky voice chirped, "wakey-wakey, rise and shine," our breakfast was laid out on the mess tables. Huge tin trays of fried eggs congealing in grease stared up at us like sightless yellow eyes. We jumped out of our hammocks and wolfed them down, swallowing hard, those of us who weren't seasick. Laflamme usually finished up whatever eggs were left. He couldn't have weighed more than one-thirty-five, but he had a monstrous appetite and took pride in the fact that he would eat anything. "Yessir, *je mange tout*, I eat it all up, including your English pussy."

Laflamme created his own version of English. He also initiated his own dress code, creating new combinations that would never have occurred to the commander. His chef-d'oeuvre, revealed at Sunday morning colours, featured the baggy white shorts that were issued for tropical wear, tied around the waist with a regulation black tie. He wore no shirt, only a starched collar with his black bow-tie issued for mess dress, and on his feet a highly polished pair of half-wellingtons. Under his cap he wore a red bandana pirate-style. It was an outfit designed to draw comment, and it did. The commander stopped in front of Laflamme with an astonished grin and passed on without a word, but Sandy as senior cadet captain assigned Laflamme extra watch duty and told him that he would not be allowed to go ashore when we visited San Diego in two days. Laflamme argued that he was merely following the mix-and-match example set by the commander, but Sandy hit Laflamme with a technicality. Half-wellingtons, though we almost all had them and wore them with our flannels and blazers when we went on leave, were not official issue and were not supposed to be worn at sea. To say nothing of the red bandana.

Laflamme did not take his punishment gracefully. The air of the mess deck was blue with cries of *calice* and *tabernacle*, but Sandy was unrelenting. The rest of us lined up on the quarterdeck in our regulation khakis and took the Liberty boat that deposited us on the jetty of a U.S. naval base. We visited American ships: an aircraft carrier and a submarine. We went downtown with a bunch of American gobs and drank weak American beer. After we'd had half a dozen each we debated what to do for the rest of the evening. Should we stay where we were and get totally pissed or head for another bar where there were said to be some very available girls?

At this point Laflamme came through the swinging doors of the bar. He was wearing civilian clothes: a double-breasted jacket and a sharp tie. He didn't deign to explain where they'd come from or how he'd managed to get ashore. Instead he launched into a pitch: a bunch of us should hire a taxi and head for Tijuana. He needed at least three other guys to share expenses. There was some enthusiasm for the project until it was revealed that the taxi fare would be at least forty dollars return. Laflamme already had a cab lined up, waiting in the street outside. Laflamme's old sidekick, the handsome René, was already committed to the project but they needed two more guys. Laflamme made a special pitch to me: "Hunter, you need this. I know what I say." I said I'd go if somebody else would. To my surprise Bruce suddenly agreed to be the fourth. Laflamme crowed like a rooster and hustled us out into the cab. We sped through the dusk toward the Mexican border as Laflamme serenaded us: *"Allons boire, oui, oui, oui. Allons boire, non, non, non. . . ."*

Laflamme seemed to know exactly where we should go. He led us unerringly to a place that looked like a saloon in a western movie. It even had swinging doors, a long bar with a rail to put your foot up on, and cuspidors. We drank a couple of beers and then switched to tequila, knocking back straight shots with increasingly drunken bravado. Within less than half an hour we were thoroughly oiled and ready for action. René had already disappeared upstairs when Laflamme lurched across the room and started up a conversation with a woman in a red blouse. "Not exactly a kid," Bruce commented. "You might say she's a *senior*-ita." He spelled it out, to reinforce the pun. Laflamme came back over to the bar and said Estrella would really like to meet us. Bruce declined to be introduced but I let Le Grand Syl lead me across the floor. It turned out that he didn't have enough money to buy the seniorita's services, but she was willing to service the two of us for fifty. Would I go halvers? Fortified by tequila, I agreed.

We followed the seniorita up the stairs and into a small dark room that contained a bed, a broken chair, and a small washstand with a basin full of dirty water. The seniorita smiled hungrily and pushed me down on the bed. She grabbed the front of my pants, undid my fly, and proceeded to give me a hand job. Meanwhile Laflamme nuzzled her left breast. She dispatched me fairly quickly and then knelt and took Laflamme's burgeoning member in her mouth. Laflamme groaned and sighed. She stood up and leaned towards him but he turned his face away. "I don' kiss when you gotta mouth full of my cream." The seniorita spat into the washbasin and took off with her fifty.

I slept in the cab on the way back to San Diego and woke to see dawn breaking as we reached the jetty. . . . René was completely cleaned out, but Bruce was able to come up with enough for the return fare. He urged the driver to hurry, knowing that the last boat left at 2 a.m. Of course we missed it. We hung around the jetty wondering what to do, until another cab full of drunken cadets drove up. They had two American sailors with them, who suggested we hire a water taxi to take us to our ship. Everybody emptied their pockets and enough money was found to finance this extravagance. Dawn was breaking as we skimmed across the harbour. Our ship had already hauled up its ladders but they lowered ropes for us to shinny up. Laflamme was cheered as he clambered aboard. At the head of the ladder Sandy was waiting for him.

For the next three days Laflamme stood extra watches and was run around the quarterdeck for an hour every morning and evening under Sandy's personal supervision. Cocky as always, he sang *"Quand je bande sur toi"* and gave Sandy the finger whenever his back was turned. Everybody's sympathies were entirely with Laflamme, but nothing would have happened had Sandy not decided to call a special meeting of cadets the night we anchored in Esquimalt. He proceeded to give us a lecture on discipline and the honour of the senior service. As he stood at the back of the quarterdeck and waxed eloquent on the necessity of maintaining proper standards of gentlemanly behaviour we gradually began to close in on him. Suddenly his confidence deserted him.

"I know you think I'm an asshole, but somebody has to be concerned with . . . with . . . with. . . ."

We did think he was an asshole. We picked him up and threw him overboard. We heard the splash as he hit the water and a rousing cheer went up.

He must have swum around to the other side of the ship and somehow clambered aboard and gone below decks. We didn't see him again. The next morning the commander addressed us briefly before we went ashore for good. "Gentlemen, it's been a pleasure having you aboard. I think you've handled the situation with admirable dispatch. I wish you all the best in your future careers."

That was it. He left after colours and sped away in his red MG. We stowed our gear in our duffle bags and headed toward the ferry that would take us back to Vancouver, back to our homes across the country. Some would come back the next year and finish their training; others would find other things to do. Almost none of us would have professional naval careers, certainly not me. But I'd learned something about Canada, and a few things about myself. And maybe I was just a little bit closer to being a man. Whatever that was supposed to mean.

TROOPING THROUGH THE GROVES OF ACADEME

I chose to study English literature at university. It was my best subject in high school and I aspired to be a writer. In those days there were no creative-writing courses. Writing was not seen as a profession or indeed a way to make a living. It was something you did in your spare time and probably hid under your mattress, like girlie magazines or condoms, lest your parents find out and punish you. A bit to my surprise, my father did not object to my course of study. He knew I had no head for figures and he wanted me to get a university degree, in part because he had not. He had also been indoctrinated by his mother with the idea that literature, especially the poetry of Wordsworth and Tennyson, was uplifting, not that he experienced the uplift himself, though he could quote Sir Walter Scott and Robert Burns on occasion.

Once enrolled in my courses, I immediately started skipping lectures to pursue other interests. But I knew I was going to have to write essays and exams if I was going to stay at university, which I was determined to do, so I read most of the books prescribed. In my first year this involved Shakespeare, whose work I already revered. The chance to do an intensive study of the characters of Hamlet, Antony and Cleopatra, and Falstaff was welcome. Because I approached these characters as an actor, my professors were intrigued, even if what I was writing was not exactly what they were looking for.

We also read American literature, which I flippantly characterized as "a contradiction in terms." I quickly changed my attitude. In that first year I discovered Walt Whitman, Herman Melville's *Moby Dick*, Emily Dickinson, Henry James's *Portrait of a Lady*, T. S. Eliot, F. Scott Fitzgerald's *The Great Gatsby*, and William Faulkner's *As I Lay Dying*. I already knew about Ernest Hemingway, Truman Capote, Carson McCullers, and Tennessee Williams. It started to dawn on me that I was a North American and my sensibility was much closer to my American cousins than to my British ancestors. This discovery was encouraged by my professor, Gordon Roper, a gentle and sympathetic man who would continue to be supportive during my university career and long after. He was a sort of post-Socratic teacher, constantly asking questions of his students and entertaining their answers seriously, often more seriously than they deserved.

The next year I was exposed to Beowulf, with whom I didn't connect, and

Chaucer, with whom I did. Chaucer's vigorous use of language, vivid perception of character, and delight in bawdy incident greatly appealed to me. We
read texts from the seventeenth and eighteenth centuries, and I tasted the
delights offered up by Marlowe and Ben Jonson, Walter Raleigh and John
Donne, Jonathan Swift and Henry Fielding, John Dryden and Alexander Pope.
Our guide in this literary journey was Professor Arthur Barker, a saturnine and
intimidating figure who at one point summoned me to his office and said, "Mr.
Hunter, you want too much. You must learn to make choices." His words still
resonate in my ears.

In my third year I resolved to take my academic work more seriously. I had
achieved fairly high seconds and established myself on the social and theatrical scenes. I had also bid goodbye to my boyhood friends: Dick had gone to
Spain with his new bride, while Jimmy had taken up the challenge of studying
theology in Edinburgh. I had made Trinity friends — Tony Bourne, Alastair
Grant, Crickey Ketchum, and Peter Russell — but I was not on really intimate
terms with any of them. Into this semi-vacuum stepped Robert Troop. He had
been in my English classes since first year, but as neither of us attended
lectures regularly we hadn't seen much of each other. I remember on one
occasion a history professor, taking attendance, called out "Mr. Troop? *Is* there
a Mr. Troop?"

I don't remember when I first realized that Troop was interested in culti-
vating my friendship, but at some point it registered. I was both surprised and
flattered. Troop was physically unprepossessing; he had lank, dirty blond hair,
a round face like a pie, thick glasses, a short, stocky body, and a slight stoop. I
knew he was bright, though he rarely spoke in seminars. He had two familiars,
Guy Upjohn and Henry Selby, both of whom I knew slightly. They had begun
reading classics, but had been asked to transfer to other courses, which they
did. In those days these things were handled in a gentlemanly fashion, without the ignominy of outright failure. (In my first two years I took philosophy as
a minor option. I was delighted with Plato and Aristotle in my first year, but
mystified by Hobbes, Locke, Hume, Spinoza, Leibniz, and Kant in my second.
It was conveyed to me that I would be given a bare pass on the exam I obviously should have failed, on the clear understanding that I would drop philosophy, to which I willing acceded.)

One afternoon Troop invited me to his house for supper. He drove a little
red MG convertible at dazzling speed up the hill and into the driveway of a

yellow-brick mansion. We went into the drawing room furnished with eighteenth-century English chests and overstuffed chairs covered in chintz. Troop put on a recording by Schnabel of Beethoven's sonata, opus 110. I mentioned that I could play the adagio, so Troop led me to the Steinway and I executed the movement fairly credibly. While I was playing his father came in and they both praised my efforts. I had been accepted. Mr. Troop then quizzed us about Joyce's *Ulysses*, which he greatly admired. He could and did recite several passages by heart.

Dinner followed in the dining room, where Mrs. Troop dominated the conversation with sharp questions about my family and personal life peppered with strong and often unconventional opinions on whatever topics presented themselves, from the art of Botticelli to the frequency of bowel movements. Both the Troop parents were short and round; as they sat at either end of the long polished mahogany table, served by a Hungarian houseman, they reminded me of the elephant characters Babar and Celeste. The meal was delicious and ended with a wonderful torte filled with cream and hazelnuts, which the senior Troops declined. They watched as Robert and I dug in, peeling half of a pear each with pearl-handled fruit knives and forks.

I would spend many evenings at the Troops' house in the next two years. Marjorie, as her five children invariably called her, proved to be a delightfully eccentric woman, interested in everything and anything she encountered, from birds to baronets, string quartets to soufflés, *Vogue* to venereal disease. She had pithy if not particularly profound comments to offer on all these subjects. She was animated and flirtatious, delighted to tell me she was excited by my "bedroom eyes," and prophesied I would be the next Leslie Howard. She had many enthusiasms and protegés besides me, one of whom was a stone-deaf European conductor, whose ambition to lead the Toronto Symphony she tirelessly promoted ("after all Beethoven was deaf, wasn't he?"). Another was a male dancer who, though talented, had just missed being a midget. Marjorie's conversational flow was unstoppable; I would sometimes call the Troop house and be treated to a twenty-minute barrage of her opinions and observations, at the end of which she would say, "And now, dear boy, you must let me go," and hang up before I could ask for Robert.

I got to know Robert's siblings. He had an older brother, Peter, a shy and rather hesitant law student, and a sister, Susan, known to the family as "Poon," a talented pianist who spent a good deal of her time shoplifting. Another sister, Deborah, nicknamed "Beege," was a pretty and vivacious girl whom my brother started to date in his last year at high school. Prudence, or "Wudge," was the rather indulged baby of the family who was sent by Marjorie to study Italian and live with a princely family in Rome. She wrote home that the palazzo where she was staying was cold and drafty, the plumbing didn't work, and the servants were drunken and incompetent. Her father wrote back that she was obviously being exposed to real Italian culture, and as that was what he was paying a good deal of money for her to experience, he hoped she would make the most of it.

George Troop was a senior executive with Brazilian Traction, a large Canadian company with extensive interests in South America. He was a close colleague of Walter Gordon and Grant Glassco. All three men had trained, like my father, as chartered accountants, but they were much more urbane, well-travelled, and interested in the arts and politics. They entertained one another and a few close associates: Gladstone ("Bill") and Ella Murray, the parents of Ann, the actress I worked with in *Tartuffe* (he was head of the CBC); Ellie Mae and Haldane Wickett (Haldane was a lawyer who speculated in mining stocks and whose son Tom I knew from the navy); and Bertie and Flora Mortimer, the parents of Grania and Maureen, both of whom I already knew. Grant Glassco's son, Bill, and Walter Gordon's daughter, Jane, would, when they married a few years later, become my good friends. Because I had connections with most of these families, I was readily accepted. I would get the reputation of being part of the "old money" set in Toronto, which I did nothing to discourage but understood I did not really deserve. But I enjoyed being with these people and their freewheeling and essentially unpretentious enjoyment of a good time. I learned that socially the important thing is to consort with people whose company you enjoy.

George Troop provided a good model. He was intelligent but not overly ambitious. He had reached a position where he could enjoy himself on his own terms. He was extremely knowledgeable about music and literature, given to rather low-key and sardonic observations that contrasted sharply with the extravagant pronouncements of Marjorie, whom he obviously found highly amusing and indulged both socially and financially. He often brought home interesting dinner guests: international bankers, explorers, artists, and adventurers. Marjorie amused them while he observed them, and the world in general, with good-humoured and tolerant equanimity.

The other major figure in the Troop household was Andrew, the Hungarian houseman, who was given to sudden outbursts in which he would sob dramatically and say things like, "In Hungary I am baron and here I am butler." He went out almost every night after dinner. His wife Helene, the cook, would produce a ritual flood of tears, and then the minute he was out the door, she would dry her eyes and go upstairs to bed.

One night Robert and I arrived at the house to find Andrew setting out rather later than usual. He was wearing raffish dress clothes and an assortment of medals and decorations. He invited us to join him at the Hungarian Club. "Beautiful girls. No pants," he promised, leering salaciously. We drove Andrew to a restaurant called the Czardas, and were greeted there enthusiastically by his cronies, many of whom were similarly bedizened with extinct orders and distinctions. We sat at long tables, knocking back slivovitz. Toasts were drunk, glasses tossed over shoulders. A Hungarian band played ever more furiously as girls in gypsy dress leaped up on the tables and kicked wildly, sending food and drink in all directions. And yes, some of them wore no pants. It was a memorable introduction to Hungarian culture.

Robert and I began to spend more and more time together. We listened to music and drank coffee and smoked cigarettes. We read and discussed the works on our courses: Milton, Spenser, Shakespeare, Blake, Wordsworth, Byron, Keats, Shelley, Jane Austen, the Brontës, Thackeray, Dickens, Meredith, and Trollope. Our interest in literature grew as we began to explore these texts in depth, whereas we had previously skimmed much of the material we were expected to digest. Our investigations of this terrain were certainly not solemn, not even serious, but we let ourselves become open to what we were reading. This fed our imaginations and our still unrealized literary ambitions, perhaps more than we understood at the time.

We were guided through the masterworks of the nineteenth century by two professors. Milton Wilson was a large, amiable man who seemed willing to entertain any unusual interpretation and actively encouraged us to be unorthodox. But Philip Child was a true original in his own right. A novelist himself, he wandered from tangent to tangent, savouring whatever passing insight presented itself. He frequently strayed from the subject he had set out to discuss, and it was a considerable challenge to follow his thought processes as he flitted like some ancient whimsical butterfly across the literary landscape, occasionally delivering a mild aphorism or newly discovered pun as he chain-smoked his way through his lectures. He frequently had two cigarettes going at once and on one occasion borrowed a cigarette from a student with his right hand while he flicked ash from the one in his left into an ashtray where two stubs were still burning. His students had great affection for him, even when they didn't understand eighty percent of his discourse.

At the end of our third year, Robert went off to England with his mother and sisters. Marjorie was enamoured of everything English. She drove a Jaguar and cooked on an Aga stove. She collected Chippendale furniture and Georgian silver and swooned like a schoolgirl over Kathleen Ferrier and Wendy Hiller, Peter Pears and Laurence Olivier. She was what would later be called a culture vulture, and for her culture meant England: stately homes, daffodil-dotted meadows, cathedrals ringing with soaring plainsong, household cavalry trotting down the Mall.

Robert returned the next autumn with the sole ambition of getting back to England as soon as possible, where he envisaged building a career as a writer, any kind of writer. But in the meantime he and I found an outlet in that weekly rag I've mentioned before, which came out every Monday morning: *Salterrae*. The title was inspired by the college football yell:

> We are the salt of the earth, so give ear to us
> No new ideas will ever come near to us
> Orthodox, Catholic, crammed with divinity
> Damn the dissenters, Hurrah for old Trinity.

Sentiments about as far from our own convictions as possible, they were meant of course to be voiced with more than a pinch of irony.

In our final year, our relationship centred on its writing, which occupied us most of every Sunday. Troop would arrive at my room in Whittaker House; we would go out for breakfast and make notes over scrambled eggs and toast. Troop would then man the typewriter (he was a much superior typist) and we would start to compose. We commented on various college activities and each week offered an original literary gem, usually parodying one of the authors we had studied. Troop had a gift for pithy epithets, and these peppered our work. Unfortunately there seems to be no existing archive of our efforts, but I can offer a few examples, still lodged in my memory:

From our existentialist issue:

> Jean-Paul Sartre
> Met a tartre,
> She blew a fartre,
> And broke his heartre.

From our classical Greek issue, a description of Alcibiades, attributed to Socrates:

> The finest, friendliest, fruitiest fart that ever felt a foreskin.

From our Christmas issue:

> Christianity hits the spot,
> Twelve apostles, that's a lot.
> Holy Ghost and the Virgin too
> Christianity's the thing for you.

From our Easter issue:

> Enter Mary Magdalene in high dudgeon.
> She searches the tomb then leaves in the dudgeon which is lowered
> for her convenience.

From a parody of Arthur Miller's *The Crucible*:

> The scene is set in Salem. In a corner a witch is quietly burning.

Title for a gossip column about our sister college, St. Hilda's:

> Snatches snitched from Snilda's.

Troop had a real bent for the scatological. His humour was undergraduate, yes, but then we *were* undergraduates after all. Our scabrous wit seemed to appeal to our peers, and even though Troop had a healthy scorn for many of our contemporaries, he also had a gift for close friendship with the people he liked. And any friend of Robert's soon became a friend of the whole group. We hung out together: Henry Selby, Guy Upjohn, Don Vipond, and my old friend Tony Bourne. Unlike me, Troop was an adept player of games. His shambling gait and abstracted air were deceptive. He played a skilled game of golf and was a crack shot at billiards. He more or less supported himself on bets he won playing these two games. (In spite of his parents' affluence, he never seemed to have any pocket money, although he regularly raided his mother's purse, aware that she was an extravagant spender who kept little or no track of her cash outlays.) Troop played bridge with Vipond and chess with Tony. I was occasionally involved in these games but soon learned I was no match for him.

The game we became known for was hockey. It was necessary for all undergraduates to rack up a certain number of athletic credits in order to graduate. I began in my first year to do a life-saving course, but in my first attempts to rescue an enormous guy who was floundering around in Hart House pool I almost drowned. I abandoned this class and found myself at the beginning of the third year with no credits and no inclination to play team sports. Troop was in the same situation. We were approached by one of the men in our year, Fran Sutton, who made it his business to organize teams for people like us, and we discovered that we could accumulate credits more quickly playing hockey than any other game. The college already had an A team and a B team. Fran Sutton created a C team for which Troop and I recruited some of our friends.

Our games always began with two of us steering the goalie, who couldn't even stand up on skates, to the net. There followed a series of scrimmages in which we often fell to our knees or on our backsides. Our play was punctuated by endless whistles as the referee attempted to enforce the rules, which many of us never mastered. Fran egged us on, hollering encouragement from the bench. There was little or no question of us winning, but we stuck it out through three periods, gaining points for endurance.

At our first games a few friends came to cheer us on, but soon the word spread. Such was the comic impact of our sheer ineptitude that we built a fan base, and attendance at our games increased beyond anything we might have imagined possible. We usually played at noon, and many of our claque brought sandwiches and coffee. Eventually my brother and his friends began to come over on their lunch hour from University of Toronto Schools. Today, fifty years later, these games are still remembered with a fond chuckle. Our final performance took place when we were challenged by a team of girls from St. Hilda's. Needless to say, they trounced us royally.

My collaboration with Troop was without any feelings of rivalry or resentment. I considered his writerly gifts superior to my own, and the fact that many of our readers considered *Salterrae* to be primarily Troop's creation, although I was nominally the editor, did not ignite feelings of jealousy. I was used to having friends more gifted than I: Dick's superior talents were evident to me from an early age, and Jimmy was not only funnier but older. I would continue throughout my life to pair up with people of greater talent. I think I hoped that some of it would rub off on me, and it probably did. Hanging out with these people increased, rather than diminished, my self-confidence.

Troop would blossom as a serious writer sooner than I did. His first novel, *The Sound of Vinegar*, was published in London and Toronto in 1963. It had a Toronto setting and chronicled the sexual and other adventures of a medical student and his developing relationship with an older Jewish woman, a rather daring story for the time. It was well reviewed by Robert Fulford and sold modestly. In 1967 he published *The Hammering*, which was set in London, where he had taken up permanent residence with his wife and two sons. It was a more complex work, a study of a troubled middle-class marriage, which had some success in Britain and was optioned by Peter Hall to be turned into a film, but it was never made. Robert's wife, Liz, was by then also writing novels, the most popular of which was *Woolworth Madonna*, which was also supposed to be a film and was in fact broadcast as a BBC radio drama. Robert's third novel, *Bobesco*, about the life-crisis of a middle-aged internationally renowned pianist crossing the Atlantic on a luxury liner, received little notice and proved to be his final published novel. All three books are comic and sharp-edged, but they did not prove to be significant to a wide audience.

I have known a good many writers, successful and otherwise, and it remains a mystery why some of their creations catch on with the public while other well-written, acutely observed works come and go without gaining much public recognition. Of course part of the reason is sheer original talent, but it would also seem to have something to do with timeliness and the fact that there is only so much room in the literary firmament. There is also an increasing tendency for publishers, reviewers, and the media to confine their interest to people who are major stars. Yet occasionally people do suddenly flare into prominence in their seventies and even eighties. The only course is to keep going, as Tennessee Williams stated long after his own lustre had faded.

Robert and I would continue to get together when I was in London and have drunken lunches embellished by the recycling of bits of nonsense fondly recalled or new quips minted on the spur of the moment. In the '70s and early '80s, Robert and I worked as journalists with some success. At a lunch one day in the old Café Royal, I remember Robert saying, "I've become the foremost property writer in England, which isn't what I meant to do at all," to which I replied, "Yes, I know what you mean. I always saw myself as an artist, but the fact is, I've become a professional gossip." Ah well. Sic transit gloria *Salterrae*.

A week after our graduation, Selby, Troop, and I set out in a Volkswagen Beetle to drive across Canada and the northern United States, then up the Fraser Valley to the Yukon, where we would work for the summer for the Yukon Consolidated Gold Company. Troop's father was a director and had got us the jobs.

We packed sleeping bags, a tent, a kerosene stove, and various cooking utensils. But the fact was we were none of us experienced campers. The first night out we had a tasty fry-up of sausages and potatoes, prepared by Troop, who was a rather accomplished cook in a rough and ready sort of way. We washed it down with a plentiful supply of beer and then found ourselves unable to pitch the tent, a large canvas affair with supporting guy ropes that were meant to be secured to wooden pegs driven into the ground. We had neglected to bring the pegs or anything to hammer them in with. We climbed into our sleeping bags and passed a fretful night trying to keep the mosquitoes at bay.

The next day we bought yards of netting, and that night Selby draped it from the trees to form a graceful canopy under which we could sleep unmolested. Shortly after midnight it started to rain, not just a delicate shower but a torrent. The netting fell down on us as we lay in our sleeping bags getting thoroughly drenched. The mosquitoes attacked with a vengeance and I have a vivid memory of Selby, festooned in soggy netting, dragging it into the lake and watching it float away before we piled into the car and tried to sleep sitting up in the tiny bug. Troop kept quoting the words of the Bard: "cramp'd, cabin'd and confin'd." Thereafter we found cheap motels to sleep in and increasingly ate in greasy diners.

As there was still no highway along the north shore of Lake Superior, we crossed into the United States at Sault Ste. Marie and proceeded along the south shore to Duluth. We then headed for Yellowstone National Park, where we stood watching the geyser, Old Faithful, erupt on cue. We drove through the badlands and on to the coast, passing through real cowboy country, where people ate steak three times a day and had no truck with paper money but traded with silver dollars. We stayed in Vancouver with a friend of Troop's father, who took us out for a good meal, then headed up north on the Alcan Highway, much of which proved to be just one notch above a dirt road, pitted with potholes and sometimes washed out by floods or avalanches.

Eventually we arrived in Dawson City, which was virtually a ghost town, its wooden houses and dance halls literally collapsing into the street. It featured one restaurant, which displayed a sign: "If you don't eat here, you don't eat." Inside there was a collection of rough-looking whiskered men, known locally as "the old-timers," men who had come to the Yukon in the Gold Rush of '97. Some had made fortunes and others not, but they were all more or less destitute now and many owed substantial sums. Unless they paid off their debts, the Mounties wouldn't let them leave. There were only two ways out: by airplane or down the Alcan Highway. The RCMP policed access to both. No one could make their way through a thousand miles of bush, so they were stuck in Dawson. What they lived on was a mystery that was never explained.

We were welcomed to the city by another old-timer, Mr. Baird, the chief accountant of the Yukon Consolidated Gold Company. He was a vigorous man in his late eighties, with keen, sharp eyes and a thin-lipped grin. An Australian, he had arrived in 1897 and staked out a claim on one of the creeks. He set up camp, walking fifteen miles to his site with a 100-pound pack on his back, and then back again, for twenty days so that his little camp was provisioned for the summer season. By the end of the first summer he had used up his resources and found nothing. But he was too proud to go home empty-handed, so he stayed on through the long dark winter and the following year he went to work for another Australian who had forty men on his crew. Every day he fired the slowest man. Mr. Baird never got fired but worked his way up to foreman, while also staking out several new claims of his own.

He saved his earnings, broke away from his employer, and set up his own camp, employing more and more men as his claims began to produce gold. One day he fell down a shaft and fractured his leg. The doctors amputated. While in hospital he studied accounting by correspondence. When he got out he went back to running his own operation until the Yukon Consolidated Gold Company opted to buy up all claims. Mr. Baird held out for a good price and the post of chief accountant. He was a millionaire but had no intention of not working. At the age of eighty-eight, he still stumped across the compound on his wooden leg every morning and put in an eight-hour day. His evenings were spent playing bridge. When asked, he would say the first day he got up and didn't feel like working, he would retire and return to his native Australia, buy a Rolls-Royce, and tour around the country in the company of a pretty nurse who was willing to drive and play cards.

As we got to know Mr. Baird, we discovered he was widely read and could discuss literature, politics, and theology. He welcomed us with a throaty chuckle and his eyes lit up when he discovered we were bridge players. Actually Selby and I were not very accomplished, but Troop was a crack player, and because of this we were entertained regularly in the evenings by Mr. Baird, whose lively stories and generous offerings of whisky made our evenings bearable over the next month.

The days were anything but enjoyable. I don't know what I had expected, but life in a mining camp was not my idea of a rewarding or enlightening experience. Every morning we hauled ourselves out of bed, sat down to a hearty meal of meat and potatoes followed by pie, and then were trucked out to the mud flats where we manned picks, shovels, and steam hoses. Under the supervision of the "straw boss," a big dumb brute of a man, we broke up the ground to make way for the dredges that would follow us and scoop up the gold nuggets in the frozen riverbed. We went back to the camp at six for a meal indistinguishable from breakfast.

The camp was set up to house some sixty men who lived in dormitories and spent their evenings in a sort of lounge where they could drink beer and listen to the radio if they chose. Apart from a couple of Australians, the men were all recent immigrants: half were German, half Italian. The Germans were young and ambitious, eager to speak with us and improve their English. They questioned us about Canadian politics and social customs. The Italians rarely attempted to speak English. They sang Neapolitan songs and played *scopa*. The two groups had little contact and we had a sense that each despised the other. It was my first experience with recent immigrants, and I felt little rapport with either group. In the navy I'd connected with other Canadians my own age, and we'd formed a bond making fun of the senior service's pretensions and flouting its ridiculous rules. But these men were older and more embittered, and there was nothing in the daily work to bind them and us together. In fact they resented us because we had our little car and could drive into Dawson for the evening. They didn't have that option. They were stuck in the camp till the end of the season and would then have to make their way in a new country to which they clearly felt no real connection.

At the end of a month, I'd had enough. Troop and Selby opted to stay on because they would get a substantial bonus if they lasted three months. They could then go to England. I had started out with the same goal but thought there must be an easier way of achieving it. I collected my pay and decided to head for home. I would hitchhike down the Alcan Highway and across the Prairies. Troop got permission to drive me out to the highway on a sunny morning, and we said goodbye. I stuck out my thumb and waited.

There was not a lot of traffic on the road. Sometimes it would be twenty minutes between cars. Finally, after perhaps three hours, a car stopped up ahead of me. I ran up to it. Two men were sitting in the front seat: a big, burly guy behind the wheel, and a slight, rather foxy-looking guy in the other seat. He gave me a sharp look and asked me where I was headed. I told him Toronto. "Hey, you got a long way to go. Okay, get in." I put my hand on the back door handle. "No, in the front. You can sit between us." He got out and I hopped into the front seat, throwing my knapsack over into the back. He got back in and his friend started the car. We were squeezed up against each other, but in those days it was not unusual for three people to sit in a front seat. "This way we're gonna get acquainted. Name's Hal." He held out his hand and we shook.

For the next two or three hours Hal did the talking. He and the driver were not close buddies, but they had decided to hook up to share expenses: gas, motel rooms, etc. They were headed for Vancouver. They could make it in two days with one overnight stop. Gord, the big guy, would do most of the driving. He liked to drive. Hal described himself as a promoter. He promoted all kinds of things: concerts, sports events, you name it. He could sell anything if he got the right angle. He'd made a star out of his wife, an opera singer, before she upped and left him. She wasn't willing to look after him sexually. Give him complete satisfaction, if I caught his drift. I didn't, but I let him ramble on. I shared a few puffs of the cigarettes he offered me, then lay back and closed my eyes.

I woke up and realized I had a hard-on: not an unusual occurrence at the time. The car was stopped. Hal smiled and said, "We're going to take a dip in the hot springs. They're famous. So take off your duds." We got out of the car and Hal stripped down. I was reluctant, but I peeled off down to my underwear. "Hey, look at you. Very impressive." And he waded in. We paddled around in the oozy, sulphur-smelling waters, which were warm and soothing. I swam away and then back again. Gord had disappeared. Hal felt me up under the water. "Don't worry, kid. I won't hurt you." We got dressed and got back into the car. As we'd gone off the road I didn't see any alternative.

We drove on until it was completely dark, and then stopped at a motel and roadside diner. We had steaks washed down with beer. Hal insisted on paying, and he entertained us with gossip about which Hollywood stars were sleeping together. Did I know Errol Flynn liked fooling around with men? They booked a room with two beds. Gord bedded down in one. I said I'd sleep in a chair. "Don't be silly, kid," said Hal and headed into the bathroom. By the time he came back Gord was snoring and I was sitting on the other bed, having taken off my shoes and socks. Hal pushed me down on the bed and climbed on top of me, attacking with eager relish, licking, stroking, squeezing, sucking, exploring my body in a way I had never before experienced, all the time utter- ing little groans of pleasure. I responded without thinking: I lay back and let him do what he liked. I had no idea how long it lasted.

I awoke in the morning tingling with pleasure but at the same time feeling dirty, degraded, and violated. I got up and went into the shower. After a few minutes Hal joined me. He proceeded to close in, "Kid, you're fabulous. You're the best. Come to Vancouver and stay with me for a month or two." I jumped out of the shower and quickly started to dry myself. "What's the matter, kid? You loved it. Don't try to tell me you didn't. I could tell." I headed into the bedroom where Gord was still asleep. I dressed as quickly as I could and headed out the door. Hal started after me, a towel around his waist, but I ran out to the highway. I stuck out my thumb and started to walk down the road. An hour later I was still standing there when Hal and Gord drove past. Hal gave me a look that said, "Okay, kid, it's your loss," but they didn't slow down. I waited another hour and a half for my next ride.

It took me ten days to get back to Toronto. The other men who picked me up included a cowboy who insisted on giving me a ticket to the Calgary Stampede, a totally francophone Métis who invited me home to meet his family on a farm in Saskatchewan, a travelling piano salesman, and an itinerant folksinger. Once or twice I thought they might try to make a pass at me, but none of them did. I arrived home with most of my earnings intact.

I spent a few weeks at home, going to Stratford to see Christopher Plummer and a cast of French Canadians that included Gratien Gélinas and Jean Gascon in *Henry V*. Perhaps it was this that gave me the inspiration to go to Quebec for the balance of the summer and fall. My father was keen to recruit

me for his paper company, so I agreed to do a three-month training apprenticeship in a paper mill. I chose to work for Rolland Paper in Saint-Jérôme.

Though I had a superficial acquaintance with Montreal, I knew nothing
about rural Quebec. It was rumoured to be totally under the thumb of Roman
Catholic priests and corrupt politicians. My initial experience did little to
dispel this notion. Before the Quiet Revolution Saint-Jérôme was a company
town. The big industry was paper-making, and the Rolland mill dominated
one bank of the river. On the other side were the houses of the Rolland family,
splendid mansions spread out alongside each other, distanced from the small
houses and cottages of the workers. The Rollands were benevolent but patri-
archal. They had built the principal church and the hospital. They employed
half the population.

I boarded with a working-class family that lived in four rooms. They rented
one of them to me while the parents and seven children lived in the other
three. The wife cooked, and scrubbed, and shopped, and washed, and
mended. Every day she fed her younger children at five, and her husband and
older sons and me at six. She never sat down to eat with us but waited on the
table and cleaned up afterwards. The first night I was there I offered to help
with the dishes. She roared with laughter. A man washing dishes: what a droll
idea. After dinner the family watched television: *Les Plouffes*, *Le Pays d'en haut*, *la
Lutte* (wrestling). And of course, on Saturday night, hockey: *les Canadiens*. On
Sundays they went to Mass. The women prayed inside while the men stood
outside and gossiped or joked, entering the church at the crucial moment of
the elevation of the Host. They ignored the sermons of the parish priest, who
told them which stores they should shop at, which bars they might drink in,
which television shows they might watch, which politicians to vote for. Then
they went home and had the big meal of the week, sometimes the only one at
which meat was served.

In the paper mill I was treated with respect filtered through a kind of mocking tolerance. I was known to be the son of an important customer. They were
curious about the ways of English-speaking Canada in much the same way we
were curious about the customs of the Chinese. It was a world apart that they
did not expect ever to experience directly. They spoke no English but were
polite when I attempted to speak to them in French. They spoke a thick
patois with a regional accent. My first day on the job one of my co-workers
asked, "*Aym-tsu-tsitte?*" I would eventually come to understand he was saying

"*Aimes-tu ici?*" meaning, "Do you like it here?"

But they were unfailingly friendly. The family always asked me to join them around the television set in the evenings, and my co-workers would include me in their drinking parties at the local taverns. The Rollands were an enormous family and some of them invited me to their houses. Lucien, the president, was an elegant figure, intensely curious and a wonderful listener; he had studied at Harvard rather than Laval. His brother, Roger, was the family intellectual and a close friend of Pierre Trudeau. Another brother, Lantier, was a playboy who on his occasional visits to the mill was invariably accompanied by a stunning model.

André Rolland, the purchasing agent, took a particular shine to me, and as soon as the hockey season began he invited me to a Canadiens game at the Forum in Montreal. We drove in his convertible at about 130 miles an hour until a police car overtook us, siren screaming. André rolled down his window. The policeman gasped, "*Ah, M. Rolland, excusez-moi,*" and sped away into the night. On the way home we stopped at a roadhouse where we drank till 4 a.m., served by buxom *filles*, with whom, André assured me, I could arrive at an *arrangement*.

My work at the paper mill was not onerous but involved regular testing of the quality of the paper that was being manufactured. Rolland still had small machines that made paper from shredded rags in the traditional manner, as well as high-speed machines. I learned that making paper, like making wine, was a process that was at once simple and highly complex; minute adjustments in temperature and the addition of certain small elements were crucial. It was still, in some sense, an art. I felt I was learning something both technically and socially. My three months in Saint-Jérôme were happier and more satisfying than my month in the Yukon.

Most weekends I visited Montreal, staying with my Uncle Merritt and Gwen in the town of Mount Royal. Like the French Canadians, they knew how to enjoy themselves. They spoke no French, but they went to good restaurants, skied in the Laurentians, and their house was full of conviviality and laughter. They were open, hospitable, good-humoured, and non-judgmental. I came to see them in a very different light than that shed on them by my parents.

As my French improved I began to go to French theatre, particularly to see Gratien Gélinas, who revived his *Fridolinades* at the Monument National. It was my first experience of penetrating the plateau in the centre of Montreal, and although the rue St. Denis lacked the glamour it has since acquired, I tuned into its special character, its easygoing, fun-loving ambiance. But mostly I was captivated by Gélinas. I had first seen him in *Ti-Coq* at the Royal Alex in Toronto in 1948, at the instigation of Dorothy Goulding. His performance as the cocky little soldier who comes back from the war to find his sweetheart has married someone else had a bittersweet pathos at once funny and touching.

I came to see Gélinas as the Charlie Chaplin of Quebec, a *naïf savant* who epitomized the plight of the little guy who stood up to the corrupt and dehumanizing forces around him. Like Chaplin he created his own characters, wrote his own scripts, directed himself and his fellow actors, made his own world. His persona as Fridolin, a gauche, outspoken habitant clown whose wry perspective threw into sharp relief the chicaneries and hypocrisies of politicians and businessmen, spoke directly to his fellow Québécois. Like the singer La Bolduc he was both fearless and sly, using the language of the streets to make his points, provoking laughter and then undercutting it with pathos.

I would see Gélinas's later plays — *Bousille et les justes*, *Hier les enfants dansaient*, *La Passion de Narcisse Mondoux* — which extended the territory he explored in *Ti-Coq* and paved the way for the plays of Michel Tremblay. But this early experience of Gélinas, with his audacity, his nervous, volatile energy, his sudden switch from mocking comedy to emotional vulnerability, made me understand the range of possibilities available to someone who could simply tap into the world around him at many levels: mockingly satiric, fearlessly questioning, unashamedly giving way to deep and disturbing feelings. Later I would try to capture the story of his contemporary, La Bolduc, for English-speaking CBC audiences. I wish I had also had a chance to tell Gélinas's story for that audience.

In late November, as I was finishing off my apprenticeship at Rolland, I received a letter from the Department of External Affairs. In the spring of my last year, just before finals, I had written the entrance exams for the foreign service, almost as a joke. I knew very little about current affairs but I did know how to write exams, so it was not a total shock when I was informed that I had passed the initial barrier and should proceed to an interview. For three hours I was confronted by a panel of senior diplomats who grilled me on the issues of the day: the Soviet threat following the death of Stalin; the situation in Indochina, where the French had just pulled out; the growing conflict in the

Middle East with the rise of President Nasser in Egypt. I knew very little about any of them but I parried the probing questions as nimbly as I could. I was aware I was not exactly dazzling them, but I was somehow managing to stay afloat in the sea of my own ignorance.

In addition to members of the Department of External Affairs, the examining panel always included an outsider, who in my case was Joe McCulley, the warden of Hart House, the big jovial Irishman who had always treated me kindly in the past. Skillfully he deflected the questions I simply could not answer. Several times I felt I should come clean: "Gentlemen, I'm sorry I'm wasting your time. Good day." But thanks to McCulley's interventions, it never quite came to that, and I finished the interview, as it were, bloody but unbowed. And now, six months later, here was a letter offering me a position in External Affairs as a junior foreign-service officer.

I hurried home to Toronto and consulted various mentors: Joe McCulley, Tom Symons, Reginald Seeley. They all said the same thing: "They may have made a mistake, but for God's sake take their offer. You could have a brilliant career as a diplomat." And so I wrote to the department, accepting their kind offer but pointing out I was committed to working in Quebec to improve my command of French. Would they defer my appointment for six months? Under the circumstances, they would.

My father was not pleased, to put it mildly. He thought he had me in his clutches, that I would join the paper company, no doubt bringing my brother in alongside me when he graduated. But I told him I had to prove myself on my own terms. I went back to Saint-Jérôme and finished the last month. But of course I did not intend to stay there for the good of my French. I would use my deferment to go to Europe, visit my friends, and absorb as much old-world culture as possible. In early December I booked passage on the SS *Corinthia* and set sail on the high seas.

AULD LANG SYNE

I was a total and committed Anglophile until I actually went to Britain. It was December and bitterly cold when I sailed from Montreal. My cabin mate was a seedy Englishman called Rex, who started drinking the minute he rolled out of his bunk at eleven in the morning. He stumbled around in a bleary haze giving everyone his stock greeting, "Hello, my dear *people*," frequently clutching at their lapels for support. Our first night alone in our stateroom he let me know that he was "available for a spot of dalliance," but his scrawny bepimpled body held no allure and I pretended not to hear his invitation, though I did accept a good belt of whisky from his tarnished silver pocket flask.

Down the hall were three Canadian nurses who were much more fun. They asked me into their cabin when I passed it on my way to breakfast the next morning. They brushed their hair and adjusted their bra straps without embarrassment as they gabbed away. (I supposed their nursing experience had obliterated all need for what was at the time considered natural feminine modesty.) We went to breakfast together and they asked me to sit at the same table. Eating was to be the principal activity available to us for the next six days, and we got off to an impressive start with stewed figs, finnan haddie, and an assortment of scones, muffins, and biscuits lashed with bitter marmalade and gooseberry preserve. The nurses assessed the other tables for suitable dating material and declared the pickings slim. "You're the best thing I've seen so far, kiddo," said Nancy, giving me a broad wink. "Even if you are practically jailbait."

"I'm twenty-three and a half," I volunteered.

"Don't tell me, I don't wanna know. Anyway I'm putting in my dibs right now. You got that, girls? The kid's mine for the first night on-board." She whinnied happily and punched me in the shoulder. Looking around the dining room, I didn't see any better prospects. I slathered jam on a scone and held it out to her; she leaned over smacking her lips and took a big bite out of it, nibbling my fingers provocatively in the process.

Up on deck I looked across at the hills of the north shore of Quebec, bare and remote in the bleak grey light of December. I was aware of someone standing beside me, a round little face tilted up and smiling quizzically. I'd met

Lizzie in Ottawa a few weeks before, when I was visiting a cousin who worked in the same office as her brother-in-law. She had told me she was sailing home to England about the same time I was, and here she was on the same ship. I was happy to see her. We chatted amiably as we strolled on the upper deck and she asked me to lunch at her table.

In the dining saloon Lizzie introduced me to her cabin mate, a rather formidable English professor who specialized in the poetry of Shelley, particularly his Italian period. The head steward approached and told me in no uncertain terms that I had been assigned to a table and that was where I was supposed to stay. But when Lizzie favoured him a charming smile and pointed out that there were two unclaimed places at their table, he reluctantly gave in. The professor lady was a bit frosty, but she warmed slightly when she learned I had studied under Northrop Frye, whose book on Blake she pronounced "Really quite a respectable piece of scholarship." We ate watery soup, tasteless haddock, and overcooked mutton while she offered up tidbits of gossip about a certain scholar at Lady Margaret Hall whose interest in her female students was not confined to their intellectual development. They had gone together on a walking tour in the lakes and she *knew*.

After lunch, Lizzie and I continued to explore the ship together, enjoying its then-unfashionable art-deco decoration, peering through glass doors at the faded splendour of the first-class lounge, disparaging its library (Lizzie was a professional librarian), and ending up in the third-class lounge for tea. Most of the other passengers seemed to be lower middle-class Englishwomen returning home after visiting their married daughters in Lethbridge or Medicine Hat. They were a glum-looking lot, huddled in their cardigans and tweed skirts; they brightened only marginally when the ship's three-piece orchestra swung into a spirited rendition of various Second World War standards:

Keep the home fires burning
While our hearts are yearning —

After dinner, the string trio regrouped as a dance band under the leadership of Bert, a mouthy Cockney crooner who encouraged and indeed goaded us into getting out on the dance floor. Nancy needed no urging and, grabbing my arm, charged out into the empty space determined to display her prowess. The Charleston was enjoying a revival, and she gave quite an exhibition of finger snapping, ankle twisting, and knee knocking. I was also fairly adept at this dance, and we were instantly hailed by Bert as the reincarnation of Rogers and Astaire. He hadn't much sense of period, but that was the least of my worries: I didn't want to be tied to Nancy. Fortunately she had already spied bigger game in the person of the ship's doctor, a handsome thirty-five-year-old whom she had met somehow during the afternoon and for whom she had "hot pants," as she confessed to me while we downed a couple beers after we left the floor and tried to catch our breaths. He had promised to pop into the tourist class and buy her a drink around ten. I tactfully left her alone and went in search of Lizzie. She seemed pleased to see me but declined when I suggested we try a rumba.

"I don't think I have the stamina."

"Would you rather go for a stroll up on deck?"

"Yes, please."

We looked up at the stars and I identified various constellations, putting to good use my study of astral navigation when I was a naval cadet. "You do have quite a repertoire of party tricks," said Lizzie with an impish little smile.

"You bet," I replied putting my arm around her shoulder and giving it a squeeze. It was cold on deck and we were soon wrapped in each other's arms.

During the next two or three days I managed to fill in the time between meals talking, walking, and drinking. I ate sometimes with Nancy and the nurses and sometimes with Lizzie and the Shelleyan scholar, whom we dubbed la Professoressa. The head steward eyed me with a certain grim satisfaction. "You're a bit of a lad, aren't you? Well, one of them will get you in her clutches and then I daresay you'll be dancing to a different tune."

Once we got out into the Atlantic, the sea became very rough and most of the old ladies stayed in their staterooms puking and groaning piteously. I avoided my cabin as much as possible. Rex threw up regularly; he advocated whisky as the best cure for seasickness, but it was unclear whether his upset stomach was caused by the ship's rolling and pitching or an overdose of Dewar's. One of the nurses succumbed to seasickness, which gave Nancy an excuse to visit the doctor. She decided to feign dizziness and suggested she move into sick bay. The doctor agreed, but as he was rarely there her ruse did little to advance her romance. I visited her sitting on the edge of her bunk as she alternated between fury and despair. I suggested she make a miraculous recovery for the costume party that was to mark our last evening at sea.

This festivity proved to be a sorry affair. I wore my pyjamas and dressing gown and sported a foot-long cigarette-holder, a prop I'd appropriated from a college play. Rex wore two towels, one around his middle and the other fashioned into a turban. He had started to black his skinny frame with shoe polish but soon gave up, so his face and chest were mahogany brown but the rest of him was a sickly white. The nurses had made themselves wigs out of yellow and orange wool with long braids and wore aprons and big bows in their hair. I wasn't sure whether they were supposed to be French maids or Swiss misses, but they were clearly determined to have a good time.

"What we chiefly need, my dear people, is lots of good old bubbly," said Rex. He ordered two large bottles of sparkling cider, which rapidly disappeared. Bert implored us to dance but the ship was pitching so violently it was almost impossible to walk across the floor, let alone waltz or cha-cha.

After a bit the doctor joined us, wearing his white mess-jacket.

"Divine outfit," chirped Rex. "I say, this isn't exactly the fête of the season, what?"

"If you think this is dead, you should look in on the first class. I've had more fun in the morgue." He gamely asked one of the nurses to dance; they were stumbling around together when Nancy made her entrance. She had draped a sheet around herself and tied it with a length of rubber hose that looked as though it might be part of some apparatus used for administering an enema. A stethoscope hung down between her legs. On her head she had tied a large bedpan. She saw the doctor clutching her erstwhile colleague and lurched toward me with murder in her eye. "Okay, kid. Let's cut a rug."

The orchestra was desperately scraping out a tango: "Jealousy," appropriately enough. I grasped Nancy and we lurched about until one enormous wave sent us all flying across the floor and crashing into a bulkhead. I picked myself up but Nancy lay immobile, groaning piteously. "You'd better have a look at her. I think she's really hurt herself," I said to the doctor.

"I'm sick of the silly goose and her trumped-up maladies. Cart her off to sick bay and tell her to get over it. I have other fish to fry."

With the help of her two friends I managed to get Nancy up on her pins and steer her down the hall. I left them together to divest Nancy of her medical paraphernalia and get her bedded down, while I made my way back to the salon where Lizzie was sitting with Rex and the remains of a bottle of whisky. He poured me a generous slug while the band thumped out "Just One of Those

Things." Bert stopped singing when he got to "So farewell, dear, and amen," and made a sad little speech ending up, "I can't go on. This is the worst frigging cruise I've ever been on. In twenty years I've never seen such a load of dead-beats. . . ."

"I say, old chap, buck up. Let me pour you a whisky," said Rex, tottering over to the piano, bottle in hand. Lizzie and I repaired to the library for a little serious smooching. We were interrupted by the steward, who announced he was about to lock up for the night. "Get lost, will you? Who do you think is going to pillage this collection of well-thumbed thrillers and dog-eared romances?" He stood there jingling his keys till we left. It was too cold to go up on deck, so we made our way down the ladder and into Lizzie's stateroom, which was in darkness. The Professoressa was snoring gently but suddenly sat bolt upright just as I managed to negotiate the hooks of Lizzie's brassiere. "What do you imagine you're doing, young man?" she demanded.

"Just think of me as one of those bits of many-coloured glass staining the white radiance of eternity." She didn't think this was witty and ordered me out. There was more snoring to be heard in my own cabin. I realized that Rex was not alone in his bunk and thought he might be consoling Bert. There were still about three fingers of whisky left in the bottle. I downed it and slept like a log.

Next morning I woke with a splitting headache and watched through slitty eyes as Rex's companion rolled out of the bunk and hurriedly got into his clothes. As he donned his white mess jacket with a groan, I realized it was not Bert but the doctor. He tied his bowtie with deft precision and left without a word. I rolled over and went back to sleep.

An hour later there was a knock at the door. It was one of the nurses. "That bastard of a doctor finally turned up after spending the night with some slut, and it turns out Nancy has a concussion. I thought maybe you'd help us with the bags. We're supposed to get on a train in half an hour." So we must already be in port. I said I'd do what I could as soon as I'd finished my own packing. While I was stuffing dirty socks and underwear into my suitcase, Rex sat up in bed. "I seem to have been ravished. It wasn't you, dear boy, I suppose?"

"As a matter of fact, no."

"Pity. I really quite fancy you, you know. Perhaps we could get together in London."

"I'm going to Scotland."

"My dear, how chilling. I think I must return to the arms of Morpheus. Ask the steward to knock me up in another hour, would you?" He lay back and was snoring again seconds later.

My head continued to pound as I organized the nurses' bags and got them up on deck. I stood by the rail and saw the Liver birds looking down through the slanting rain as Nancy was carried ashore on a stretcher. Lizzie stood beside me, a bright little smile on her lips. "Right then, happy Christmas. See you in London in two weeks. Ma and Pa always give a big party on New Year's Day. You'd better come to that." We got a cab and held hands till we got to the train station. I helped her get her bags onto the train and stood watching as she pulled out of the station. Then I found my own train and clambered aboard. My mouth was dry and burning and the rest of me was wet and freezing. I vowed never to touch whisky again. I wished I were back home in bed in a nice, overheated, suburban Canadian bungalow. Visions of hot buttered popcorn and fizzy, friendly Coca-Cola danced in my head as I sped through the grey drizzle toward Edinburgh.

But the next morning the clear air of Edinburgh was as sharp and stinging against my skin as broken glass. I was to stay with my old friend Jimmy, who was in the process of turning himself into a Presbyterian minister at New College. The building might have been new in about 1560. Its cavernous rooms were drafty and unheated. I thought this might be because they were deserted during the Christmas break, but Jimmy informed me that the Scots thought of heating as some sort of new-fangled aberration that would soon pass, an opinion confirmed by the housekeeper, Miss Elsie Hay, as she welcomed me into her parlour where she presided over tea. She offered me her homemade scones, which Jimmy informed me were famous for their lightness. Miss Hay made a self-deprecating grimace and inquired about my ancestry. She was gratified to learn my Martin relatives were from her own city. The Hunters came from Ayrshire and that evidently was acceptable, though she said wistfully, "I suppose then you haven't the language."

"The language?"

"She means Gaelic," explained Jimmy. "Miss Hay speaks Gaelic, 'braid Scots,' and English."

"Aye, but then I'm educated, ye see. Most of the young today can't manage any of the three. They're entirely ignorant, and vain of it."

"'Vanity, vanity, all is vanity,'" said Jimmy.

"'What profit hath a man of all his labour which he taketh under the sun? One generation passeth away and another generation cometh, but the earth abideth forever. The sun also ariseth.'"

"Mr. Hemingway agrees with you."

"Aye but if he must quote the guid Book, he maun do it correctly. Well, I can't sit here all day blathering. I don't suppose the supper will be making itself. It's a fine bright day. Ye'd best take a brisk turn around the town before we tuck in."

"I thought we'd eat downtown and give you a break, Miss Hay."

"Is your friend one of those American millionaires, then? Nay, I thought not by the look of his boots. Ye'll be back here sharp at seven." And she marched out with the tea tray.

Over the next week I picked up the rhythm of life in Edinburgh, alternating between meals with Miss Hay and walks through the city with Jimmy. Miss Hay's meals were excellent: good meat well but not overcooked, root vegetables treated with respect and imagination, and a good deal of baking. There were delicate, flaky crusts for meat pies and fruit tarts; oatmeal bread that she baked every third day, rising at six to knead the dough; and of course her famous scones. Miss Hay displayed an astonishing versatility with a very limited range of ingredients; at the same time there was nothing flashy about her culinary creations, and although she liked to be complimented, she disparaged her materials or deflected my praise by quoting scripture. Indeed, she and Jimmy had made a game of this. "The flesh of this bird is a thought dreich," she would say, arching her heavy brows critically.

"'All flesh is grass,'" chirped Jimmy.

"'All flesh is *as* grass,'" she corrected and continued, "'and all the glory of man as the flower of grass. The grass withereth and the flower thereof falleth away.'"

"'But the word of the Lord endureth forever.'"

"Aye," said Miss Hay with satisfaction and wiped her pepper-coloured moustache with a starched napkin.

We had spent the day looking up at the city's castle-crowned profile from the neatly manicured gardens of Princes Street, and then looked down on it from the mist-blown heights of Arthur's Seat. We had walked the Royal Mile, sticking our noses into little medieval closes and yards and peering up forbiddingly dark 400-year-old staircases. We explored the austere splendours of

Holyrood House, still haunted by the ghost of Mary, Queen of Scots. In grade school my head had been crammed with English history, but I knew nothing of the history of the lands of my ancestors, the Scots and the Irish, except for the melodramatic events in the life of the lovely, wilful girl who dared to challenge the joyless precepts of John Knox and paid for it with her head. Her story had been lined out for us by our grade-four teacher Miss Ferrier. Miss Ferrier was a highly strung, red-haired, and opinionated woman, a sort of low-key Canadian version of Miss Jean Brodie, and she obviously identified with the ill-fated queen.

The room in Holyrood where Rizzo was murdered in Mary's presence turned out to be about the size of a small clothes closet. "What do you suppose she and Rizzo were doing together in such close quarters?" I asked.

"He was instructing her in the meaning of the Song of Solomon. 'Behold thou art fair, my love, behold thou art fair.'"

"'Thou hast doves' eyes within thy locks: thy hair is as a flock of goats that appear from Mount Gilead.'"

"Very good, my son. We'll make a preacher of you yet."

"No fear." I dodged Jimmy's sales pitch. "I think we should visit your friend Archie on the way back to the college."

Archie was the barman at a pub in the New Town. As soon as we appeared he reached under the bar and produced an unlabelled bottle from which he poured two generous shots of single malt whisky, giving us the Gaelic toast, "Slàinte mhath." The initial taste was a mixture of tar and cough medicine, but it slid down the throat like molten gold and warmed the innards better than anything else I had encountered in this chilly town. Jimmy kept me company. He was not ashamed to be seen in a pub; he explained that the Scots might be strict moralists, but they were concerned with the salvation of the soul rather than the purity of the body, which was doomed to destruction anyway. This presumably was what was meant by predestination. In any case Archie was a Highlander and a Catholic and he enjoyed teasing Jimmy with such questions as, "Can your reverence tell me why Presbyterians don't like to fuck standing up?"

"I don't know. Tell us, Archie."

"Because it might lead to dancing." He cackled with glee and poured us another generous tot.

On Christmas Eve we went to a service in St. Giles' Cathedral. There was a huge procession led by splendidly robed beadles bearing golden maces, choristers and chaplains in scarlet cassocks, and moderators with lace cuffs and jabots. The congregation included many men in full Highland dress, with kilts and braided jackets, and women swathed in tartan. Trumpets rang out and voices swelled as they lit into the twenty-fourth psalm:

> Ye gates, lift up your heads on high
> Ye doors that last for aye
> Be lifted up, even so the King
> Of glory enter may.

The hallelujahs bounced off the vaulted ceiling and I understood what my great-aunt Suz Martin meant when she said, "The Scots may not have much, but they have their pride and that's all they need."

On Christmas Day we went to the church where Jimmy was assistant and afterwards had dinner with the minister and his family. He was a gravely genial man whose name was also Martin, and he queried me about my education. Finding I had gone to Trinity, he asked about Father Fairweather, whose theological writings he'd studied.

"The man has some brilliant insights but I'm forced to conclude he's a *fanatick*."

"You think he should be burnt at the stake?"

"No, but a taste of the ducking-stool might do him no harm," he said with just a hint of a twinkle. "I hear you went to St. Giles last night. I daresay it was very grand. I'm told their services are somewhat higher than a pontifical Mass, but then I'm Free Church, you know." I had imagined that the Presbyterian Church was a coherent and unified body, though my boyhood experience of the Elders of my father's church should have prepared me for the divisions and debates, the rancours and animosities that divided the adherents of the Church of Scotland from the Covenanters, the Free Church, the Wee Frees, and the numerous other sects. The minister recounted the controversy that had raged over the serving of communion and his efforts to reconcile the teetotallers, the sanitary reformers, and the fundamentalists. He now offered the sacrament in four forms: common cup, alcoholic; common cup, non-alcoholic; individual cup, alcoholic; individual cup, non-alcoholic. The service took two hours, but in the end everyone was satisfied, although there had recently been a debate about the quality of the sherry used: there were those who thought that locally distilled elderberry wine would be more suitable and the money saved could be expended upon good works. The minister warmed to his subject and I could see that this was indeed the very stuff of the ministerial life. Tempting as it would have been to see the look on my father's face when I told him I had decided to become a minister of the Lord instead of going into his business, I knew I wouldn't last six months.

I told Jimmy as much as we walked home to the college through a chilling mist. "Anyway I'm not a believer."

"You might be if you gave God half a chance."

"What's that slogan? Let go and let God?"

"Aye, there's a lot in it."

"God doesn't want a lightweight like me."

"Who are you to think you know what God wants?"

"I may not be much, but I'm all I've got."

"'Pride goeth before destruction.'"

"'And a haughty spirit before a fall.' I sound like Elsie Hay."

"You might do worse."

"I've no doubt I will."

Without Miss Hay to restrain us (she had gone to her brother's in Fife for Christmas Day) we polished off half a bottle of whisky before turning in and slept in the same bed for warmth.

The next morning we made our own breakfast and went to the pretty seaside town of Cramond for lunch. We had been asked to a Boxing Day party by the young people of Jimmy's parish, and we made our way to a fine old Georgian house in the New Town after dinner and were welcomed at the door by Morag and Jeannie, two fresh-faced sisters who led us to an upstairs room where a circle of young people sat on the floor. A young man with tousled hair and a guitar sang folk songs in imitation of Ewan MacColl: "The Gypsy Laddie," "The Three Ravens," "The Bonny Earl o' Moray," "Sir Patrick Spens," and "Lord Randall." There wasn't a cheerful number in the lot, but the singer had an appealing catch in his voice, and the girls in the room gazed at him with shining eyes and restrained desire.

After the singing, Jeannie and the singer held hands while Morag broke out the refreshments: cider, shortbread, and some excellent fruitcake. "Martha and Mary," whispered Jimmy as he went to help Morag. She then supervised the clearing away of furniture to make room for dancing. I looked on while the others performed for a bit and then Morag came over and offered to lead me through the Dashing White Sergeant. I found it difficult to follow the intricate patterns, but Morag was very good-tempered about it. She made light of my awkwardness, and when she twigged to my pent-up exasperation she asked me to help her carry more cider up from the kitchen. It proved to be down two flights of stairs in the basement and startled me with its plainness. There was a stone floor, a wooden table, and a small gas range. I'd never been in a kitchen without a refrigerator, but then the kitchen itself was so cold that the water in one of the bowls on the table had a thin skin of ice on it. I remarked on this and she smiled.

"You get used to it. After a wee while the blood thickens."

"I don't think I'm going to stick around long enough for that."

"Ah, Jimmy will be stricken. He's been talking of your visit since October. He thinks you have the making of a minister."

"He doesn't know me as well as he thinks."

"He's very partial to you, Martin."

"I suspect you're more than a bit partial to him."

"I'll not deny it. He's a braw laddie and far ben with the Lord. A bit slow to come to the boil, but — well, it does no good to greet and girn, does it?" And she led the way back upstairs.

Walking home, I broached the subject of Morag to Jimmy. "She's a fine lassie but I can't support myself, let alone a wife."

"I hear she's a lawyer. Maybe she can support you."

"Don't be daft. This is Scotland, my son."

Elsie Hay was waiting for us with the whisky bottle. Jimmy refused and headed for bed, but I stayed up to take a dram with her. "Scots wha hae," I said, raising my glass.

"I'm glad you're here. You've bucked him up. He's a good lad but he needs reinforcement."

"I'm off to London in the morning."

"I'm no' surprised. Ye're a rover, I see that."

"'To strive, to seek, to find and not to yield.'"

"That's no' Walter Scott."

"Tennyson."

"Ye'll no' find what ye're seeking in England, laddie."

"You think not?"

"There's a lot of Scot in ye."

"And a lot of Irish."

"But no English, am I no' right?"

"Not that I know of."

"I thought not. Ye're what we call a lad o' pairts. You'll make your way in the world, right enough. *Slàinte mhath.*"

She raised her glass and drained it and we went off to our beds. I said good-bye to Jimmy as I was leaving early in the morning. We would go our separate ways but remain friends, and five years later he would take up a post in Western Canada. For twenty-some years he would minister to a congregation in St. John's, Newfoundland. There he found a wife and fathered four children. He would finish his ministry in Montreal at the Church of St. Andrew and St. Paul (locally referred to as the A&P), the largest and richest Presbyterian church in Canada. When he took up the appointment he said to me, "If I'd been called to this church when I was thirty-five, I'd be insufferably conceited and grand, but after twenty-five years on the Rock, I can take it in my stride." And he did.

AWAY DOWN IN BLIGHTY

The next day I was speeding south on the Flying Scotsman, my only souvenir a bottle of whisky that Archie had pressed into my chill-blained hand on Christmas Eve. I was met at King's Cross by Judy Cunningham. I knew she was in England but I hadn't spoken or written to her for well over a year. She was thin and elegant in a smart tweed suit with a little toque hat. She wore long suede gloves and high-heeled suede pumps that made her seem six feet tall. With her was an even taller Englishman named Lionel. He suggested he might drive us to the Ritz for tea. It sounded good to me.

On the way there, Judy chattered about her life in London. She had come over with her friend Judy Gianelli for a year. They called themselves Judy One and Judy Two: she was Judy Two and Gianelli was Judy One. Knowing Gianelli I was not surprised; she would have to be Number One. She was at LAMDA, the drama school, while Judy Two was on a teacher's exchange program, but she had found teaching in the London slums with no proper equipment, books, or even toilets just too wearing. She was working at Harrods for the Christmas rush. She had trouble making change but the customers liked her, so she had been kept on at the artists' supplies counter, selling monogrammed pencils to countesses and gold-filled fountain pens to moustachioed colonels with twinkles in their beady blue eyes.

Several of her well-born customers had taken pity on the poor colonial girl and invited her home for tea. One woman, Shirley, had in fact taken her in hand. "My dear, you're very sweet and pretty and I do think you're quite marriageable. But we'll have to do something about that *appalling* accent and you must learn not to wear suede gloves. Nothing but kid." Shirley had introduced Judy to several suitable young men, including Lionel, who was a cousin of the queen. This was conveyed while Lionel was having a word with the head waiter. The lobby of the Ritz appeared to be full, but somehow a table was found for us. We had tea and then champagne cocktails while Judy bubbled on and Lionel eyed her with a mixture of amused condescension and controlled curiosity.

Suddenly it was seven o'clock. Judy and Lionel were going on to the theatre with some friends and wondered if they could drop me somewhere. I said I thought not and collected my luggage from Lionel's car.

"I do hope we'll see you again," he said, with the first hint of warmth or sincerity he'd sounded in the whole afternoon. He climbed into the Daimler and they drove off.

I rang my friend Troop. I'd got his telephone number from his parents in Toronto before I left. I had written to him to say I was coming to England, but received no reply. Nonetheless when he came on the phone he sounded delighted that I was in London and asked me to come round at once to Earls Court to the flat he shared with our friend Selby. As I had two bags I allowed myself the extravagance of a cab.

Troop and Selby's flat was a large, damp basement room furnished with one comfortable chair, a rickety table, and a large, lumpy bed. An alcove contained a gas range, a cupboard stocked with chipped and ill-assorted crockery, and a bathtub. The toilet was off a landing on the outside stairs. It was a splendid porcelain object decorated with blue and green dragons, bearing the mark of Josiah Wedgwood. Above it hung a pull with a heavy gilded tassel. The water in the bowl had a thin skin of ice on top.

Troop seemed pleased to see me and even more pleased when I produced Archie's whisky. He found two more or less clean glasses and I poured each of us a generous shot. Troop stood at the stove concocting a sort of mixed grill of refried potatoes and onions, canned peas, sausage, bacon, and leftover bits of mutton from a four-day-old roast. He informed me he was working for a publishing company, writing jacket blurbs, copy-editing and proofreading, while Selby taught supply in a secondary mods school. They spent most evenings at the local pub or playing Beethoven sonatas. Troop had taught himself to play the violin, and Selby had recently acquired a battered cello. Now I was here we could have a go at some of the trios. Troop had always encouraged me to play his piano; the fact that I hit one wrong note in four and couldn't manage a tempo faster than andante molto didn't bother him. He loved the idea of making music and would rather saw away himself than sit and talk about the performances of Gilels and Rostropovich, though he did a good deal of that too.

By the time Selby arrived, half the whisky was gone and the pan was full of black bits of burnt onion. Over dinner it was settled that I'd bunk in with them at least for the next couple of weeks. They were frankly eager for me to chip in on the rent and food money and pointed out that I could have the flat to myself during the day to pursue either literary or amorous activities. It was Troop's fantasy that there would be plenty of both.

Having finished the whisky we headed for the pub and drank Guinness till closing time. We met some Australians and other Canadians and a rather pretentious Argentine, all of whom had come to London to find the well-spring of their culture and ended up doing essentially menial jobs for pay they wouldn't have considered accepting at home. We parodied Oxford accents and made some disparaging remarks about the royal family, but our Anglophilia was obvious. Through thickening fog we wove our way home and all three bedded down together, Troop rightly pointing out that the only way to survive an English winter was not to sleep alone. My body heat was just as welcome as my weekly rent.

During the next two weeks I strove to accommodate myself to London: the damp, the cold, the unending greyness. I tried staying in bed for a whole day, but as it was warmer outside than in our basement I decided it was better to get up and go out. I soon learned it was both cheaper and more appetizing to eat at home than in pubs or any of the restaurants we could afford. Troop was an able cook and Selby seemed actually to enjoy doing dishes; he had lived in boarding schools since he was little and enjoyed the unaccustomed chores of domesticity. I assumed responsibility for shopping. On my first outing I bought a dozen potatoes but then discovered I was not going to be given a bag to put them in. I stuffed them in my pockets and walked home, returning with a string bag to hold other necessaries. I soon came to realize that I was quite a capable shopper, a skill learned from my mother. Somehow I had unconsciously absorbed her techniques for evaluating the ripeness of vegetables and fruit, comparing the prices and qualities in rival stores and recognizing a bargain when I saw it.

I was determined to soak up British culture in London. I tried to knock off at least one monument a day and did the standard spots: Westminster Abbey, St. Paul's, the Palace, the Tower of London, Madame Tussauds. The first two kindled an interest in architecture and history that sent me off to explore the remaining Christopher Wren churches, the Chelsea Hospital, the Old Royal Naval College and Queen's House at Greenwich, Chiswick House, Burlington House, the Soane Museum, and the Catacombs of Highgate Cemetery, as well as the remaining traces of medieval and Tudor London that had survived the Great Fire: Hampton Court; the George Inn in Southwark; and St.

Bartholomew the Great, a half-timbered wine bar in Holborn that had been operating since the days of Pepys.

Several evenings I went to the theatre, sitting in the gods for less than a quid. I saw the great stars in their current offerings: Olivier allowing himself to be upstaged by Marilyn Monroe in *The Prince and the Showgirl*, Gielgud putting his languid elegance at the service of Noël Coward's fading wit in *Nude with Violin*, Guinness trivializing his talent in a Georges Feydeau farce *Hotel Paradiso*. I condemned them all as passé. What impressed me was the saucy invention of newcomer Joan Plowright in Eugène Ionesco's *The Chairs*, the electrifying intensity of Helene Weigel and her visiting Berliner Ensemble in *Mother Courage*, the physical dexterity and startling imagery of Jean-Louis Barrault and Madeleine Renaud in Paul Claudel's *Christophe Colomb*, and the tough-talking rant of Jimmy Porter in *Look Back in Anger* as he sounded the death knell of the effete style and hollow technique of the theatrical knights.

I pronounced on these matters in the pubs of Earls Court and the smart little hole-in-the-wall bistros of Knightsbridge where I sometimes had supper with the Judies at a cheap eatery called the Soup Kitchen: a change from their accustomed outings with their high-born admirers, dancing the night away at the Savoy or the Café de Paris. They returned my hospitality by inviting me to supper in their rented flat in Victoria, where for me and an old classmate from Trinity they produced a very English meal of kedgeree followed by trifle. Roly was one of the people I had studiously avoided at college. He had a preposterous accent filtered through a stutter; his enthusiasms included Wilde, Beardsley, and Ronald Firbank, and he apparently never washed. He was at London University doing an MA on George Gissing, about whom I knew nothing. I had absolutely no wish to be enlightened. I was horrified to think that the Judies identified me with Roly, but hearing that this was the first time he had been invited anywhere for dinner since his arrival in England seven months earlier, I softened sufficiently to give him my phone number. This was a mistake.

Roly called me repeatedly and I finally invited him to dinner in Earls Court. Troop and Selby made merciless fun of him, mimicking his stutter and holding their noses when they walked past him. This didn't seem to discourage him, and he stayed on long after the meal was over. Finally we offered to entertain him by playing a Schubert string trio, which we had never before attempted. He lasted until the scherzo, and then rose and took his leave. After that, whenever he called, whoever answered signalled the others to start scraping away in the background. Eventually the calls stopped.

Domestic life in Earls Court was amiable enough. Troop, Selby, and I formed a fairly successful ménage à trois. We each had a goal and worked at something related to it: Troop wrote in his spare time and worked for a publisher; Selby taught and attended night classes, hoping to complete an MA in classics; I got casual work as an assistant stage manager, took voice classes, and began writing a play. I thought of it as a searing indictment of domestic life, but in fact it came out more like warmed-over Coward or Shaw than school of Osborne.

We spent a couple of evenings together each week sawing and thumping away on our instruments, then hitting the local before closing time. Besides being bonded by the joys of music making, Selby and I genuinely appreciated Troop's cooking, and I think they both enjoyed the fact that I kept the place relatively tidy and supplied with essentials like toilet paper and shampoo. At home I had always thought of myself as a slob; it was only when I escaped my meticulous family that I realized I was probably the fourth-neatest person in the world. Above all, Selby enjoyed having a home. Though we didn't realize it, I think Troop and I were happy parenting Selby, relishing his inordinate pride in our dingy little digs. He even faithfully read my father's letters; I found this weekly relaying of the weather conditions back home and the state of my relations' health deeply boring, but since Selby savoured every detail Father's efforts were not totally wasted. I would later come to realize that one is rarely appreciated by the person one sets out to impress, but rather by those one views as marginal.

When we three were together, we worked endless variations on a few old jokes and fantasized about our love lives for each other's benefit. Troop was shyly pursuing a sharp-tongued North-Country girl called Betty, who worked in his office. He hadn't got any further than taking her out for coffee, but he was working up the nerve to invite her to an upcoming Elizabeth Schwarzkopf concert. Selby had somehow met a red-haired American girl who was studying piano at the Guildhall. She came to dinner one night and charmed us utterly. She had a high white forehead that made her look a bit like Good Queen Bess and a husky southern drawl that suggested the young Tallulah Bankhead. Troop outdid himself serving up a lamb pilaf followed by Cherries Jubilee. I provided a bottle of Beaune. She played Chopin on our rickety upright, and Selby suggested we should reciprocate by playing for her, but Troop and I knew better. We pooled our slender supply of pound notes to send her home in a cab.

My own love life was less straightforward. I spent occasional theatrical evenings with one or both of the Judies. We always seemed to have a good time, but there was a holding back on both sides, a sense that none of us wanted to make any clear choice that would compromise our ambiguous three-point equilibrium. We were intrigued by the possibilities of flirtation. They went out with other "beaux," and I had renewed my acquaintance with Lizzie. I phoned to apologize for missing her parents' Christmas party, but she informed me they were all so sick they had postponed it and instead were having a Twelfth Night party. She would be delighted if I could make it.

I turned up at her Hampstead house at two in the afternoon. It was a tall Regency building whose main floor was a double drawing room that contained about eighty people, all of whom were holding champagne glasses and talking at the top of their voices. Their breath could be seen rising in little wisps. "We only open up these rooms in the winter when we have forty people or more and the body heat is sufficient to counteract the chill. I can get you a whisky if you like, but I suggest you try Pa's champagne. He gets it specially from a tiny vineyard nobody's ever heard of. Come and meet Hubert. He's a novelist." She propelled me toward a handsome blond man, who I was happy to see was standing close to the fireplace. As I backed toward the warmth he suddenly focused piercing green eyes on me and asked me if I knew anything about the High Arctic.

"I spent a couple months in the Yukon last year." I edged backwards and felt a welcome glow on my calves.

"Did you travel by dogsled?"

"No, but I hitchhiked two thousand miles down the Alaska Highway."

"Really? Splendid fellow," chimed in a white-haired man with a beaky nose. He pulled a pipe out of his mouth, trailing a thin string of slobber that fell on his waistcoat. "I don't suppose you'd like to review a couple of books for me?"

"I could, certainly."

"Excellent. Come to lunch with me Tuesday at the Reform Club. Will you come as well, Hubert?"

"No, actually I'm against reform."

"You would be, of course. Pity. The port's really rather fine just now. One o'clock, shall we say?" And he turned away to talk to someone else.

"Who's that?" I asked Hubert.

"Our host. Zed, to his intimates."

"Imagine him asking a perfect stranger to lunch, just like that."

"You may be sure he knows who you are. He's a shrewd old bird. Now about the Arctic, I'm thinking of using it for a book. I should go and see it, but I haven't the time or the scratch. There can't be many people up there. A few Eskimos, what?"

"I believe there are a lot of Americans setting up radar systems to warn against Soviet attack."

"Perfect. You know about these things then?"

"Not really. I have a friend in the Department of Northern Affairs you could write."

"Northern Affairs. Rather a fetching title, hmm? Look, I'm a bit fagged. Had sex with three different people in the last twenty-four hours. How about meeting me for a drink sometime? Here's my card, give me a call. I could take you to an amusing literary pub in Soho, if you like."

He wandered away and Lizzie reappeared. "What did you make of Hubert?"

"He asked me to have a drink with him. I suppose I should read one of his books first. Are they good?"

"I wouldn't know. Everybody who comes to this house writes books. I couldn't possibly read all of them."

"Your father's asked me to lunch. He said something about reviewing books for him."

"Good old Pa."

"Does he run a magazine or something?"

"Didn't I tell you? He's literary editor of *The Telegraph*. Let's go downstairs and see if we can rustle up something in the kitchen. If I have any more champagne, I shall keel over."

Down in the kitchen we met Lizzie's mother, who was wearing an apron over a tweed suit. She handed us lobster sandwiches. "For the favoured few," she said tartly.

"You been upstairs, Ma?"

"Gracious no. Anyone I want to see knows enough to come down here and get something to eat. The rest can stagger on home and good riddance."

"I feel a bit unsteady myself," I admitted.

"A good brisk walk is what you need, my lad. Up Primrose Hill and back again."

So we set out into the winter twilight. I wasn't sure whether Primrose Hill was some sort of euphemism but it turned out to be a real place. Up on top of it we sat on a bench looking out over the city and necked for quite a long time. I didn't have the nerve to put my cold hands on Lizzie's bare skin. In spite of her warmth I felt the chill seeping through my clothes and into my bones. Finally I stood up and stamped my feet. "I've got to go somewhere warmer." We walked to the nearest pub and ordered two pints of Guinness. Lizzie raised her glass. "Nice having you in London. Settling in then?"

"I think so. You want to come to dinner and meet Troop and Selby?" I was eager to show her off.

"You think I'll pass muster?"

"They're not very judgmental. They're Canadians."

"All right. I must go home and help tidy up. There's always masses of debris after Pa's parties. And he'll be having a kip."

"While the women do the dirty work."

"Man's prerogative. At least in this country. I expect you could get used to it." She gave me a twisted little smile.

We walked arm-in-arm to the tube station and locked ourselves in a long embrace, while passersby smiled at us appreciatively. For all their love of decorum, it surprised me the way English lovers kissed and fondled each other in public. I supposed it must have something to do with their supreme confidence in their superiority and knowledge of what constitutes acceptable behaviour. If you make the rules, then I guess you're free to break the rules. I shivered all the way home on the tube. As I walked down the Earls Court Road my nose was dripping. The flat was empty but I felt too miserable to go to the pub. I started to get undressed and discovered I had burnt the back of my trousers standing in front of Zed's gas fire. I left them on, pulled on another sweater, and got into bed fully dressed.

The next morning I awoke and sneezed my head off. I was alone; either Troop and Selby had spent the night out somewhere, or they had got up and dressed and gone off without waking me. I felt terribly groggy. I had planned to go to see Doctor Johnson's house but I wanted company. Then I remembered Lizzie's father's invitation. At the Reform Club, sitting across from Zed, as he insisted I should call him, I had a sense of facing a predator, maybe a courtly old fox. We were drinking a very pale sherry as a wheezing old waiter set plates in front of us containing what looked like a sort of cold fish pie. I plunged my fork into it and Zed eyed me quizzically over his half-glasses.

"I think you'll find a spoon the most efficient implement for dealing with this." Obediently I made the switch. "They do this rather well here, though it's not quite as good as a dish they serve on the Basque coast. No one understands piquancy better than the Basques." He chuckled and stuffed a spoonful into his mouth, adding a fresh splotch to his already vividly stained waistcoat. I squelched my sneezes as best I could and dug in.

Zed launched into a highly seasoned monologue about Mediterranean food, which he acknowledged was his "great passion." Since the war he had been one of the evaluators of a certain region of the Languedoc for Michelin. This involved going to France and, with three colleagues, eating two enormous meals each day for a week, driving over bumpy roads between repasts in a tiny *deux-chevaux*, and groaning the night away in dusty provincial hostelries. "I'm meant to go again in April but I don't know that my liver will be able to stand the strain. After our trip last year I felt like one of those geese chained up to a post. I had to spend four days in bed eating nothing but milk-pudding. Horrible."

The lunch proceeded at a stately pace. An egg dish, a cold vegetable dish, some cheese, and then a savoury. Each one was accompanied by a different wine, which Zed identified and discoursed upon. Finally we were offered rust-coloured pears and a glass of port. "You won't taste anything like this except in one or two of the clubs. It was laid down twelve years after Waterloo. I have a few bottles that are almost comparable which I bought when the Earl of Strathmore sold off most of the cellars at Glamis. Sadly I couldn't afford to bid on his claret."

I swallowed with the utmost concentration, though whether my taste buds were responding to the wine, or my imagination to Zed's words, I couldn't be sure. He questioned me about Canadian investments and I burbled as knowledgeably as I could about the state of our economy. I spoke of the emergence of a modern, more assured Quebec, which appealed to his Gallic sympathies, citing the work of Gratien Gélinas and Roger Lemelin, the only two French-Canadian writers I'd actually read.

Apparently satisfied with my performance, he led me out of the club and we took a cab back to his office in Fleet Street. It was tiny and piled with books to a height of about five feet, with a narrow path from the door to the desk. He selected four volumes about the Canadian North and handed them to me, suggesting I cover them in about two hundred words. The fee would be two quid and he could give me the name of a bookseller who would pay me half the market price of the books if I didn't soil or tear the jackets. He lit up his pipe as he dismissed me. "We must get you launched, my dear boy." He pulled his pipe from his mouth, and a long festoon of saliva glistened as he waved me a friendly farewell.

On the tube I noticed one of the books was by Pierre Berton; the other authors I'd never heard of. I started to read, and by the time I reached Earls Court Station I had finished two chapters and exhausted my interest. All that reading for a measly two quid. But after all, how much could I say in two hundred words? Each book would get two sentences at most. The sensible thing was to skim through them quickly to get the flavour, compose a few choice phrases and a snappy ending, hand it in, and collect the loot. I took the books to a pub and scampered through them in the time it took to demolish a pint. Then I went home and knocked out my notice on Troop's old Olivetti. Succumbing to the combined effects of sherry, Chablis, claret, Graves, port, and lager, I rolled into bed and slept until I smelled Troop frying up bangers for supper. Between sneezes I read him my piece and he waxed enthusiastic, "Huntie, you're well on the way to being the Ken Tynan of the literary world."

The phone rang, and Judy Two reminded me that I was supposed to be accompanying them to the ballet at Covent Garden the following evening. "Black tie. We're in the dress circle. A gift from Lionel who has season tickets. He's in Morocco at the moment."

"No can do. I left my penguin suit at home."

"Then you'd better go to Moss Bros. See you in the lobby at a quarter to seven."

But it turned out that Selby had brought his dinner jacket with him and it wasn't such a bad fit, so feeling distinctly woozy I made my way through the pouring rain and, appropriately attired, met the two Judies, who looked stunning in cocktail dresses with big bouffant skirts. We were joined by Roly, who had in fact hired his outfit and looked distinctly seedy. To cover his malaise he immediately launched into a tirade about the inferiority of ballet to opera as an art form. We climbed up to the dress circle; our seats were excellent. The first ballet was *Job*, based on the Blake drawings. As I watched the naked dancers, their bodies painted to look like the muscular seraphs I had seen in the Tate, I began to shiver and imagine myself transported into some idealized world where everyone shimmered like stars in the morning sky.

"What you need is a good stiff brandy," said Judy One and marched me off to the bar. I had two doubles during the intermission and felt distinctly warmer during the first scene of *Petrouchka*. Indeed, as I watched the coachmen and nursemaids capering, I began to feel as if I were literally on fire. Then I started to shake uncontrollably. I gripped the arms of my seat as hard as I could but began to realize the whole row was shaking. I tried to concentrate on the elegant little steps of Fonteyn's dancer. She seemed to be dancing far away, on another continent, and yet even the tiniest movement was sharp and clear. She was perfect: self-contained and inviolable as Helpman postured his theatrical way through his hopeless passion as the clown puppet.

The lights came up and I found both Judies looking at me like birds of prey. "I think I need another brandy," I said.

"Nonsense," said Judy One, "take his other arm." The two women grabbed my elbows and marched me downstairs while Roly followed, stuttering incomprehensibly.

They hailed a cab, pushed me into it, and gave the driver instructions to drive straight to St. George's, Hyde Park Corner. Once there I was bundled into a wheelchair, pushed down a long corridor, stripped of my finery, and installed in a bed in a large ward. The whole process seemed unreal, like an extension of the ballet, a sort of gruesome third act devised to follow the two fantasies we'd seen. The nurses and interns seemed almost to pirouette and leap about while in the background ghostly figures performed a carefully orchestrated composition of coughs and wheezes. In my delirium I transformed the sounds of a respiratory ward into an artwork complete with a sort of stylized choreography. The parade of doctors and nurses through the ward seemed as ritualized as a procession at Westminster Abbey, with crucifers and acolytes holding their crosses aloft and swinging their censers. It was to be three days before I awoke early one morning and saw my surroundings through normal eyes. By then the fever had passed and I was, I was assured, out of danger.

"It was a close thing for twenty-four hours. You're a very lucky young man," said a pretty but severe young nurse, looking down at me from above the starched white bib of her apron. "And now that you're out of danger, you can get back on your pins. Up you get."

I put my legs over the side of the bed and stood a bit shakily. The nurse gave me her arm and promenaded me through the ward, which contained perhaps thirty beds, all of them occupied by men ranging in age from sixteen to eighty. The nurse greeted them by name and they replied cheerily, "Good morning, Nurse Birckett."

She kept hold of my arm and marched me back to my bed. "I'd say you're well on your way to recovery. Tomorrow you can start to make yourself useful. This ward doesn't run itself, you know."

"What do you expect me to do? Empty bedpans?"

She ignored this sally. "Can you make tea?"

"Yes."

"Very well. We'll start with that."

For the next fortnight I made tea every morning for the whole ward. I was awakened at six by the sound of horses' hooves. From the window beside my bed I could look down and see troopers of the Household Cavalry exercising their mounts, one man and eight horses clattering across Knightsbridge and down Rotten Row. I would put on my flannel dressing gown, go to the tea station, and get to work. All the inmates took tea, some weak, some strong, some with milk, some with double sugar, one with a slice of lemon, and so on. One old geezer, who turned out to be a baronet down on his luck, demanded Ovaltine; an aging priest wanted hot chocolate; and a rather elegant young man named Patrick insisted on green tea.

I was aided and abetted in my labours by the man in the next bed. He was called Mick Geoghen, but in spite of his Irish name he was a cockney who had worked since the age of twelve as a barrow boy at Covent Garden. He was full of quips and taught me a lot of rhyming slang. He showed me snapshots of his family. "That's me old trouble," he said, pointing to a heavy-set woman who looked as if she'd stepped out of a Giles cartoon. "Fine figure of a woman. Weighs twenty-two stone."

"She's older than you, isn't she?"

"Not much. How old d'you think I am then?" Mick was thin and fit-looking in a wiry sort of way with a full head of sandy-coloured hair. I said I thought he might be in his mid-forties. He chuckled with delight. "I'll be fifty-seven next Guy Fawkes day. I'm a great-granddad. This here's little Mick, named for me and just as much of a scrapper." He pointed with pride to a pugnacious-looking three-year-old. After Mick and I had served early morning tea to the entire ward and washed up, we got back in bed and played cribbage. He usually beat me, but I was used to this from playing with my father at home.

At ten o'clock in the morning came rounds, a ceremony that was to the medical profession what changing the guard was to the military. It involved about twenty people: nurses, interns, and residents, all led by the chief physician, Sir George Hunter, grandson of the founder.

He marched up to me the first morning I was fully aware and said, "Well then, Hunter, back with us, are you? I suppose you know you had double pneumonia and pleurisy." He put his stethoscope to my chest and cocked his head to listen to my breathing. "Where do you hail from?"

"Canada."

"Family been there long?"

"Since 1797."

"And before that?"

"Somewhere in Ayrshire, I believe."

"Yes, that's where we're all from. Where are you living in London?"

"I've been staying in a bed-sitter in Earls Court."

"Well we can't have you going back there till we get those lungs cleaned up. You'll be here a fortnight anyway. Probably longer. Nurse Birckett, keep a sharp lookout for this young man. He'll need a bit of exercise. Keep him from going doo-lally. We wouldn't want to send him home to the colonies in damaged condition, would we? On we go now, mustn't lollygag." And he marched his troop away.

Nurse Birckett returned after lunch wearing a dark blue cape over her starched uniform. "Up you get, then, and get dressed. We're walking out together. Not my idea. Sir George's orders. You'll find some suitable clothes in the closet next to the loo."

Once outside the hospital, Nurse Birckett lost a lot of her starchiness. Her name, it turned out, was Margaret, and she had grown up in Wiltshire, where her passion was her horse, Firefly. She had done eventing and won several ribbons before she had a nasty fall that caused several broken ribs and a dislocated shoulder. While she recuperated in hospital, a new passion was born: nursing. It was not an easy life: twelve-hour shifts, six-day weeks, hospital food, living in a dormitory that offered no more privacy or comfort than our ward, but she loved it because she felt she was "doing something for the first time in my life. Mummy's never done anything except arrange a few flowers and pour tea. The sheer idleness of Mummy's life depressed me so awfully I made up my mind to get away and do something. Anything. And now I have. What do you do, by the way?"

"I review books for the *Daily Telegraph*."

"Doesn't sound much."

"I'm training to be a theatre director."

"Golly, how do you do that?"

"Keep my eyes and ears open. Can I buy you tea?"

"Very well. And then we must go back. I've got reports to make out."

Walking out with Nurse Birckett became part of my routine. Four afternoons a week we set out and strolled in the park for half an hour, and then had tea together before returning to St. George's. And I began to have visitors. Troop appeared, bringing me what he said was a care package. It turned out to contain a scrabble set, my favourite sweater, a jar of olives, a pound of butter, and a bottle of Scotch. All of them would come in handy. Troop sat on the edge of my bed looking quite pleased with himself.

"What's up?" I asked. "Somebody give you an advance on your novel?"

"The fact is, Huntie, I've got laid." Apparently after the Schwarzkopf concert Betty had asked him back to her flat and they had spent the next forty-eight hours in bed together. They were currently discussing whether she should move into the basement in Earls Court or he should move into her room in Bayswater, bright but about the size of a large broom closet. "We have to do it perpendicular."

My care package also contained two letters, one from my father announcing that he and Mother would shortly be arriving in London on the first stop in their planned tour of Europe. The other was from Dick, postmarked Seville, in which he announced that he would soon be in England. "It turns out, I'm not Goya after all," he wrote. "I've been offered a job by George Dunning in London and I figure I might as well get back to what I really know how to do: animation."

I proceeded to introduce Mick Geoghan, my tea mate, to the game of Scrabble. He caught on rapidly and soon introduced me to dozens of words I didn't know. I realized that the English facility with language is by no means confined to the upper classes: the lower orders are equally adept verbally; it's ingrained, part of their heritage. As an American friend would later phrase it, "They're really into words over there."

Another early visitor was Lizzie. "Pa was pleased with your piece. Have you seen it? It's in today's *Telegraph*." She produced a paper from her bag and handed it to me. "He's sent along a fresh lot of books, if you feel like doing another. They're about the American Southwest. I assured him you had first-hand knowledge of the area."

"I don't."

"You've got an active imagination. I daresay you'll manage. How much longer are they going to keep you here?"

"At least two weeks. I've got water on the chest."

"Better than on the brain, I suppose. I was thinking we might go to Sicily together. I have a friend who has a house there who'd put us up. It'll be spring in Sicily by now."

"Sounds nice."

"Mmm. Well then, hurry up and mend."

The next day the two Judies came clicking through the ward in their high heels, wearing hats and gloves; they had just come from some fashionable event where they had met Princess Margaret. They brought a basket from Harrods containing Scottish shortbread, French cheese, and a cluster of hothouse grapes that looked wonderful but proved to be absolutely without taste. Their big news was that Judy One had received a phone call the night before from John Saxton back in Canada who had proposed marriage. She had said she'd think about it. Meanwhile, she was having a romance with a young actor at LAMDA, Donald Sutherland, who was trying to get her to move in with him. "We're the marriageable age. Mother Nature's determined to get us hooked up with somebody."

When they left, Geoghen teased me about my fashionable lady friends. His wife had been to see him exactly once in the three weeks he'd been in the ward. "Not as I miss her, you know. It's a bloomin' 'oliday, is wot it is." We played Scrabble till he had such a coughing fit, he had to lie down and rest. His face went red and then purple and I suddenly realized he was probably sicker than he knew.

The day after, instead of walking in the park with Nurse Birckett, I suggested we visit my friend Troop so I could retrieve some of my clothes. The apartment was empty. I found a bottle of wine and by the time we finished it I was feeling quite amorous and had persuaded Margaret to shed her starch and stripes. She revealed a fine set of breasts which I duly admired and began to fondle. She suggested I shed my clothes.

"I've seen it anyway," she said, producing a condom. "Here, put this on, I've got another sixteen months before I complete my training so I can't go getting myself knocked up."

We were enjoying a post-coital smoke when Troop arrived home with Betty and a bottle of whisky. He produced a bang-up meal and then we went to the pub. It was after eleven when we finally showed up at the hospital. In spite of my inebriated state, I noticed they had put screens up around Geoghen's bed. The next morning, Sister descended on me like a mother eagle whose nest has been violated and announced that Nurse Birckett would be working in another ward for the rest of the month and I would be transferred to a convalescent hospital in Ealing in three days' time.

Two days later my father and mother arrived. The Judies had phoned them to tell them I was in hospital. My parents had been planning a trip to Europe anyway and had simply advanced their booking by two months. My father managed to get an interview with Sir George while my mother sat on my bedside. It was my duty to come home and help Father with his business. Father returned and announced that he had been given permission for me to be released from the hospital the next day, provided he took responsibility for me and saw to it that I did not go back to my cold-water flat. He would go to American Express the next morning and book me a passage back to Canada on the next ship. In the meantime I could stay in their suite at the Dorchester. After they left, I challenged Geoghen to a game of Scrabble. His playing wasn't up to his usual standard but for some reason I let him win. I was glad I had. He died that night.

The following day I managed to find Nurse Birckett and kiss her goodbye. She let me put my hands under her apron and feel her breasts one more time. "I'm glad to have met you," she said, "but you're a bit too untamed for me. It's just as well you're going back to the wilds you came from."

My father took me to lunch in Jermyn Street and then to Simpsons, Piccadilly, and bought me some decent clothes. Then in a fit of generosity he offered to take all my friends to dinner — Troop and Betty, Selby, and the two Judies. I opted for the Café de Paris and we polished off five bottles of champagne. Marlene Dietrich did her famous act and blew a kiss to my father at the end of it. He paid the bill without even checking the addition.

My parents flew to Paris the next morning. As soon as their taxi pulled away from the hotel I set out for the American Express office in the Haymarket and exchanged my steamship passage for a first-class railway ticket to Madrid. I went back to Earls Court and packed the least disreputable items of my old wardrobe in a canvas bag, climbed into my new blazer and flannels, and set out for Victoria Station.

I decided to stay over in Paris for three days and discovered it was actually colder than London, though there was some heat in my hotel. But I craved warmth and hoped to find Dick in Seville. After three days I boarded a train for Biarritz. The beach was deserted and the Bay of Biscay seemed anything but bonny-O; huge waves pounded against the jagged rocks, and the sky was grey and overcast. I got on another train, crossed over the Spanish border and proceeded at a slow but steady pace to Madrid. I walked along its stately streets, but the sky was still grey and the air chilly. I decided not to linger but to go on to Seville.

It took sixteen hours to travel the 400 kilometres between the two cities. We stopped at every village and were met by a knot of people who offered us whatever they had to sell: a bunch of spindly asparagus, or goat's curd wrapped in grubby cheesecloth. In the next compartment three nuns giggled more or less continuously. When I looked in through their window, they lowered their eyes modestly but made no attempt to conceal the fact they were drinking from an open wine bottle.

About halfway through the trip, a courtly old gentleman got into my compartment. He settled himself comfortably, nodded to me, and made a remark that I couldn't understand. I explained that I had no knowledge of Spanish and he then decided we should converse in my language, which he had studied at school. His vocabulary was distinctly Victorian in tone. He came up with words like "notwithstanding" and "perspicacity" and explained that his grammar was a bit shaky; he was not entirely secure in his command of the subjunctive. The old Spaniard was delighted to learn I was a North American. One of his "fondest aspirations" was to travel to Mexico to see the ancient pyramids. He discoursed knowledgeably about the Aztec gods and the differences between the Olmec and Toltec styles of temple decoration. He also knew a good deal about Mexican painting and gave me a critique of the works of José Clemente Orozco and Jusepe de Ribera. He particularly admired the work of Frida Kahlo, whom I had never heard of.

Presently he asked me to get off at the next station and have a drink with him in the bar. We drank *fino*, pale mouth-puckering sherry, and I screwed up my courage to ask about General Franco. The old Spaniard explained that I must not attempt to discuss politics in his country. The Spanish temperament was too fiery to support democracy, but they were too proud to admit it. He offered me another glass and I suggested that we'd better get back on the train. He looked at me with amusement and said, "They will not leave without us. I had a word with the porter." I realized I had penetrated another world, one where Anglo-Saxon attitudes seemed fully as absurd as in Lewis Carroll's fantasy.

I knew my flight from the winter was over when I saw oranges hanging from the trees lining the streets of Seville. I had an address for my friend Dick, and my train companion courteously gave me completely incomprehensible directions. I tried threading my way through the streets of the Barrio Santa Cruz, the old Moorish quarter. It looked like a set for *Carmen*, with its white and ochre walls, cobbled streets, tall iron gates, and trailing scarlet bougainvillea. As the evening shadows lengthened, intense-looking young men walked in pairs, locked in passionate argument or leaned against the black grilles that covered every window. Occasionally an inner shutter would open to reveal a housemaid in a blue-and-white uniform. In those days even the humblest Spanish girls never went out into the streets alone; their lovers wooed them through the bars. It was known as "eating iron."

I finally found the house I was looking for in Calle Abades. An old woman appeared in an upstairs window. She obviously could make no sense of my attempt at Spanish and turned away, hollering, "Manolo, Manolo . . ." A thin shadow of a man appeared and whispered through the gate. "*Vous cherchez l'étudiant canadien? Il a disparu il y a deux semaines. Personne ne sait où. Excusez-moi, je suis pressé.*" He disappeared into the interior of the house and I turned to find a member of the Guardia Civil giving me a suspicious look from under the square black hat that sat on his head like a surrealist typewriter about to tap out a report of my misdemeanours: loitering and whispered exchanges in a foreign tongue.

I stumbled along over the cobblestones and found I was being followed by a gypsy lady who tried to sell me a carnation. I gave her a peseta. She instantly grabbed my hand and began to interpret my future. "You have made a long journey. You search for the adventure, no? You will find it, *si*. You have a good heart and a good head but you must choose which is to rule. You will meet first a man, and then a lady, and another figure who is neither — a priest, perhaps."

She laughed delightedly at her own wit as a crowd began to gather around us. I offered her another peseta and she spat contemptuously. I gave her ten pesetas and made my escape, followed by her raucous voice shouting after me in Spanish. I didn't know whether she was cursing my stinginess or ridiculing my extravagance, but the crowd cackled with delight.

I headed into a bar and ordered a glass of wine, wondering where I was going to spend the night when I heard a voice: "Hey, mate, what you doin' in these parts?" In front of me stood Ivor, the blond-bearded Australian I'd worked with in the mining camp in the Yukon the previous summer. We ordered more *vino* and reminisced. Ivor suggested I come back to his hotel to see if they had a room they could rent me. They did; it overlooked a little courtyard with blue and yellow tiles and a tiny dribbling fountain. The price was roughly two dollars a day. Ivor said we could have dinner in the dining room any time after ten o'clock. He'd arranged to eat with an American writer he'd met a couple of days ago, "Sort of a Hemingway character, you'll get a bang out of him."

The dining room was gloomy, with peeling plaster walls painted a dismal green. There was one waiter, a tall man who looked like a down-at-heel duke; he wore frayed white gloves and a tailcoat that was also a dismal green. He showed us to a table where the American writer was already seated; he looked less like Hemingway than like Tennessee Williams' older and more dissipated brother. He introduced himself as "Boo" and blew a cloud of cigarette smoke at me through dirty yellow teeth. It turned out that he did know Tennessee Williams slightly, and Truman Capote more than slightly. I said I'd read *Other Voices, Other Rooms* and *The Grass Harp* and thought they were super. "Truman's supposed to be coming to Seville any moment. Poor Truman, he really is beginning to look quite strange with that huge head and that *triste* little body. Quite like Rumpelstiltskin."

Boo needed no urging to tell us about himself, "one of my *favourite* topics." He was the younger son of a prosperous old family from a small town in New Hampshire. He had decided to be a writer, and in the late '30s had actually had two stories published in the *New Yorker*. There had been talk of him going to Hollywood as a screenwriter; then the war had come along and he had gone to work for the State Department, eventually becoming a sort of undercover observer in Spain. He stayed on after 1945; he could no longer afford to live in New York. He was working on his memoirs.

Boo promised to show us Seville: the tapas bars of the Sierpes, the cafés of Triana, the Gypsy quarter across the river. "But not the *corrida*. It's *too* brutal for this little boy. I once knew a young *novillero* who persuaded me to go and see his first big fight. I sat right on the *barrera* and watched while he was gored. Too *triste. Never* again."

Ivor went to the washroom, and Boo grinned and leaned across the table, exhaling smoke mingled with a strong smell of halitosis. "Of course you know I'm queer. I was only sixteen when I went to Harvard. My brother was a senior. By the end of the first term I'd had half his classmates. When I told him years later, he didn't believe me. They're all bank presidents or corporation lawyers, married men with three or four children." He giggled and knocked back a glassful of *vino tinto*. Ivor came back and Boo suggested we might head across the river and hear some flamenco.

The streets of Triana were shabbier than those of Santa Cruz, but the twang of guitars and the clatter of castanets filled the night air. We went to several cafés and drank many glasses of brandy. Eventually we wound up sitting beside a tiny stage where a woman who looked to be in her forties danced barefoot. She wore a red dress spotted with huge polka dots and was obviously pregnant. She immediately tuned into Ivor and aimed her performance at him, finishing up by leaping onto our table and yelling at the top of her lungs something that brought down the house. "What did she say?" I asked Boo.

"Roughly translated: 'I'm wonderful, I'm the greatest. I'm seven months gone and the father is the whole of Triana.'" The gypsy grabbed Ivor's beard and pulled him to his feet. With raw Australian gallantry he kissed her as the crowd shouted encouragement.

"I think it behooves us to slip *tactfully* away." Boo grabbed my hand and we pushed through the ringing *Olés* toward the door. I looked back to see if Ivor had seen us go. "Don't worry, leave him to his fate. They understand fate in these parts." We walked back across the Guadalquivir. "I'd ask you back to my place, but I don't want to rush you. We might meet for lunch. I've a friend I'd like you to meet. Bring Ivor. Two o'clock at that little café across from the Giralda." He squeezed my hand and we staggered off in opposite directions.

At noon the next day, Ivor was still snoring and refused to be roused. I went alone to meet Boo and his friend, who turned out to be a chesty English girl called Norma with a wonderful laugh like a waterfall. She came from somewhere in Lancashire and, having got "fed up with all the folderol," had packed a knapsack and hiked her way to Seville, where she was maintaining herself by teaching English. Boo wondered how she coped with the advances of Spanish men. "I'm bigger than most of them for a start," she said, her giggle cascading merrily.

After lunch we went to see the Alcázar with its endless proliferation of geometric patterns: tiled walls, marble floors, inlaid roofs, and latticework grilles, each with its own intricate design, yet somehow harmonized. Boo instructed me, "Everything attractive in Andaluz is the legacy of the Moors. The gardens, flamenco music, even sherry. Five centuries of sadistic Jesuit repression hasn't quite succeeded in killing their sheer enjoyment of life. The Church hasn't created anything of the slightest aesthetic interest here. Even the Giralda was originally a minaret."

We walked afterwards in the Maria Luisa Gardens. Children in spotless white smocks and pinafores played while plump nurses in striped uniforms sat on the benches and gossiped. Peacocks squawked, and strutted, and occasionally a smart little black carriage drove by, pulled by a sleek high-stepping little horse. "Some *doña* from a neighbouring plantation coming into town to visit a friend or buy a box of candy. This town is still run by sporting gentry who have some idea of *style*."

"She may have her own carriage," said Norma, "but I'll bet her husband keeps her locked away behind iron bars. I don't call that style. I call it slavery."

"Jealousy will get you nowhere, *mi corazon*. You'd trade places with her in a moment, don't tell me you wouldn't. You just haven't been asked."

"That's all you know."

"I know what I know." Boo gave her sly little smile. "Time for my siesta. I'll leave you two to gawk at the passing scene. You should ask *la señorita* Norma to teach you the rudiments of Spanish. You won't make much headway in this town without it."

"I never teach anyone without charging a fee. It's a basic principle for an old pro." She laughed again and I realized she was using "pro" in the English sense: an abbreviation not for "professional" but for "prostitute."

"What fee did you have in mind?"

"It's negotiable. Suppose we start at five bob a lesson." It was less than seventy-five cents Canadian but I was trying to live on twenty dollars a week. We agreed on two lessons a week, starting the next morning.

Norma proved to be an exacting teacher and in the weeks that followed I saw a lot of her. We sometimes went shopping in the Sierpes to give me a chance to use my Spanish. I bought her some castanets and a black lace fan. In the mornings I sat at café tables drinking *cafe con leche* and writing poetry in which I tried to capture the rhythms and colours of Seville; in the early evenings Ivor and I joined the *passado*, the promenade in the streets before dinner. In those days most of the people were too poor to buy drinks and tapas; they just strolled and talked to their friends. After two weeks Ivor said he wanted to move on to Valencia and Barcelona. He asked me to go with him, but I was happy in Seville. I stayed on.

One night Norma and I took Boo to see a performance of *zarzuela*, the Spanish version of operetta. The show began at 1 a.m., and the gallery where we sat was crowded with families who had brought their children and their dinner. Every time the leading lady appeared they shouted *Olé* and *Hija de Triana*. She was a local star, a gypsy girl who had made it into the big time. In every scene she had a different costume: she changed from saucy peasant girl to wimpled medieval princess to ragged slave-girl to white-wigged courtesan.

"I can't follow the plot," I complained.

"Plot? There's no *plot*. It's fantasy in its *purest* manifestation," explained Boo as the lighting changed from brilliant fuchsia to a livid green to indicate we were now at the bottom of the sea. Our heroine was discovered strumming a guitar and sporting a mermaid's tail of glistening silver scales. We left about halfway through, at three thirty in the morning.

On another occasion we went to see a religious procession. The streets were already full of people when the huge doors of the cathedral were thrown open and red-robed acolytes appeared swinging their silver thuribles. High on a silver-handled litter stood the Virgin, decked out in lace flounces and ropes of pearls. A tear trickled from her glass eye and rolled down her painted cheek. The gathered fell to their knees and crossed themselves. I followed their example but Norma stayed on her sturdy North Country legs, her head sticking up above the crowd. The Bishop appeared, coped and mitred, and stopped in front of her. In ringing tones he demanded, "Daughter, why are you not kneeling?"

"Because I'm an English Protestant and I don't go down on my knees for any wax-faced doll." The Bishop made a dramatic gesture that might have terrified Satan and moved on as Norma's laughter spurted above the voices of the chanting priests.

After a month my Spanish was still pretty rudimentary but I was beginning to know my way around Seville. I had seen the mysterious Manolo several times. He usually nodded to me conspiratorially and hurried away, but one morning I was sitting drinking coffee in a little square and he came over to sit with me. Leaning across the table he confided, "*Je t'ai vu avec un certain monsieur americain qui s'appelle Boo. Prenez garde. Il est méchant.*" Before he got up to go, he was hailed by another young Spaniard whom he introduced as Andres and who sat down at my table as Manolo scurried away.

Andres explained that Manolo had Republican sympathies and was obsessed by the idea that the Guardia Civil were watching him. He always spoke in French so that his conversations would not be understood; this of course made him more conspicuous than ever. But Andres doubted that the police were really interested. "In Madrid, his fears might be justified, but here in Seville, no one takes politics seriously. Poor Manolo, his whole life has become a fantasy of terror. This is very Spanish."

Andres asked me if I would like to see a typical Spanish dance hall. I suggested I might bring Norma and he was enthusiastic; he also would bring a girlfriend. The dance hall was crowded with men in black suits, women in black lace dresses. A small band played music with a distinctive Latin beat. "Seville hasn't heard of Elvis?" I asked Norma. She shrugged and I led her out onto the floor. I'd managed to fake my way through some of the Dashing White Sergeant in Edinburgh, but my feet couldn't find their way through the intricacies of the *pasodoble*.

We sat out the next dance, and then Andres joined us. He had left his girl talking with friends on the other side of the room. "The *Sevillana* is more complex than it looks. But I think *la señorita Norma* has danced it before, no?" He led Norma out onto the floor and they gave a very polished performance together. When she came back I bought her a drink and she said, "Andres asked me to meet him afterwards."

"You want to? That's okay."

"What about you?"

"What about me?"

"Are you interested in girls or boys? It's obvious your friend Boo has his eye on you. Don't pretend you don't know."

"Boo's fun but he's pretty repulsive —"

"You mean if he were young and handsome —"

It was a challenge I couldn't duck. "You want me to come home with you?"

I grabbed her arm and without even stopping to wave at Andres dragged her through the swift-stepping dancers and out into the street.

The next morning I suggested we might try to find a place together. Norma laughed. "You're a keen student, but I don't see myself as a full-time teacher."

I went off to the café and scribbled furiously while my coffee turned cold. In fact I'd been waiting to hear from the two Judies, who had said they might come and join me in Spain. I'd heard nothing from them, but if they did appear, it would be just as well if they didn't find me living with Norma. I'd bide my time; in the meantime I had fresh inspiration for morning poeticizing. I wondered if I should show my efforts to Boo. He was, after all, a published writer, though I doubted whether he would be sympathetic to what I was doing. Youthful ardour probably wasn't exactly his thing.

The next time I saw Andres he asked me to come home with him. He lived in a big house in Barrio Santa Cruz; his parents were away visiting their estates south of Jerez. A manservant brought us brandy in the salon, which was full of treasures: a fifteenth-century Moroccan carpet, a marriage chest that had contained the dowry of an Italian countess who married into the family in the time of Felipe IV, leather-bound journals written by a conquistador who had gone to Peru with Pizarro. "You are the first non-Spaniard who has been in this house in four hundred years."

"I am honoured. But why?"

"Norma says you wish to see the real Spain. I like you and you are very good for Norma, I think. So, if I am able to do something for you, why not?"

"You like Norma?"

"Who would not like Norma? She has what we call *duende*. You know what is *duende*? It is the perfect gesture of the flamenco dancer, the swirl of the matador's cape as he makes the *veronica*, the passionate poetry of García Lorca . . ."

"You mean it's sort of Sevillian for style?"

"More than style. It is spirit. The spirit of *Andaluz*. You understand?"

"I think so. Anyway Norma's quite the girl."

"*Si*, quite the girl, *la Norma*." He raised his brandy glass, drained it, and tossed it into the fireplace: perhaps his own attempt to demonstrate *duende*.

The next week was the *Semana Santa*. Norma and I went to watch the famous procession of the *Penitentes*. Andres was among them. He came up to Norma and asked her to hold his candle while he whipped himself. Norma laughed as he dodged away, and explained that in Spanish "to whip oneself" is slang for knocking back a quick shot of brandy.

The following week I had lunch with Boo. He bared his yellow teeth at me in a mocking grin. "Your hero Truman Capote is in town. He's staying with the Bowles. They've taken a house here until the trouble blows over in Morocco. You'll like the Bowles. *Very* amusing people, even though she's usually drunk by noon and he's perpetually stoned on *kif*."

I'd never heard of Paul Bowles but I did know about Jane; I'd seen her play *In the Summerhouse* in New York, mainly because Judith Anderson was playing the lead. They normally lived in Tangiers, but when the old Sultan died and there were riots in the streets they decided to escape to Seville for a few months. But of course the real draw for me was Capote. "They've asked us for nine o'clock. Don't expect much in the way of food. Jane can't get lunch organized, never *mind* dinner."

The house the Bowles had rented had a pretty courtyard with a monkey in a cage. It screamed at us fiercely as we went into the kitchen, where Jane was sitting at a table among chopped onions and tomatoes, glass in hand. I told her how much I'd liked her play, and she gave me a melancholy smile.

"That's sweet of you, but really I thought it was too *recherché* for words. One can't just write for one's five hundred friends, can one? I'm afraid I've had a fight with Truman and scared him away. He's gone off to stay in the *Alfonso XIII*, the little snot. Could you pour me another shot, Boo?"

I sat and listened while Boo and Jane exchanged gossip about mutual writer friends. An Arab boy came in silently and scraped the chopped vegetables into a bowl, then started to prepare a meal. Jane paid no attention; her speech was becoming blurrier. She got up and, hanging onto the table, excused herself. Boo put his arm around her shoulders and led her out of the room. I tried my Spanish on the Arab. He gave me a dazzling smile but obviously didn't understand me. I wondered whether I should just sneak away, and so I went into the courtyard. A handsome man stood in the doorway opposite.

"You're Boo's friend?" He smiled at me and held out his hand. I went over to him. He took both my hands and squeezed them in his. He looked me in the eyes and his voice dropped an octave. "You're a writer?" I shrugged and tried to withdraw my hands but he held on. "You must come and visit us in Tangiers. We could go south and visit the Berbers. Wonderful men. Fierce, and gentle, and utterly untamed." He looked straight at me with his dilated pupils, like a cobra hypnotizing its prey. I heard Boo behind me. "Jane's gone to bed. And I gather Truman's decamped. Perhaps we should retire too."

"As you like." He released my hands, but continued to look into my eyes. "Don't forget." He disappeared into the shadows inside the house.

"Unless you're *mad* for Arab food, I think we might as well go to Don Raimundo." I wanted to stay but didn't have the nerve to say so. I followed Boo out. "I adore Jane," he continued. "She's so funny."

"Funny ha-ha or funny peculiar?" — a cliché of the period.

"Funny *triste*." Boo gave me a little grin, exposing his terrible teeth. "Like me." The monkey screamed. He too bared his teeth and I couldn't help thinking he looked a lot like Boo. Two mischievous animals. I wondered whether Boo had deliberately broken in on my encounter with Paul. I remembered Norma saying he obviously found me attractive.

We walked along together without talking. Manolo came out of the bar opposite the Giralda and I hailed him. He took a quick look at Boo and fled. "Poor Manolo," said Boo. "He was a *great* beauty ten years ago. I offered to take him to Paris. I still had a little money then. But he thought he was in love with someone else. Now look at him. *Triste, triste.*"

We had a good meal at Don Raimundo. After our second brandy, Boo blew cigarette smoke at me and said, "I think I should tell you about Norma. She had a child by your friend Andres. He offered to marry her, or so she says. But he comes from a very old family and she couldn't imagine submitting to the life his family would impose on her. She gave the child up for adoption. I thought you should know." I wondered why he'd decided to tell me this now. At least he'd levelled with me; I had to give him credit for that. On a sudden impulse I asked him if he would read my poems and tell me what he thought of them. I'd actually brought them with me, thinking I might get Capote to look at them. "You *are* a glutton for punishment. What if I tell you they're complete and unadulterated *merde*?"

"I suppose I might as well know."

"Well, hand them over." I set them on the table, got up, and walked away. Boo called me back; he was sorry, but he couldn't afford to settle the bill himself.

The next morning I sat in the hotel courtyard, torturing myself with the idea of going round to Paul Bowles' house, when a message came through that the Judies were in Seville and were staying at the Inglaterra. I walked over and there they were. They informed me they intended to spend three days in Seville. I set out to show them the city: the Cathedral, the Alcázar, the gardens,

Triana. I flaunted my Spanish, my knowledge of the tapas bars as proof of my new-found sophistication, and recounted my near brush with Capote.

Their second night in town I took them to Triana to the gypsy café. The three of us danced together, then Judy One complained of a headache and went back to her hotel. Judy Cunningham and I walked across the bridge spanning the Guadalquivir and through the romantic squares of the Barrio Santa Cruz. We held hands as we strolled along. We sat on a bench under the orange trees. We kissed, and the embers of our teenage romance suddenly seemed to rekindle. We had trouble awaking the concierge at her hotel and I asked her to come back to my room. She smiled her agreement but then the old hag appeared in the doorway and she disappeared into the courtyard.

The next day, their final day in the city, the Judies had an invitation to a lunch party given by a friend of a friend, and they managed to have me included. We went to a splendid apartment and were greeted by Doña Soriano, a vivacious woman with glittering rings, and her husband, a courtly doctor with a huge drooping moustache and a flowing Byronic necktie. They had invited several other young people and we drank *fino* in chilled glasses and ate tapas handed around by white-gloved manservants. At three o'clock we sat down to a sumptuous *paella*, a huge dish of saffron-coloured rice brimming with lobster and octopus, garnished with mayonnaise flavoured with crushed lobster shells. It was far beyond anything I had eaten in Sevillian restaurants. Doña Soriano graciously revealed her recipe: "The secret is this, you must first beat the yellows . . ." We all looked puzzled; it slowly came to me she was talking about egg-yolks.

The men discussed bull-fighting. It turned out we were going on to the Plaza de Toros after lunch. We would see Antonio Ordoñez, a young *torrero* from an old bull-fighting family in Ronda, who had won the attention of the *aficionados* earlier that year when the judges had decreed that a particularly noble bull should not be slaughtered. Antonio continued to fight the bull without his sword, miming the kill by leaping over the horns and indicating with graphic accuracy how he would stab the bull between the shoulder blades.

"You see," one of the young men explained to me, "you must not think of blood. Only of the colour and the elegant movements of the matador. It is like a dance. Like the *sevillana*, raised to a higher art form."

I also remember Dr. Soriano saying, "You must excuse me, I never go to the *corrida* now. Since they put blankets on the horses to protect them, it is nothing."

I said little and drank a lot. Sated with food and wine, we young people said goodbye to the Sorianos and strolled to the Plaza de Toros. The procession was already underway as we were shown to our seats just above the *barrera*. The young men told us we were very fortunate to be so close, where we could see everything. I realized we could also smell everything: the sweat of the horses, the bulls, and the men.

The *picadors* rode with easy grace, swinging their lances, their faces stern and concentrated. By contrast the *matador* seemed like a boy dressed up in his splendidly silly outfit of green and gold with pink stockings and dainty buckled shoes. His face was gentle and amused. He teased the bull with confidence and charm, like a polished actor, a Cary Grant of the bullring. Then suddenly the fight became serious. The bull charged and missed goring the *torrero's* thigh by centimetres. The pink and gold cape swung in ever-smaller circles, luring the bull closer until the sword struck home at the base of its huge neck. I saw blood spurt in the air. I smelled it. I fainted.

One of the young men put me in a taxi that took me back to the hotel. I threw up and went to bed. Next morning there was a note from the two Judies. They were spending a few days in Madrid, then two weeks in Paris. Why didn't I join them there? I remembered the new-found intimacy, the kisses on the bridge over the Guadalquivir. The thought of courting Judy under the bridges of Paris did a little dance in my brain.

I had breakfast and went to see Norma. I asked her about Andres and the baby. "Yes, it's true. Andres is a fine fellow, but he doesn't know what he wants. He's confused. Like you. I don't care to be tied to little boys. If that's what I wanted, I could have stayed home with my brothers." I told her about the bullfight and her laugh bubbled up. "I don't think Spain is your country somehow. If I were you, I'd move on. You're not Ernest Hemingway, are you?"

"Neither is Boo."

"Boo's tougher than you might think."

We said goodbye. I went to my hotel and packed. As I sat in the café in the station I saw Boo coming toward me. "Norma told me you're leaving. I warned you about the *corrida*, but you wouldn't listen. Such a *funny* story."

"It didn't seem funny to me. Or maybe as you would say, funny *triste*."

"You know, I wouldn't be surprised if funny is your thing. There is some wit in your little efforts, but not the *tiniest* glimmer of passion, *mon cher enfant.* Forget about being a poet." He put my little bundle of poems in my hand and grinned at me with his dirty yellow teeth. "I *hate* goodbyes. Send me a Christmas card. And *do* try to figure out what you really want. You're not going to look like that forever, you know." He squeezed my hand and was gone. I finished my coffee, dropped the poems in the trashcan, and headed for the platform.

My fantasy of conquering Europe with my precocious artistry faded. I suddenly saw I didn't belong in Spain, or England, or even Scotland. I hadn't really felt at home with the English any more than with the Spanish. I didn't even like the English very much. And it was their country after all; if I wasn't prepared to assimilate, I should go home where I belonged. Find my own life, my own voice. Just as Dick had realized he was not Goya, I was not Dylan Thomas or even Truman Capote. I remembered Professor Child saying to me with characteristic gentle mockery, "You want to go to Europe? To *find* yourself, I suppose. Yes, yes, the geographic approach to maturity."

My mind had suddenly cleared. I knew where I was going. I would get a ticket to Paris and court Judy Two along the *quais* of the Seine. I'd persuade her to go back to Canada with me. I had a job waiting for me in External Affairs that offered the prospect of new experience, a fresh challenge. And the possibility of a relationship I believed I was ready to come to terms with. I was on the brink of becoming an adult. Whatever that might turn out to mean.

THE ROAD FORKS

I was still beavering away in External Affairs the following spring. I had made it through the bleak Ottawa winter with the aid of a few weekends in Montreal and also Toronto, where I spent most of my time with Judy Cunningham, who had returned from Europe after we had had our brief fling in Seville. We went to movies and concerts as we had in our student days and afterwards necked in her living room. I became aware that I had a rival, a guy I had known at college. Not that Judy was secretive about this. I had a distinct sense that I had an edge, but also that she was not prepared to wait for me indefinitely. It would soon be summer. She told me she would be spending most of it at her family's cottage close to Ottawa. I was welcome to visit on weekends. I took this to be a positive sign.

Following Jim's departure from External, I inherited his desk and now had two actual Canadian missions to correspond with. I received telegrams daily and began to try to unravel the complicated political situations in Cambodia and Laos, both of which were ruled by royal families whose members seemed to include traditionalist princes and Communist princes. It all seemed a bit like a Gilbert and Sullivan operetta. Every week the political officers of the missions had a meeting with their counterparts from Poland and India. At the end of each meeting the Canadian commissioner sent a report of what had been discussed and an agenda for the next weekly meeting. I immediately began drafting instructions for the next meeting and sent it Arthur Menzies. He in turn sent it on to other heads of department within External and the deputy undersecretaries for revision and comment. It would be several days before these were collated and the revised document would be telegraphed to our missions in Phnom Penh and Vientiane. More often than not I would get a reply from them saying, "Unfortunately your instructions arrived too late for this week's meeting, so we said . . ."

In order to speed up the process another officer was added to the chain of command working alongside Arthur Menzies. Peter Campbell was about as unlike Arthur as possible though both were Asian specialists, or as the Brits would have said, "China hands." Peter was in his early forties. He had a ready wit, and a rather original vocabulary. He referred to children as "titches,"

· women as "ginches" and the Chinese as "slopes." Before the advent of political correctness, his sallies were accepted as being outrageous but amusing. (He was delighted when I referred to the upper echelon of the department as "the Externalia.")

Peter was at once elegant and rakish, courteous and confrontational, a sort of cross between Humphrey Bogart and David Niven. He had commanded a frigate in the Canadian Navy during the Second World War and survived being torpedoed by a U-boat, and been our last consul in Shanghai, playing cards with Russian countesses and jumping into swimming pools in full evening dress before the city fell to the Communists. As first secretary at our embassy in Washington he had publicly exposed the dunderheaded policy of the counsellor and been sent home, ostensibly because he had made improper advances to the wife of the New Zealand ambassador.

One day Peter suggested that we get together after work for a drink. He challenged me to a game of pool, during which I made a poor showing, and a game of chess after which he pronounced me a worthy opponent. Peter and I hit it off immediately and began to hang out together. We sometimes went to good restaurants but more often frequented grotty pool halls in Lowertown or Hull. Peter was a scrapper and enjoyed a fight. I remember once he showed up at a departmental meeting wearing dark glasses. I wondered whether the senior officers suspected what I knew: both of Peter's eyes had been blackened in a barroom brawl the night before.

In June Peter rented a cottage at Mulvihill Lake near Chelsea. I spent several weekends there with him, hitching a lift on Friday afternoon after work, sometimes with another young officer. Johnny was a good-looking blond guy who also had a skeptical attitude towards the department. We played chess and sometimes bridge with a guy from a neighbouring cottage, whipped up crude but tasty meals by tossing onions, potatoes, peppers, mushrooms, hamburger and whatever else was handy into a frying pan and washing it down with large drafts of plonk. We went skinny-dipping in the lake and indeed Johnny was prone to walking around the cottage completely naked. I was aware of an erotic charge in the air but there was nothing overt. I sensed that Peter was attracted to both of us, but I decided to keep my physical distance.

In July I began spending alternate weekends at the Cunningham's cottage at Marshall's Bay, sticking my thumb out at five o'clock on a Friday afternoon and usually getting there in time for a swim before dinner. Judy's parents had gone to Europe for six weeks, leaving her in charge and she and her siblings had many guests. Judy presided in the kitchen but we found time to go for walks in woods studded with wildflowers and to paddle down the creeks and snyes, where water lilies and arrowroot bloomed, kingfishers swooped down to catch their prey, and giant turtles snapped at us as we passed. In the evenings we all sat around a bonfire, toasting marshmallows. We sang, "How Could You Believe Me When I Said I Loved You When You Know I've Been a Liar All My Life" or "My Gal's a Corker, She's a New Yorker, that's where all my money goes, keeping her in style."

It was a less sophisticated ambience than at Mulvihill but I found it very easy to fit into. I was on friendly terms with Judy's brother and sister, and their friends, who were mostly five or six years younger, and so Judy and I slipped naturally into the roles of surrogate parents. I had a brief foretaste of what it would be like to be married and have children. The Cunningham family was fun-loving and easygoing, quite unlike the strict, rigid household I had grown up in.

I returned to work on Monday mornings with some reluctance. The negotiations in Phnom Penh and Vientiane seemed to have bogged down and in any case meetings became more sporadic because of the summer heat. When we had nothing more pressing to occupy us one of our duties as junior officers was to answer some of the hundreds of letters from the public that had piled up in a small room in the East Block. Many were addressed to Lester Pearson himself and varied from complaints of the extravagant expense of maintaining ambassadors in foreign countries where they rode around in chauffeur-driven cars and drank champagne for breakfast to pleas to send Canadian wheat to feed the starving Chinese and Indians.

Occasionally one of the letters contained an intelligent argument from some thoughtful person about Canadian foreign policy that deserved a serious reply. I took my handwritten replies to Mrs. Boyd, the head of the typing pool who rolled her eyes and then confided, "Not a chance. I'm only here till the end of the month, Mr. Hunter. I left schoolteaching to come here, thinking nothing could be worse than trying to pound some knowledge into the kids in grade six and seven, but I was wrong. I'm going back to it in September."

There were also letters from loonies including a number from one woman who signed herself variously Eleanor Roosevelt, Florence Nightingale, and Queen Victoria. Although the handwriting was unmistakably the same she had separate stationery printed for each of her assumed aliases. I couldn't resist writing a reply to one of her missives. I knew it wouldn't get passed on through the proper channels so I mailed it to her myself.

In early August Peter told me he was to be posted to Vientiane as Canadian commissioner. He would be leaving in mid-September. He would keep the Mulvihill cottage till the end of August; he hoped I would be able to spend most weekends there as Johnny had decided to leave the foreign service and go back to school. The next weekend was rainy and we spent most of it indoors reading. I was even more convinced Peter was seeking a more intimate relationship, perhaps replacing what he had enjoyed with Johnny. But I was reasonably sure he wouldn't make the first move. A senior officer jumping a junior could be in a lot of trouble.

The next weekend I went to the Cunnigham's cottage and learned from Judy's brother, who was a keen little gossip, that my rival had visited the weekend before and proposed. Apparently Judy had said she would have to think about it. "If you want to stay in the running, you'd better jump," he said. Judy and I didn't discuss this development, though I came close to throwing my hat in the ring with a proposal of my own.

Back in Ottawa I had a call from my father inviting me to lunch with him and my mother. We ate cold lobster and drank Chablis, I suppose as a concession to my supposed worldliness. Father left for a meeting and I was alone with Mother. She offered a bit of news about family members and then looked at me solemnly. "Your father's been diagnosed with glaucoma. He's going blind."

"When did you find this out?"

"A week ago."

"There's no cure?"

"They may be able to delay it. He's counting on you to help him, Martin."

"Meaning what exactly?"

"You owe him that."

I thought again of the Sunday school hymn: "Where duty calls or danger, be never wanting there."

Two days later I was summoned to Arthur Menzies' office and informed I would be posted as the junior officer to Vientiane in October. That evening Peter and I went on a pub-crawl.

"I assume you had a hand in this."

"I don't have any control over postings. I made a suggestion, that's all."

"Oh, come on . . ."

"We'll have fun. It's another world, the East. Different set of rules. And no Mounties breathing down your neck."

"Meaning?"

"Surely I don't have to spell it out? I'm going up to Mulvihill tomorrow. You coming up on the weekend? I thought we might go up the Gatineau. I've got a friend with a sailboat up on Lac-des-Îles."

"I'm not sure."

I usually sleep like a log but that night I barely closed my eyes. I remembered my English professor Arthur Barker saying, "You want too much, Mr. Hunter. You must learn to make choices." For years I had drifted along more or less taking things as they came. Making few commitments. Enjoying whatever adventures came my way. Sometimes seeing the next step and thinking, "That could be fun" but rarely stopping to figure out why things happened the way they did. Now I had to make a decision. Did I want adventure or the security of a long-term relationship? Freedom or responsibility? Either way I'd have regrets. Was I over-dramatizing the situation? Maybe, but I did have to make a choice.

The next two days I walked around in a haze of indecision. Then on Friday after work I took a bus to the edge of the city — and stuck out my thumb.